CONCEPTUALIZATIONS IN THE
MANUSMṚTI

CONCEPTUALIZATIONS IN THE *MANUSMṚTI*

PARNASABARI BHATTACHARYYA

MANOHAR
1996

ISBN 81-7304-154-7

First Published 1996

Published by
Ajay Kumar Jain for
Manohar Publishers & Distributors
2/6 Ansari Road, Daryaganj
New Delhi 110002

Lasertypeset by
AJ Software Publishing Co. Pvt. Ltd.
305 Durga Chambers, 1333 D.B. Gupta Road
Karol Bagh, New Delhi 110005

Printed at
Rajkamal Electric Press
B 35/9 G.T. Karnal Road, Indl. Area
Delhi 110033

To
My Grandparents

BHUPENDRA NATH
and
TARA BHATTACHARYYA

Contents

kingship is similar to the European concept of the same - Ghoshal's criticism of Bhandarkar's formulation - N.C. Bandyopadhyaya's view that the *Manusmṛti* ushered in an era of social repression and political subjugation, repudiated the secular ideals of the *Arthaśāstra* caused the perpetual degradation of the Śūdras, slaves and women, made the Brāhmaṇas highest of the created beings and the king the divine representative of Dharma and the owner of everything of earth - Beni Prasad's general outlining of Manu's polity - H.N. Sinha's emphasis on the theory of protection - K.V.R. Aiyangar's view that the *Manusmṛti* oulines the scheme of polity which is rooted in the general scheme of Hindu life - Despite his divinity the king is subordinate to the conventions and to *daṇḍa* - Altekar's view that though one of the seven limbs of the state Manu makes the king a veritable divinity - V.P. Verma's view that while Kauṭilya was in favour of primeval kingship having an elective origin Manu suggested the divine creation - J. Gonda on the king's identification with various deities - R.S. Sharma's treatment in historical perspective - Drekmeier's general observations - Spellman on Manu's insistence of king's divinity - Manorama Jauhari's study - Views of I.W. Mabbet - Prabhavati Sinha's view that Manu and other law-givers did not consider the king above law - Manu's theory of polity is only one section of his social theory - Manu compared with Plato - Treaties of Rājadharma - Their origin, branches and purpose according to the traditional view - Whether the Kṣatriyas alone could become king - Śūdras even could become kings - Whether Manu's concept of the seven limbs of the state (*saptāñga*) has correspondence with the organic theory of the Western political thinkers - View of Bhandarkar, Jayaswal, B.K. Sarkar, Anjaria, Kane and Spellman in this regard - Review of Manu's concept of *arājaka* on the basis of the views on the same expressed in the earlier and later texts - Jayaswal's view that *arājaka* meant an ideal state of nature was contested by Kane - On the origin of the state and kingship - Manu's theory of divine origin - The king is not an incarnation of God but symbolises the power of certain gods - Recommendation for the removal of the unjust and oppressive rulers - Underlying all the hyperboles, the emphasis was

claiming of a divine origin for his laws by Manu is not unnatural because ancient peoples all over the world, without exception regarded their laws as of divine origin which may be demonstrated with reference to the Old Testment, the Code of Hammurabi, the Egyptian, Greek and Roman codes - Manu's insistence on customs, rituals, etc., as part of cultural tradition is not especially religious and inconsistent with his legal formulations - Popular customs and usages as source of law - Manu's concept of law as a divine revelation coming down to the earth through human agency - Legal philosophy of Manu centred on *dharma* - The idea of *dharma* replaced the earlier - Relation between *ṛta* and law - Manu on king's right to make law - Medhātithi and Kulluka on royal edicts - On the discriminatory nature of Manu's legal procedure - Class orientation of law all over the world, ancient and modern - Approaches of Plato and Aristotle - Meanings and interpretations of the term Vyavahāra - Its four feet - Manu's classification of law under eighteen titles - Minor variations in other legal texts - Manu's insistence on justice and equity - Right judicial procedure should be followed - Manu on the constitution of the judiciary - King should normally preside - Importance attached to local usages and customary laws besides the institutes of the sacred law - Manu on evidence - Persons admissible as witnessess - Policy of investigation - Oath or ordeal - Other law-givers on evidence - Manu's emphasis on the social purpose of justice - Protection of the weaker section of the people - Caste privileges and disabilities in the case of the criminal law - Concession to the Brāhmaṇas - When law may be taken into one's own hand - Various forms of punishment - On detection of motive behind the crime - On recovery of debt - Certain debts of father are not to be repaid by his inheriting son - Rates of interest on debt - deposit and pledge - sale without ownership - concerns among partners - resumption of gifts - non-payments of wages - non-performance of agreements - dispute between owner and servants - dispute regarding boundaries - Points where Manu and Kauṭilya differ - Manu's influence on the laws of Yājñavalkya, Nārada and Bṛhaspati.

Acknowledgements

I owe the deepest debt to my revered guru Professor Pranabananda Jash for the valuable guidance and kind supervision that I received from him all along the progress of this work. But for his keen interest and affectionate goading, all these years, this study would not have been possible. I also express my deep sense of gratitude to the teachers of the Departments of Ancient Indian History, Culture and Archaeology, Modern History, Philosophy and Sanskrit of the Visva-Bharati University for their valuable assistance and suggestions. The Librarian and other staff, especially the staff of the reference section of the Central Library, staff of the Central and Departmenal office and other friends of Visva-Bharati especially deserve my sincere thanks.

I am deeply indebted to Dr. Vivekananda Jha and Dr. B.K. Pandeya and other officials of the Indian Council of Historical Research, New Delhi who, besides granting me an ICHR fellowship, have helped me in many ways. They were always very keen about the progress of my research. Late Professor J.C. Jain, the well known Prakrit and Jain scholar, was kind enough to supply me data pertaining to Jain parallels of some of the passages of *Manusmṛti.* Professor G.V. Saroja, formerly of the Tamil University, helped me by sending information on the Tamil translations of the *Manusmṛti.* Professor P.K. Agrawala of the Banaras Hindu University sent me a copy of his father V.S. Agrawala's out-of-print work on Manu. Such acts of kindness to an ordinary researcher like me reveal their greatness. Simply thanking them would not be enough. I should

also express my gratefulness to my examiners, Professor V.C. Srivastava of BHU and Professor Y.B. Singh of the Jammu University. Both have recommended its early publication.

I am also grateful to other persons who have given me opportunities to present papers or delivering lectures on Manu at various seminars and conferences, thus encouraging me a lot. They are Professor Nisith Ranjan Roy, Director, Institute of Historical Studies, Professor L.K. Tripathi, formerly Dean, Faculty of Arts, Banaras Hindu University, Dr. G. Subbaiah of Visva-Bharati, Professor Gautam Chatterjee of Paśchimvaṅga Itihās Saṃsad, and Professor B.N. Mukherjee of Calcutta University.

To Dr. Ranabir Chakravarti of the Department of Ancient Indian History and Culture, Calcutta University, my gratitude knows no bounds. I am also grateful to Professor Bhaskar Chattopadhyay of the Department of History and Dr. Dipak Chatterjee of the Department of Sanskrit, Burdwan University. Dr. Gautam Sengupta, Director, State Archaeology, Govt. of West Bengal, Dr. Asim Kumar Chatterjee of the Department of AIHC, Calcutta University, Dr. Ranjit Sen of the Department of History, Rabindra Bharati University, Professor Buddhajivan Chakravarti of the Department of Bengali, Presidency College, for their valuable assistance in many ways. My thanks are also due to my typist Sri Kamala Kanta Das. Sri Ramesh Jain and Sri Ajay Jain of Manohar Publishers & Distributors deserve my sincere gratitude for the interest they have taken in publishing this work.

Joraghat PARNASABARI BHATTACHARYYA
Chinsurah 712101

Abbreviations

ABORI	Annals of the Bhandarkar Oriental Research Institute.
Ait. Ār.	*Aitareya Āraṇyaka.*
Ait. Br.	*Aitareya Brāhmaṇa.*
ALB	Adyar Library Bulletin.
Āp. Dh.S.	*Āpastamba Dharmasūtra.*
Āp. Gr.	*Āpastamba Gṛhyasūtra.*
Āp. Sr.	*Āpastamba Śrautasūtra.*
Ar.	Āraṇyaka, added after the first name of the text.
ASWI	Archaeological Survey of Western India.
Āśv. Gr.	*Āśvalāyana Gṛhyasūtra.*
Āśv. Sr.	*Āśvalāyana Śrautasūtra.*
Av.	*Atharvaveda.*
Baudh. Dh. S.	*Baudhāyana Dharmasūtra*
Baudh. Gr.	*Baudhāyana Gṛhyasūtra.*
Baudh. Sr.	*Baudhāyana Śrautasūtra*
Bib. Ind.	Bibliotheca Indica.
Br.	Brāhmaṇa, added after the first name of the text.
Br. Up.	*Bṛahadāraṇyaka Upaniṣad.*
Ch. Up.	*Chāndogya Upaniṣad.*
CHI.	Cultural Heritage of India.
CII.	Corpus Inscriptionum Indicarum.
Dh. S.	Dharmasūtra, added after the first name of the text.
Ep. Car.	Epigraphia Carnatica

Ep. Ind.	Epigraphia Indica.
ERE	Encyclopaedia of Religion and Ethics.
Gaut. Dh. S.	*Gautama Dharmasūtra.*
Gr.	Gṛhyasūtra, added after the first name of the text.
Hir. Gr.	*Hiraṇyakeśī Gṛhyasūtra*
IHQ	Indian Historical Quarterly.
Ind. Ant.	Indian Antiquary.
IPQ.	Indian Philosophical Quarterly.
Jaimini	*Pūrvamīmāṃsā Sūtra (PMS)*
JGJRI	Journal of the Ganganath Jha Research Institute.
JGRS	Journal of the Gujarat Research Society.
JIH	Journal of Indian History.
JBBRAS	Journal of the Bombay Branch of the Royal Asiatic Society.
JAOS	Journal of the American Oriental Society.
JESHO	Journal of the Economic and Social History of the Orient.
JBRS	Journal of the Bihar Research Society.
JOI	Journal of the Oriental Institute.
JRAS	Journal of the Royal Asiatic Society.
Kām.	*Kāmandakīya Nītisāra*
Kauṭilya	Kauṭilya's *Arthaśāstra.*
Manu	*Manusmṛti*
Mbh.	*Mahābhārata.*
Mit.	*Mitākṣarā* Com.
Nir.	*Nirukta.*
OH	Our Heritage.
Pāṇini	*Aṣṭādhyāyī of Pāṇini.*
Pār. Gr.	*Pāraskara Gṛhyasūtra.*
PMS	*Pūrvamīmāṃsā Sūtra* (Jaimini)
PTS	Pali Text Society.
Pu.	Purāṇa, added after the first name of the text.
Rām.	*Rāmāyaṇa.*

Rv.	*Ṛgveda.*
Saṃ.	Saṃhitā, added after the first name of the text.
Śāṅ. Gr.	*Śāṅkhyāyana Gṛhyasūtra.*
Śat. Br.	*Śatapatha Brāhmaṇa.*
SBE.	Sacred Books of the East.
Sr.	Śrautasūtra, added after the first name of the text.
Taitt. Br.	*Taittirīya Brāhmaṇa.*
Taitt. Saṃ.	*Taittirīya Saṃhitā.*
TLL	Tagore Law Lectures.
Up.	Upaniṣad, added after the first name of the text.
Vāj. Sam.	*Vājasaneyi Saṃhitā.*
VS.	*Vedānta Sūtra.*
Yāj.	*Yājñavalkya Smṛti*
ZDMG	*Zeitschrift der Deutschen Morgenlandischen Gesellschaft.*

Chapter I

Studies on *Manusmṛti*: The Historiographical Perspective

Western interest in *Manusmṛti* derived its principal impulses mainly from the impelling necessity of ruling a country which differed significantly from the norms of Western social and religious behaviour and practices and partly from an antiquarian viewpoint with a condescension that ancient India could achieve some standard in the development of its civilization. It was no less a person than Warren Hastings, the actual founder of the British rule in India, who recognised that the sovereignty of England in India would be secure only if the rulers understood how to treat the social and religious prejudices of the natives with all possible considerations. Thus he had got a work compiled by a number of Brahmaṇas out of the ancient Indian law books, under the title of *Vivādārṇavasetu* (Bridge over the Ocean of Disputes) containing everything important about the Indian law of inheritance, family law and the like. It was first rendered from Sanskrit into Persian and the latter version was translated in English by Nathaniel Brassey Halhed in 1776.[1]

Sir William Jones, who came to India in 1783 as a Puisne Judge of the Supreme Court, also shared the view of Warren Hastings and held that even the best intended legislative provisions would have no beneficial effect unless they were congenial to the disposition and habits, the religious prejudices and approved ceremonial usages of the people for whom they were enacted, especially when that people universally and sincerely believed that all their ancient usages and established

rules of conduct had the sanction of an actual revelation from heaven. This was precisely the circumstances under which Sir William Jones brought out his translation of the *Manusmṛti* which was published in 1794.[2]

Sir William Jones regarded the *Manusmṛti* as one of the most important records of the Hindu antiquity. According to him the style and the metre of *Manusmṛti* are widely different from the language of the metrical rules of the later Sanskrit language. From this point of view and also from a parallel chronological study of the Latin writings of different ages, he came to the conclusion that the *Manusmṛti* should be slightly older than the Five Books *(Pentateuch)* of Moses and hence it should be assigned to c. 1280 B.C. Jones found reasons to support Dara Shukoh's contention that Manu, the first of the created beings, could be no other than the progenitor of mankind whom the Jews, Christians and Muslims attributed the name of Adam.[3] According to him, the name of Manu is derived from *man,* meaning 'mind' or 'to understand'. His work thus contains the understanding of the doctrines of the Vedas and that is why he is highly honoured in the Vedic tradition in which it is said that 'whatever Manu has pronounced is a medicine for the soul'. In later *Smṛti* texts of Bṛhaspati, Vyāsa, Parāśara and Nārada, Manu's authoritativeness is firmly established.

Jones also refers to the Indian tradition, as was known in his time, that Brahmā taught his laws to Manu in a hundred thousand verses and it was subsequently handed down by Manu to Nārada who abridged it in twelve thousand verses and gave it to a son of Bhṛgu named Sumati who reduced the verses to four thousand. Jones believed that, there was further abridgement since the present text consists only of two thousand six hundred and eighty five verses. He refers to the commentaries on Manu made by Methātithi, Govindarāja, Dharaṇīdhara and Kulluka. He himself used Kulluka's commentary which according to him, was the shortest, yet the most luminous, the least ostentatious yet the most learned, the deepest yet the

most agreeable commentary ever composed by any author, ancient or modern, European or Asiatic. Regarding the contents of the *Manusmṛti* the assessment of Sir William Jones was as follows:

> It is a system of despotism and priest-craft, both indeed limited by law, but artfully conspiring to give mutual support though with mutual checks. It is filled with strange conceits in metaphysics and natural philosophy, with idle superstitions and with a scheme of theology most obscurely figurative ... the punishments are partial and fanciful, for some crimes dreadfully cruel, for others reprehensively slight and the very morals though rigid enough on the whole, are in one or two instances, unaccountably relaxed. Nevertheless, a spirit of sublime devotion, of benevolence to mankind, and of amiable tenderness to all sentient creatures, pervades the whole work, the style of it has a certain austere majesty that sounds like the language of legislation and extorts a respectful awe. The sentiment of independence of all being but God, and the harsh admonitions, even to kings are truely noble.[4]

Since 1813, numerous reprints of the text of *Manusmṛti* with and without Kulluka's commentary appeared at several times in India, but they were all uncritical. The first with Kulluka's commentary was published from Calcutta in 1813. This was printed by Colebrook's protégé, Baburam, but it was full of serious misprints. Two editions appeared in Europe, in which a critical restoration of the text had been attempted. The first was in 1825 by Sir G.C. Haughton, whose edition of the text was made on the basis of a careful comparison of nine manuscripts, obtained from various parts of India. It was enriched by critical and explanatory notes. He also edited the English translation of Sir William Jones, of which mention will be made later. Haughton's edition of the text of Manu was acclaimed as,

> one of the most beautiful monuments of true philosophical research, combined with sound criticism that Hindu literature has to boast of.

Haughton held that,

> the institutes of Manu are not only revered by this unvarying race of men as they were by their primeval forefathers, but have moreover contributed to preserve, in pristine force, opinions, usages and maxims, which by a law, which reverses in the moral, what is observed in the material world, have only grown the stronger by the use of ages.[5]

The second European edition of the *Manusmṛti* was done by Loiseleur Deslongchamps in 1830-33. He also made a French translation of the text which was published from Paris in 1850. It agreed tolerably closely with that of Sir William Jones. We have already had the occasion to refer to Haughton's edition of Sir William Jone's translation (1863) in which Haughton has recorded the variations and a few misinterpretations at the end. According to him the discrepancies in question must have arisen from some variations in the readings of the manuscripts consulted by Sir William Jones.

Different types of study on the *Manusmṛti* also began to come to light simultaneously. A sociological and historical approach to the study of *Manusmṛti* was initiated by Raja Rammohan Roy who held that the laws of Manu contained the essence of the Vedic tradition and therefore should be given precedence to all other Śāstras. In his own words,

> the ancient saints and holy teachers and their commentators ... agree that Manu is better acquinted than any other lawgiver with the spirit of the Veda.

In many of his writings, especially in those pertaining to the practice of Satī, rights of the Hindu females, Hindu laws of

inheritance etc., published between 1816 and 1832 he made frequent references to the codes of Manu and interpreted them in a sociological perspective, based on a sound historical understanding, quite uncommon at the age in which he lived and worked.[6] In 1849 Weber and Stenzler[7] suggested that a set of teachings handed down in a mass of floating verses, of rules and observations, which were later crystallized in the shape of *Manusmṛti,* formed the substratum of the earlier Indian norms of social and individual behaviour governing the life and conduct of the people. The metrical *Manusmṛti* did not begin all of a sudden and at a given date. They also held that the germs of the *Manusmṛti* lay in the older Sūtras and these were later collected and arranged for the convenience of instructions. This approach was subsequently rendered into a stratificatory theory by Max Müller and others.

The first Indian who made an English rendering of *Manusmṛti* in 1850 was Tarachand Chakravarti. In 1858, J. Muir gave model translations of numerous passages of the *Manusmṛti.*[8] Muir at first collected a series of texts from the *Ṛgveda* which speak of Manu as the progenitor of mankind and the first institutor of religious rites. Then he adduced a number of legends and notices relating to Manu from the Brāhmaṇas and other works next in order of antiquity to the hymns of the *Ṛgveda.* The most interesting and important of these legends is that of the Deluge as given in the *Śatapatha Brāhmaṇa* which he has compared with the later versions of the same story, found in the *Mahābhārata,* the *Matsya, Bhāgavata* and *Agni* Purāṇas. Next he has given legendary accounts of the origin of castes, among the descendants of Manu, on the basis of the Purāṇas. So far as the text of the *Manusmṛti* is concerned he has given translation of some portions of the first and twelfth books. While dealing with the account of the system of the Yugas, Manvantaras and Kalpas, he has made frequent references to Manu and some of his commentators.

The structural theory indicated by Weber and Stenzler was given a complete shape in 1850 by F. Max Müller.[9] According

to Max-Müller the systematic cultivation of the sacred sciences of the Brāhmaṇas centred in the ancient *sūtrakaraṇas*, the schools which first collected the fragmentary doctrines scattered in the older Vedic works and arranged them for the convenience of oral instruction in *sūtras* or strings of aphorisms. The sacred laws were included in them. The Sūtra treatises on law covered the whole range of topics contained in the metrical Smṛtis. Max Müller insisted on the *Mīmāṃsā* tradition, which declares that originally each Vedic school or Karaṇa possessed a peculiar work on Dharma. While the Dharmasūtras possess a considerable antiquity, the metrical Smṛtis cannot be equally ancient. It is therefore very probable that each of the metrical Smṛti is based on a particular Dharmasūtra. The *Mānavadharmaśāstra* in particular may therefore be considered as a recast and versification of the Dharmasūtra of the *Mānavasūtrakaraṇa,* a subdivision of the Maitrāyanīya school, belonging to the Black *Yajurveda.*

Although Max Müller was severely criticized by some later scholars for expounding this theory, since no trace of a *Mānavadharmasūtra* could be shown, nor could any connection between the *Mānavadharmaśāstra* or *Manusmṛti* and the school of the Mānavas be established, his hypothesis possessed two strong points. First of all, it supplies a rational theory of historical development. Secondly it agrees with certain facts which the explorations of Vedic literature had brought to light. When Max Müller formulated his theory, the precise relation between the Dharmasūtras and the Gṛhyasūtras was not clearly understood and their impact on the Dharmaśāstras was almost impossible to ascertain. But later textual studies were able to clarify many points. For example, the *Viṣṇusmṛti,* notwithstanding the difference in the style of the introductory and concluding chapters, shows a special resemblance of its contents to those of the *Kāṭhaka Gṛhyasūtra* and it seems quite likely that the work is only a Vaiṣṇava recast of a text of the *Kāṭhaka* school. Such comparative studies, to a certain extent, support Max Müller's theory that in the post-Vedic times some

ancient works dealing with a variety of subjects were converted into generally binding law codes, either by simply taking them out of their connection with the Śrauta or Gṛhya Sūtras or by adding extra matter. With respect to the conjectures especially connected with the *Mānavadharmaśāstra* the former existence of a *Mānavadharmasūtra*, in prose mixed with verses, may be inferred by the discovery of some quotations in the Dharmasūtras of Vasiṣṭha and others.

But the earlier attempt to connect the *Manusmṛti* with the *sūtrakaraṇa* of the Mānavas did not prove successful. In fact, there is hardly any data for the sweeping generalisation of Max Müller that all genuine Dharmaśāstras are nothing but more modern texts of earlier Sūtra works on *Kuladharma*. One main plank of this theory that the continuous employment of the Śloka metre was unknown in the Sūtra period has now been exploded. The recovery of the writings of the so-called Mānavas has not furnished any fact in support of the supposed connection. Rather it has raised difficulties, as it appears that the doctrines of the *Mānavagṛhyasūtra* differ very considerably from those of the *Mānavadharmaśāstra*.[10] It was held by Jolly and Bradke, in favour of the hypothesis of Max Müller, that a close affinity existed between the *Viṣṇusmṛti* and the *Manusmṛti*, as was found between the *Kāṭhaka* and *Mānava* Gṛhyasūtras and between the *Kāṭhaka* and *Mānava* Saṃhitās. Hence the Vedic original of the *Manusmṛti* may be supposed to have belonged to the Mānava school.[11] But this argument has become much weakened as Bradke himself has pointed out that the *Viṣṇusmṛti* is not the original *Kāṭhaka* Dharmasūtra which suggests that just as the *Viṣṇusmṛti* is not a recast of the *Kāṭhakadharmasūtra* so also the *Manusmṛti* cannot be the recast of the *Mānavadharmasūtra*. But the controversy did not stop here. Many more arguments were put forward by the supporters and opponents of Max Müller's theory to prove or disprove the former existence of a *Mānvadharmasūtra* as the precursor of the metrical *Manusmṛti*, as we shall see later.

A fitting introduction to *Manusmṛti*, especially meant for

Western readers was provided in 1875 by Monier Williams.[12] According to him, although standing in a manner at the head of post-Vedic literature, it is connected with the Sūtras. Probably the compilation we now possess is an irregular compendium of rules and maxims by different authors, which existed unwritten for a long period of time and were handed down orally. Monier Williams, however, was not very much interested in theoretical stratification of the text. He assigned the date round about the 5th century B.C. to the text. In support of this dating he says that the gods mentioned in the *Manusmṛti* are chiefly Vedic and the fourfold caste system is that of the *puruṣasūkta*. There is no direct allusion to Buddhism, though many of Manu's precepts are decidedly Buddhistic having frequent parallels in the *Dhammapada*. Nor there is any allusion to Satī, nor to the worship of Viṣṇu and Śiva which from a statement of Megasthenes may be inferred to have prevailed in India soon after Alexander's invasion. Nor is there any mention of the stories of the *Mahābhārata* and *Rāmāyaṇa*. At the same time the former epic often contains verses identical with those of Manu. These are probably either taken from Manu or derived from a common source.[13] Monier Williams analysed and arranged in a connected manner of the contents of the *Manusmṛti* offering prose translations of selected passages and pointing out in a general way the characteristic features of (i) its sacred knowledge and religion, (ii) its philosophy, (iii) its *ācāra* or social rules and caste organisation, (iv) its *vyavahāra* or criminal and civil laws and rules of government, (v) its system of *prāyaścitta* or penance and (vi) its system of *karmaphala* or future recompenses of acts done in this life. He also gave specimens of the most striking passages under the last four heads in a metrical English translation.

The next important work was the English translation of *Manusmṛti* by A.C. Burnell which was edited and completed by E.W. Hopkins in 1884.[14] After Sir William Jones and Haughton, J. Jolly made annotated German translation of some portions of the *Manusmṛti*. A complete Marathi translation of the same

was made by Janardan Vasudev Gurjar which was published from Bombay along with the Sanskrit text in 1887. The first Tamil translation of *Manusmṛti* was made by Ramanujachariyar in 1865, and the second by Gurusamy Mudaliyar in 1896 under the title *Manutarma Cattiram.* Burnell made in his translation and interpretation little use of Rāghavānanda, more of Medhātithi and most of Kulluka. All the variant readings quoted by Loiseleur in the notes to his edition of 1830 - readings gathered from a number of manuscripts - were compared with what was found by Burnell in his own manuscripts and that is why this volume has a greater historical importance. In a valuable and thought-provoking introduction (which the author could not complete and the editor Hopkins did not elaborate further) various problems regarding the text have been outlined and discussed. According to Burnell, the *Manusmṛti* is no original treatise but a versified recension of an older treatise in prose. He believes with Max Müller that it is to be traced back to a Sūtra work belonging to the Mānavas, one of the six subdivisions of the *Maitrayanīya* School of the Black *Yajurveda.* He holds that although the *Mānavadharmasūtra* has not yet been recovered and is probably lost forever, there can be little doubt that it was turned into verse which later became the actual *Manusmṛti.* He confirms the views of Whitney[15] that

> Out of the last two (*Gṛhya* and *Dharmasūtra*) especially the last, come by natural development the law books (*Dharmaśāstra)* which make a conspicuous figure in the later literature: the oldest and most noted of them being that called by the name of Manu (an outgrowth, it is believed of the Mānava Vedic school); to which are added that of Yājñavalkya and many others.[16]

According to Burnell, the *Manusmṛti* is later than the Sūtra period and this conclusion furnishes the first element to fix the date of the text. Medhātithi lived about A.D. 1000 and this

circumtance fixes the lowest possible date at about A.D. 500. The striking fact is that it is in a very simple and modern language and in *śloka* verse. The most modern form of compound words are freely used.[17] Compared with the older Dharmasūtras, two important additions are seen at once in the text. The first and twelfth chapters form an explanatory philosophical framework to the whole. The seventh chapter is an abstract of the polity and conduct of life and affairs for kings, such as is found in the *Rājadharma* section of the *Mahābhārata.* Such matter is entirely foreign to the original Dharmasūtras. The philosophical additions are also very characteristic. The dialogue introducing the substantial matter is quite in the style of the *Purāṇas.* From this, Burnell has come to the conclusion that the text, as it is, was compiled between the first and fifth centuries A.D. and that it is a popular work intended for kings and similar persons and was not originally intended for the use of the Brāhmaṇas. He also holds that the final form of the text was rendered about A.D. 500 under the Cālukya sovereign Pulakeśī (the Cālukyas are said to belong to the Mānava Gotra) and that the text belongs to an outgrowth of the old Brahmanical literature which was intended for the benefit of the kings of the Deccan and South India where the Brahmanical civilization had begun to extend itself. The text belongs to the second class of law books: that is to say to the books which were intended to popularise the earlier *Dharmaśāstras,* and for practical use in tribunals. The most superficial examination of the text proves at once that the Vedic literature in its entirety, even down to a late Sūtra, as well as later developments, were known to the compiler. Burnell's approach towards *Manusmṛti* was to a certain extent biased, especially when he says,

> We meet with so much that it is inhuman, and such a hideous and cynical contempt for the human body that we are tempted to believe that these books are the insane ideal of crazy fanatics or the foolish reveries of besotted ascetics.[18]

A similar contemptuous approach, as we shall see later, was maintained by E.W. Hopkins, who was not only associated with this work of Burnell but also made independent studies on *Manusmṛti*.[19]

Two new and critical editions of *Manusmṛti* appeared in 1886 and 1887 respectively. The first was by Rao Saheb V.N. Mandlik, which was published from Bombay, and second was by J. Jolly which was published from London. But the most important work, which is as yet unsurpassed, though not actually free from historical criticism was its English rendering with a detailed and critical introduction and extracts from seven commentaries by G. Bühler. It was published in 1886 in the *Sacred Books of the East* series.[20] The views of Bühler therefore requires to be treated in some greater detail. According to him, though the texts of the Dharmasūtras have not always been preserved in perfect purity, they have evidently retained their original character. They do not pretend anything more than compositions of ordinary mortals based on the teaching of the Vedas. They are manuals, written by the teachers of the Vedic schools for the guidance of their pupils. At first they were held to be authoritative in restricted circles and they were later acknowledged as sources of the sacred law applicable to all. But the metrical Smṛtis on the other hand are surrounded by clearly fictitious traditions and by mythological legends which either may have grown up spontaneously or may have been fabricated intentionally in order to show that these works possess divine authority and hence have a claim to implicit obedience on the part of all. Thus in the *Manusmṛti*, it is narrated how the great sages approached Manu, the descendent of the self-existent Brahman, and asked him to explain the sacred law. Agreeing to their request, he taught the institute to the ten sages, whom he created in the beginning and then transferred the work of expounding to Bhṛgu, one of his ten mind-born sons.

In the *Manusmṛti* itself Bhṛgu is often named as narrator; sometimes Manu is specially mentioned as author of certain rules. According to Govindarāja's interpretation some pupils

of Bhṛgu recited the work which had descended through an unbroken line of teachers. This indicates, according to Bühler, a triple exordia instead of a double one, and our *Manusmṛti* does not contain the original words of Bhṛgu, but a recension of his recension, such as handed down among his pupils. Medhātithi and Govindarāja held that Manu was a particular individual well versed in the Vedas, while Kulluka, though he admitted the human character of his Śāstra, declared Manu to be a manifestation of the supreme soul. On the question, how the Smṛti can be called the *Mānavadharmaśāstra*, Medhātithi says (1) that Brahman produced multiple of injunctions while the work itself was composed by Manu and (2) that even if it was composed by Brahman it goes by Manu's name as is the case with the Ganges (born in heaven and known as Haimavatī). Narada and Kulluka say that it was Brahman's or Prajāpati's work abridged by Manu. According to Bühler Medhātithi's and Kulluka's assumption that our *Manusmṛti* is meant in the passages of the Vedic texts, which refer to Manu requires very strong proof, as the language and part of his doctrine by no means agree with those of Vedic times. Even the Puranic and Smṛti reference to Manu prove the existence of the general belief that Manu was the first law giver of India, their evidences are of little use because their antiquity is doubtful and several recensions of Manu's laws are admitted.

Bühler supports and supplements the view of Max Müller that the *Manusmṛti* is based on a Dharmasūtra of the Mānavas. According to him the conflicting decisions on certain points of the rituals and of the law as recorded in our *Manusmṛti* may refer to actual lawbooks which preceded the text. Three passages allude to their existence in general terms. The first occurs in the definition of the Śruti and Smṛti; by the former (revelation) is meant the Veda, and by the later, tradition, the institutes of the sacred law.[21] The second occurs in the text[22] where a Dharmapāṭhaka (one who recites the institutes of sacred law) is named among the members of a *pariṣad* or assembly entitled to decide difficult points of law. The third

passage is perfectly explicit, as the word Dharmaśāstra is used in its plural.[23] Here the existence of many earlier lawbooks is plainly acknowledged. The character of the institutes of the sacred law known to the author of our *Manusmṛti* may be inferred from some other passages which reveal an acquintance with the *Aṅgas* of the Veda. Further in the name of the *Aṅgas* the *Kalpa* literature finds clearcut mention.[24] The *Kalpa* denotes collectively those Sūtras of the Vedic school which teach the performance of the Śrauta sacrifices. If according to the Hindu tradition all Sūtrakaraṇas formerly possessed Dharmasūtras and in some existing Kalpas, the Dharmasūtras are closely connected with the Śrautasūtras, it becomes exceedingly probable that our *Mānavadharmaśāstra* is later than some of the *Dharmasūtras*. This conclusion is further corroborated by those passages of the *Manusmṛti*, where the author quotes the opinions of the individual predecessors.[25] Bühler also says that, there are passages in the *Vasiṣṭha Dharmasūtra*[26] which prove the former existence of a *Mānavadharmasūtra* and that the *Śāṇkhyāyana Gṛhyasūtra* has a faint reference to the *Mānavadharmasūtra*. More important is the evidence of the *Kāmandakīya Nītisāra* in which the opinions of the Mānavāḥ occur twice and of Manu once. In one case the doctrine attributed to the Mānavāḥ agrees with the teachings of our *Manusmṛti*. The view of Jolly and Bradke that there is no special agreement between the *Manusmṛti* and the *Mānavagṛhyasūtra* has not been rejected by Bühler but he says that it is possible to adduce some more passages not mentioned by the aforesaid scholars in which the *Gṛhyasūtra* shows a special affinity with the Smṛti. In conclusion Bühler mentions a certain agreement between the *Maitrāyana-Brahmaṇopaniṣad* and the *Manusmṛti* and holds that this may also point to a connection of the *Manusmṛti* and of its original with the Mānava school. These arguments of Bühler have been severely criticised by some Indian scholars - especially by Ganganath Jha and P.V. Kane - as we shall see later.

Next Bühler has raised four important questions: what

circumstances led to the substitution of a universally binding *Mānavadharmaśāstra* for the manual of the Vedic school? Why was so prominent a position allotted to the remodelled *Smṛti*? How was the conversion effected? When did it probably take place? As regards the first question Bühler thinks that the *Mānavadharmasūtra* was converted into a metrical Smṛti by a special school of legal experts. The Vedic schools first systematised the six sciences (the Vedāṅgas) for the sake of specializations. He refers to Patañjali's *Mahābhāṣya* which hints that at the time of its composition the Dharma was taught not only in the Vedic, but also in special schools. Possibly, the word Dharmaśāstra, which occurs occasionally in his Bhāṣya[27] may also point to manuals studied by the special schools. The special law schools produced the first and the most ancient division of the secondary Smṛtis on the basis of older Dharmasūtras, and one among these schools, which though cannot be further specified, turned the *Mānavadharmasūtra* into our *Manusmṛti*.[28] Bühler disagreed with the view of Hopkins that the adherents of the Vedic Mānava school had undertaken the revision of their *Dharmasūtra*.[29] In that case they would not have forgotten to mention such ceremonies as those which according to their *Gṛhyasūtra* must be performed on beginning the study of particular portions of thier *Saṃhitā*, and they would have allowed *mantras* belonging to the *Maitrāyani -śākhā* to stand. The absence of all distinctive marks of any Vedic school in our *Manusmṛti* can only be explained on the hypothesis that it was remodelled by persons for whom minute details had no interest and who concentrated their attention on those rules which they considered essential for all.

The second question raised by Bühler was concerned with the reasons which led the special law schools to select just the *Mānavadharmaśāstra* among the large number of similar works. According to Bühler the reason for this selection and the conversion of it into the metrical *Manusmṛti* was the name of Manu and the myths which clustered round this name. In

Vedic mythology, Manu is the eponymous of the human race. He is the progenitor of mankind and is therefore naturally considered as the founder of social and moral order, as a ruler of men, and as a Ṛṣi to whom sacred texts were revealed. The Manu legends are sufficient to show why the special law schools should have directed their attention to the *Mānavadharmaśāstra* and chose that in preference to other similar works. As soon as the identification of the author of the *Mānavadharmaśāstra* with the father of mankind was made, the *Manusmṛti* naturally obtained a particularly high position and was accepted as the paramount authority on the sacred law. Moreover the Vedic legends contain the origins of the seemingly contradictory statements of the Smṛti regarding Manu. When he is represented there as a descendent of the self-existent Brahman and a Prajāpati who takes a prominent part in the creation or as a Ṛṣi and as a king of the remotest antiquity it implies that the codes of Manu should have a divine sanction. The Manu mythology did not even cease to take various forms even in the Epico-Puranic period.

The third problem how the conversion of the *Mānavadharmasūtra* into our *Manusmṛti* was effected involves, according to Bühler, three questions : (1) Which portions of our *Manusmṛti* are ancient and which are later additions? (2) Whence have the additions been derived? (3) Whether they have been added at one time or successively? According to Bühler, in the attempts to distinguish between the old and the modern elements in our *Manusmṛti* we must be guided by the analogies which the other existing *Dharmasūtras* furnish. From this point of view he held that the whole first chapter must be considered to be a later addition. The chapters II - VI seem to represent with tolerable faithfulness, the contents of the corresponding sections of the anticipated *Mānavadharmasūtra*. Very different is the case of the next three chapters (VII - IX) which treat the duties of a king and of civil and criminal law. These sections probably bear only a faint resemblance to the corresponding portions of the original work. But in all these

chapters a considerable number of verses belong to a later period. The rules on times of distress given in the tenth chapter differs considerably from those of the Dharmasūtras, as they include also the theory of descent of the mixed castes. The eleventh chapter is again, like chapters II-VI, in all probability a faithful representative of the corresponding portion of the *Mānavadharmasūtra*. The XIIth chapter according to Bühler is certainly due to the author of the metrical version. Its contents are partly foreign to the *Dharmasūtras* and partly repetitions. As to the second question whence this large amount of additional matter has been taken, Bühler holds that a clue to the solution of this problem is furnished by the peculiar relation of the *Manusmṛti* to the *Mahābhārata*. The relative position of the two works might induce to assume with Rao Sahib V.N. Mandlik[30] that the *Mahābhārata* had a direct influence on the final redaction of the *Manusmṛti* and that the author of the latter appropriated from the former large number of identical verses which in the *Mahābhārata* are not ascribed to Manu. Bühler also supports the view of Hopkins that the materials on which both works are based were not treatises on law and philosophy but the floating proverbial wisdom of the philosophical and legal schools which already existed in metrical form. Thus the question whence the editor of our *Manusmṛti* took his additional material agrees very closely with Hopkins's hypothesis that the law book is a conglomorate of the *Mānavadharmasūtra* and of the floating sayings attributed to Manu, the father of mankind.

The answer to the next question, whether the conversion of the *Mānavadharmasūtra* was effected at one time or by degrees and whether Bhṛgu's recension has to be considered as the immediate offspring or as a remoter descendent of the Sūtra, according to Bühler, depends on two circumstances. First, it is a common habit of Indian authors to place conflicting opinions, supported by authorities of equal weight side by side and to allow an option, or to mention time-honoured rules, legal customs and social institutions, and afterwards to disap-

prove of them; and secondly, as our *Manusmṛti* is in any case a recast of an earlier Sūtra that fact alone is sufficient to account for contradictions. As regards the second argument, the assertion of the *Nāradā-smṛti*[31] that Manu composed a *Dharmaśāstra* in 100,000 verses which was successively reduced by Nārada to 12000, by Mārkaṇḍeya to 8000 and by Bhṛgu's son Sumati to 4000 verses might be important for the history of Manu's lawbook. Abridgement of larger works are in literature as common as expansion of shorter ones. It is certainly not true that Nārada's version of Manu's laws is more ancient than that of Bhṛgu. Against the genuineness of Narāda's story we may also adduce the Pauranic statement according to which Manu's laws were remodelled first by Bhṛgu, next by Nārada, next by Bṛhaspati and next by Aṅgiras.[32] While there is no proof for the opinion that the modern portions of the *Manusmṛti* have been gradually added one to the other, or that the present text is one of the last links in a long chain of metrical recensions, there are several points which tend to show that our *Manusmṛti* is one of the first attempts at remodelling a *Dharmasūtra.* According to Bühler, *Bhṛgu's* Saṃhitā was the first and most ancient recast of a Dharmaśāstra attributed to Manu. This *Bhṛgu samhita* certainly existed in the 2nd century A.D. and seems to have been composed between that date and the 2nd century B.C.

Bühler also has made an analytical discussion on the commentaries on *Manusmṛti.* Among the commentaries, he used those of Medhātithi, Govindarāja, Sarvajñanārāyaṇa, Kullukabhaṭṭa, Raghavānanda and Nandanācārya as well as an anonymous *tippana* contained in a Kashmir manuscript of the *Manusmṛti.* Regarding the *Manubhāṣya* of Medhātithi, Bühler says that it is not merely a gloss which paraphrases every word of the text, but its aim is to show the general sense of Manu's dicta to elucidate all really difficult passages and to settle all doubtful points by a full discussion of the various possible interpretations and of the opinions, advanced by others. Medhātithi displays a great amount of learning, carefully uses

a number of more ancient commentaries and demonstrates a full acquaintance with the Vedic literature, grammar, Mīmāṃsā, Dharmasūtras and other Smṛtis, Vedānta and the *Mahābhārata.* He avoids undue quotations, enhances the value of his explanations by illustrating Manu's rule from instances taking from everyday life and takes a much more independent position towards Manu than the other commentators. But his weakness is that he cannot decide between conflicting interpretations and very often vacillates for which he is criticised by Kulluka. Next, after the *Manubhāṣya,* but probably at a considerable interval, followed the *Manuṭīkā* of Govindarāja. It is very concise, and in the main an abstract of Medhātithi's *bhāṣya.* Govindarāja appropriates whatever seems to him most valuable from Medhātithi's *bhāṣya* and discards the greater number of his predecessors' optional explanations. He adds explanation of those words on which Medhātithi does not comment and sometimes puts forward opinions not traceable in the earlier works. Sarvajñanārāyaṇa's *Manvarthavivṛti* or *Manvarthanibandha* was composed in the 14th century A.D. It confines itself only to the elucidation of selected difficult passages and words, written with the avowed intention of undoing the works of his predecessors. The well known *Manvarthamuktāvalī* of Kullukabhaṭṭa, was composed in the 15th century A.D. According to Bühler, it is little more than an improved edition of Govindarāja's *Manuṭīkā.* Kulluka has copied very large portions of the earlier works, sometimes verbatim and sometimes very insufficient extracts. But in certain cases Kulluka's independent remarks or criticisms of earlier works are useful. The *Manvarthacandrikā* of Rāghavānanda is mostly based on Kulluka's commentary, though the author's exposition of the philosophical portions of the text is mostly independent, interpreted in the line of Vedānta. The *Manuvyākhyāna* of Nandana is a very short commentary which mostly repeats and explains only a few words or phrases of the text.

E.W. Hopkins was for a long time associated with the study

of *Manusmṛti*. His first work on the mutual relations of the four castes according to the *Manusmṛti* was published in 1881. Hopkins also held that the *Manusmṛti* was a metrical recast of an earlier *Mānavadharmasūtra*. He completed Burnell's unfinished translation of the *Manusmṛti* and inserted some of his own views in the former's introduction to his work. In 1891 he published a lengthy article 'Professed Quotations from Manu found in the *Mahābhārata*'[33] which requires a detailed review in the present context. It should be remembered that the connection existing between the *Manusmṛti* and the *Mahābhārata* and the importance of the latter for the history of the institutes of Manu had long been recognised. Weber[34] pointed out that the *Mahābhārata* contains not only a number of quotations from Manu, some of which are found either with or without variations in the existing Smṛti while others are not traceable, but also a considerable number of verses, not attributed to Manu. He inferred from these verses that the existing *Manusmṛti* could not have been extant in its present shape even at the period to which the later portions of the *Mahābhārata* belonged. Another conclusion, based on the agreement of numerous *ślokas*, especially in the twelfth and thirteenth Parvans of the great epic, with verses of the *Manusmṛti* was drawn by Rao Sahib V.N. Mandlik[35] that the latter was to a large extent based on the former. According to Hopkins their number is thirty-three among which seventeen are traceable, five being verbal quotations, the rest agreeing in doctrine only. His explanation for the untraceable quotations is not that they have been taken from an older recension of the *Manusmṛti*, but that a floating mass of unwritten sayings of Manu existed, some of which were incorporated with Dharmasūtra of the Mānavas in its revisions, while others were not. He also noticed that our *Manusmṛti* contains many verses which occur also in the *Mahābhārata* without being attributed to Manu as well as some which are ascribed to other authorities. According to Hopkins, the references of Manu's verses are hardly found in the earlier part of the epic. However, they are mostly available in the

didactic epic, which must be a later addition. Manu's verses are not put into the code all at a same time; most of them are adopted at a later stage and for this reason the citations are not generally found in the text. The thirteenth book has eleven citations of which ten agree with the statement of the present code while the other books of the epic agree only in one-third with the present text. He refutes Bühler's argument that the authors of some portions of epic knew the existence of a *Mānavadharmaśāstra.* But he says that it is the very character of the epic that it contains ancient legends from all sources. The pseudo-epic, i.e., Anuśāsana Parvan which is supposed to refer to a *Mānavadharmaśāstra,* is not a Śāstra but a Sūtra. His conclusion is that the extant *Manusmṛti* is distinctly earlier than the later epic but later than its earlier portions.

The next important work on *Manusmṛti* was by J. Jolly which was published in 1896 as the first part of the Encyclopaedia of Indo-Aryan Research.[36] Jolly also holds that the *Manusmṛti* was related to a Dharmasūtra of the Mānava school, but he is not absolutely free from doubt. He also says that the *Manusmṛti* marked some type of specialization. How early the authority of this work spread over the whole of India is best shown by the commentaries composed in various parts of the country. It cannot also be doubted that the present *Manusmṛti* is essentially the same as it was thousand years ago. Manu is heavily drawn upon by later lawgivers like Bṛhaspati and Nārada. The Burmese and Japanese law books are no less dependent on *Manusmṛti.* Kumārila is more important as a witness because the ancient commentary often cited by him frequently refers to our *Manusmṛti.* The inscriptions too corroborate this, at least in so far as they mention Manu at the head of the teachers of law. In this connection may be mentioned a Valabhi inscription of the 6th century A.D. The relation between the *Manusmṛti* and the *Mahābhārata* has also been discussed by Jolly who holds that the *Mahābhārata* represents an older state of things and that their agreement cannot be the result of borrowing but goes back to a common

source. Even the Dharmasūtras are full of verses which are again seen in Manu. There might have been a large mass of memorial verses in existence from an early date, a section of which was culminated in the establishment of sacred laws. The theory that the transition from the Sūtra form to the Śloka form was connected and coeval with the transition of the sacred law from the Vedic Caraṇas to special schools of Dharma has a certain amount of probability. The time of the origin of our *Manusmṛti* and the *Mahābhārata* is approximately the same. As the *Mahābhārata* at the time of its revision was considerably extended in view of the advancement of Brahmanism so the Dharmasūtras too received a great deal of accretions in conformity with changes in socio-religious ideals. Since the Sūtra works were made for committing to memory, they had to be as concise as possible. Thus in these texts the laws were treated in a stepmotherly fashion. This accounts for the emergence of elaborate *Dharmaśāstras,* not meant for simple memorizing, but for guiding the practical aspects of life. As in its contents, so also in the arrangement of the subject matter, the *Manusmṛti* exhibits a remarkable advance on the Dharmasūtras. The eighteen titles of law and their classifications are based on actual life. Jolly also has dealt with the parallelisms between the *Manusmṛti* and the *Mānavaśrāddhakalpa,* compared the Gṛhyasūtra and Śrautasūtra of the Mānavas and made cautious remarks in regard to the uncertainty about Manu's relation with the so-called Mānava school. According to him the evidences yield only a certain degree of probability to the supposed relationship between the *Manusmṛti* and the Vedic Mānavas and hence it is perhaps more advisable to reserve the final decision on this question till the discovery of decisive manuscript materials.

So long we were discussing the views of the Western scholars. Indian scholars did not lag behind in critical and thought-provoking study in the *Manusmṛti.* We have already had the occasion to refer to the English rendering of the *Manusmṛti* by Tarachand Chakravarti which was published

during the fifties of the 19th century. A very handy volume of English rendering was done by M.N. Dutt which was published in 1908. It was done in a very lucid language intelligible even to the lay readers with critical notes and comments. Besides the technical terms which have been carefully explained in the foot notes, extracts from the commentaries have been supplied, though Kulluka seemed to be his special favourite. Dutt was inspired by the national awakening of his time and he believed that a careful study of the *Manusmṛti* is

> "fraught with immense value and profit not only to the students and practitioners of law but to the general readers as well. They will, by such a study, be not only able to form an estimate of life and conduct, so glorious and eminent in themselves, of the ancient Hindus, but will also be able to regulate their own conduct in the same light and on the same line with such healthy innovation as the environment under which they now live so urgent requires. True regeneration of the Hindus depends mainly upon the regulation of their life and conduct upon national lines. And nowehere can they find greater light and help in forming their national life anew that in the Saṃhitās."[37]

Dr. Bhagavan Das who made Manu the subject of his lifelong study and preached his doctrines all over the world with a missionary zeal in his *Science of Social Organisation or the Laws of Manu in the Light of Ātmavidyā* (2 vols. 1910)[38] tried to show that a time-befitting re-interpretation of Manu would be able to serve as a guide to solve the problems of modern times. According to him the *Manusmṛti* lays down the right principles of a healthy and all-comprehending social organisation in which

> individualism and socialism are duly combined and balanced, the life of the individual and the life of society as a whole are both organised and interwoven as warf and

> woof, to subserve clearly visualised aims of life diligently seeking to ensure general welfare, deliberately planned to provide spiritual as well as material bread in appropriate quantity and measure to all and each.

K. Sundararama Aiyar in his *Dharma and Life* (2 Vols. 1924) has also tried to vindicate the modernity of Manu's ideals and assert that much of the animus against *Manusmṛti* in our day is due to imperfect comprehension of its real teachings. But there were Manuvilifiers as there were Manuphiles. B.R. Ambedkar, for example, held that the *Manusmṛti* was the most reactionary legal text which directed melted lead to be poured in the ears of the Śūdras, decried their aspirations, impaired their self-respect and perpetuated their social, religious and political slavery. On December 25, 1927 after adopting a resolution at a conference held at Mahad, Ambedkar made a bonfire of the *Manusmṛti* as a protest against the agelong torture and discrimination of the backwards inflicted by the members of the upper castes. Commenting on this event his biographer wrote:

> December 25, 1927 is therefore a red-letter day in the annals of India, as it was on this day that Ambedkar burnt the old Smṛti and demanded a new one to reshape the Hindu code governing the life of so vast a people. Mahad thus became the Wittenberg of India.[39]

The biggest work on *Manusmṛti* was done by M.M. Ganganath Jha in five volumes, containing English translation and extensive expository and comparative notes, which was published between 1922 and 1929.[40] According to Jha, it has been a fashion with all writers on *Manusmṛti* to devote several pages to the discussion of the claim "set up by its author to be the first legislator". Such attempts are like "beating the air" because the *Manusmṛti* as known to us is not he work of Manu himself, but "Bhṛgu's version of the institues of the sacred laws

proclaimed by Manu". Thus we have hardly any justification for fastening upon Manu the merits and demerits that we discover in a reflected version of his work. As such no Hindu who views the question of the origin of *Manusmṛti* with the 'eye of faith' need be perturbed by the reviews that have been written for proving the indebtedness of the *Manusmṛti* to the *Mānavadharmasūtra* or to other law books that went before the *Smṛti.* As a parallel example, he says that Sureśvara in his great *Vārtika* is supposed to be expounding the teachings that he received from Śaṅkara. But this does not mean that the *Vārtika* is a verbatim report of the lectures delivered by the master to his favourite pupil. According to Jha, Jaimini formulated in his Sūtra (I.1.2.) the three propositions that (1) what is good for man can be learnt from the Veda (2) it can be learnt from the Veda only and (3) whatever the Veda says must be true. The supreme authority of the Veda is based upon its own eternal and immutable character; but the Veda, at the same time, bears signs of being distinctly progressive - taking into account the varying conditions of time and space. This same progressive spirit and desire for adapting the law to the changing conditions of life gave rise to the *Smṛti.* It cannot, however, be denied that the Smṛtis mark the second stage in the development of Hindu law. But they were accepted as having authoritative character, when the people were convinced that these texts contained nothing new; they only put into simple and clearer language what was already contained in the Veda.

The next significant contribution to the study of *Manusmṛti* is an article entitled 'The Age of Manusaṃhitā' by B.K. Ghosh which was published in 1927.[41] Various theories were formulated regarding the age of the *Manusmṛti,* some of which have been stated earlier. Max Müller wanted to bring it down to the 4th century A.D. Bühler however arrived at a different conclusion and formulated a rather too wide limit of the age of *Manusmṛti,* between the 2nd century B.C. and 2nd century A.D. K.P. Jayaswal dated it around 150 B.C. According to B.K. Ghosh, a careful study of the quotations from the *Manusmṛti* in

other works should show that the actual date of *Manusmṛti* lies rather beyond the arbitrary barriers of time limit. From two considerations, each exaggarated to an unreasonable degree, Manu has been denied his due. (1) A large mass of popular parables constituting the 'Spruchweisheit' of ancient India has been bodily incorporated into the *Manusmṛti* and therefore many of the verses in the quotations might really have been taken from this source and not necessarily from the *Manusmṛti* itself. This hypothesis is more or less correct : (2) The other consideration is that our *Manusmṛti* was formerly composed in Sūtras, so that many of the quotations which cannot now be traced in the extant text of the *Manusmṛti* may refer to the earlier Sūtra work attributed to the Mānava school, a view which we have already had the occasion to deal with. According to B.K. Ghosh we have as yet no proof of the existence of a *Mānavadharmasūtra*, which, when versified became the *Mānavadharmaśāstra*. He says that one step further can be reached and it may be proved that a metrical *Manusmṛti* was in existence before 300 B.C., at least before the *Vasiṣṭha* and *Baudhayāna* Dharmasūtras were composed. He refers to a verse found in both *Rāmāyaṇa* IV. 18.38 and *Baudhāyana* II.1.16 - a fact which leaves no doubt that both the authors concerned are in this case directly quoting Manu independently of each other. It is interesting to note that the first half of this verse in the *Rāmāyaṇa* is identical with the first half of the verse as found in Manu VIII. 316 while the 2nd half is somewhat different. Baudhāyana on the other hand has the second half in common with Manu while the first half is somewhat different. This, Ghosh thinks, can be explained only on the hypothesis that both *Rāmāyaṇa* and Baudhāyana have drawn upon *Manusmṛti* about the same time and each wrought minor changes in the verse in its own way. *Rāmāyaṇa* VI. 18.30 expressly says that Manu had proclaimed the following two verses (*ślokas*). This shows that the author of the *Rāmāyaṇa* knew no Sūtra work of the Mānava school but rather a metrical work of the same. Other quotations from Manu in works of a

quite different nature have an important bearing on this question. Manu has been quoted in works of the Śikṣā category, e.g., the *Māṇḍukī Śikṣā* etc. Ghosh also says that the work of the Mānava school referred to by Kauṭilya was not the hypothetical *Mānavadharmasūtra* but quite a different work of the same school (perhaps the *Mānava Arthaśāstra*), though by anonymously quoting two verses (VII. 105; XI. 181) of Manu Kauṭilya betrays his acquaintance with the metrical *Manusmṛti*. According to him the *Manusmṛti* is most popular and universally accepted because is is perhaps the most ancient work of the Smṛti literature and also because at a very early date like that of the *Rāmāyaṇa* it was composed in popular verses agreeable and accessible to the general public, when the law books of the other Vedic Caraṇas were still composed in the unusually stiff prose of the Sūtras and could therefore hardly interest the general public in them.

Among other important works on the *Manusmṛti*, K.P. Jayaswal's Tagore Law Lectures on *Manu* and *Yājñavalkya* (1928) are concerned with the analysis of the jural ideas of the two works. Its contents will be discussed in the seventh chapter of the present volume. The work contains many thought-provoking ideas which the historians should take notice of, though it has been vehemently criticised by P.V. Kane and U.N. Ghoshal. Kewal Motwani's *Manu in Hindu Social Theory* (1934)[42] claims to present Manu's social theory in terms familiar to the students of modern sociology and is in effect an attempt to vindicate its sociological soundness even when judged by western standard. According to him the code of Manu is unique because it is not merely theoretical. It is operative and has remained operative through many centuries. Today it still remains the legal and social background of our oldest functioning culture. The celebrated Vedantist Hinrendranath Dutta in his Bengali work *Manur Varṇāśramadharma* (1942)[43] has raised certain important questions regarding sovereignty, form of government, mutual relation of a people, relation between the state and an indi-

vidual, social stratification, nature of class division, relation between man and woman, marriage, education, relation between workers and their masters, aristocrat and the down-trodden, and rich and poor, the economic infrastructure, conflict between social production and individual appropriation, state control on production and distribution, taxation, interest, shares of profit, etc., and held that Manu's answers to all these questions are more rational and sensible than those of most modern social scientists. He quotes the view of Neitzsche that the *Manusmṛti*

> epitomises the experience, the precautionary measures, and the experimental morality of long ages; it settles things definitely ... To draw up a law book like Manu's is tantamount to granting a people mastership for the future, perfection for the future - the right to aspire to the highest art of life.

K.V. Rangaswami Aiyangar in his *Aspects of the Social and Political System of Manusmṛti* (1949)[44] attempted to reconstruct the sociology of *Manusmṛti* in a more critical way, though his conclusions are sufficiently in agreement with those of the previous authors. According to him the best minds of India have made it for centuries the subject of study and comment so that its light may create illumination for future ages. Not a century has passed without a great commentary on *Manusmṛti* being composed. Today except among those who have made a close study of *Manusmṛti* there is often lack of appreciation of its cardinal importance and wisdom. This is due to several causes, the most important among which is unfamiliarity with the technique of the composition of the Smṛtis and of the habitual form of expression that have passed in India from common life to literary works. The *Manusmṛti* has a plan, unity and order like any carefully composed work of literature. Aiyangar's work consists of six lectures, the first dealing with the supposed rivalry between the Dharmaśāstra and Arthaśāstra

traditions, the second with the problems which the students of *Manusmṛti* confront, the third with the background against which the teachings of Manu and the Hindu social system have to be viewed, the fourth and fifth with the basic ideas of Varṇa and Āśrama and their bearing on social life and the last with the salient features of the political system and ideas described in the *Manusmṛti.* According to Aiyangar, the *Manusmṛti* must be read in its literary context, i.e., along with the work of the class in which it enjoys primacy and authenticity. It is not an isolated work. A great part of it is a restructuring of the material of the Sūtra literature, which forms an adjunct to the Vedic. But Aiyangar's work is not designed as a defense of Manu or of the social and political ideas contained in the *Manusmṛti* or of its claim to rest on a semi-divine authority. He has endeavoured only to present the salient features of the social and political ideas as found in it and of Indian society as understood for centuries by those who drew their inspiration from this source.

The most extensive use of *Manusmṛti* in historical and sociological perspectives was made by P.V. Kane in his multi-volumed *magnum opus.*[45] The first volume was published in 1930 and the last volume in 1962. Owing to this long time gap there was need of a revised version of the first volume, which contained Kane's own views about the *Manusmṛti.* The revised version was published in two parts in 1968. Though in many cases he changed some of his views, his observation on the *Manusmṛti* remained quite unchanged as it was presented in the 1930 edition. In a chapter entitled "Mānavadharmasūtra - Did it exist?" Kane tried to refute the theory put forward by Max Müller, Bühler and others. While dealing with the views of Max Müller we have already referred to Kane's argument that there is nothing to prove that all genuine Dharmaśāstras are modern recasts of the earlier Sūtra works on *Kuladharma.* Even the argument that the continuous employment of the Śloka metre was unknown in the Sūtra period, which was once believed to be valid, is not tenable now-a-days. In favour of Max Müller's theory Bühler has suggested that (i) the *Vasiṣṭha Dharmasūtra*[46] contains four Sūtras which

may be regarded as adopted from the hypothetical *Mānavadharmasūtra*; (ii) there are other quotations in *Vasiṣṭha* attributed to Manu which contradict the present *Manusmṛti* and thus have a bearing on the earlier Sūtra work; (iii) a fragment of Uśanas which quotes an opinion of Manu is in prose Sūtra style; (iv) the *Kāmandakīya Nītisāra*[47] while referring to the Vidyās according to the Mānavas to be studied by a king probably refers to the *Mānavadharmasūtra* and not the *Manusmṛti*. According to Kane, *Vasiṣṭha* IV. 5-8 on which Bühler relies have nothing to do with any hypothetical *Mānavadharmasūtra*. It has also not been reasonable for Bühler to argue that because the *Vasiṣṭha* quotes a Mānava *śloka* which is not in the extant *Manusmṛti*, it must have been taken from an earlier *Mānavadharmasūtra*. His reliance on a fragment of Uśanas which is corrupt is not worthy of consideration. Regarding the Mānavāḥ of Kāmandakī who simply paraphrased Kauṭilya it may be said that the views ascribed to the Mānavas in the said text have some difference with those found in our *Manusmṛti*, Kumārila, Śankara, Viśvarūpa and others have employed Mānavāḥ for *Manusmṛti* and not for any *Mānavadharmasūtra*. The analogy of the works of the schools of Āpastamba and others, so much stressed by Bühler, can furnish no proof. Indian authorities like Kumarila nowhere mentioned the *Mānavadharmasūtra* as studied by the followers of the Black *Yajurveda*, though he mentions Baudhāyana and Āpastamba as studied by them. He places *Manusmṛti* even higher than the *Gautama Dharmasūtra*. According to Kane, existing materials are not sufficient to establish that a *Mānavadharmasūtra* once existed.

A separate big chapter on the nature and contents of the *Manusmṛti* has also been provided in the said volume of Kane. This chapter at first deals with the references to Manu in the Vedic texts, the Epics and Purāṇas and in some important Smṛtis. Then the problem regarding the composition of *Manusmṛti* has been dealt with for a second time with reference to the theories of Bühler and others. A descriptive content of the twelve chapters has been added which has been supple-

mented by reference to the extent of literature known to Manu. Kane also has made a serious objection on Bühler's attempt to refute the claims of Manu to be regarded as the first legislator. Kane is very much critical about the theory of Hopkins, according to which the Manu-verses found in the Manu treatise were simply caught up and drawn from the heresay of the whole Brāhmaṇa world. According to Kane, doctrines utterly at variance with the Mānava treatise are palmed off upon us with "Manu said" doctrines. Hopkins's view that a floating mass of unwritten sayings of Manu existed, some of which were incorporated into the Dharmasūtra of the Mānavas in its revisions has been declared by Kane as uncalled for. According to Kane such views are "baseless and purely subjective remark and wild theories". Regarding "Manu said" (*Manuravravid)* Kane says that since Manu was famed as the lawgiver of ancient times, and since some practices and rules had changed in the course of centuries, later writers wanted changes according to their lights to be recognised but if they had stated them in their own names, little weight would have been attached to them. Therefore they probably hit upon the plan of saying in some cases that the views propounded by them had the authority of Manu.

Kane has made detailed discussion in regard to the age of *Manusmṛti* from external and internal evidence. According to him this question is bound up with other problems, viz., whether there are earlier or later strata of the extant *Manusmṛti*, whether the *Manusmṛti* was recast several times or once only, what relation exists between the *Manusmṛti* and the *Mahābhārata.* By critical analysis of the literary sources which mention *Manusmṛti*, Kane has shown that writers from the 2nd century onwards, if not earlier, looked upon the extant *Manusmṛti* as the most authoritative Smṛti. This position it could not have attained unless several centuries intervened between it and these writers. Therefore it must be presumed that the *Manusmṛti* had attained its present form at least before the 2nd century A.D. The next question whether the *Manusmṛti*

contains earlier and later strata has been viewed by Kane from the position that the original *Manusmṛti* in verse had certain additions made in order to bring it in a line with a change in the general attitude of people on several points. But all these additions must have been made long before the 3rd century A.D. as the quotations from Bṛhaspati and others show. He also has pointed out that the text of *Manusmṛti* is the same with very few exceptions at least from the 6th century onwards as the quotations in the *Tantravārtika* and *Śaṅkarabhāsya* on the *Vedāntasūtra* and the commentaries of Medhātithi and others show. According to Kane whether the *Manusmṛti* has undergone several recasts does not seem likely and the evidence adduced in support of the theory that the *Manusmṛti* suffered several recasts is quite inadequate. The occurence of several conflicting passages, according to him, can be well explained on the theory of a single recast and it has also to be borne in mind that Sanskrit writers down to the most recent times are in the habit of placing side by side conflicting opinions without actually preferring a particular view to others.

It should be noted in this connection that from the middle of the nineteenth century quotations from Manu and their interpretation formed an important aspect of legal literature. It was probably due to the fact that the European legal practitioners, as well as their Indian counterparts, were required to know the basic contents of the Dharmaśastras in general and *Manusmṛti* in particular, and their commentaries, especially for their professional interest. In this connection reference may be made to the works of Thomas Strange (1830), West and Bühler (1867- 69), Sir Gurudas Banerjee (1878), J.D. Mayne (1878) V.N. Mandlik (1880), J. Jolly (1888), G.C. Sarkar (1891), P.N. Sen (1918), K.P. Jayaswal (1928), Radhabinod Pal (1938), N.C. Sengupta (1953), L.Sternbach (1965-67) D.M. Derrett (1968), etc. Likewise the *Manusmṛti* has been extensively used in numerous works on ancient Indian polity, specially important being those authored by K.P. Jayaswal, N.N. Law, U.N. Ghoshal, Beni Prasad, N.C.

Bandyopadhyaya, P.C. Basu, C. Chakravarti, R.K. Mookerji, K.M. Panikkar, K.A. Nilakantha Sastri, C.P. Ramaswami Aiyar, K.V.R. Aiyangar, B.B. Naik, J.J. Anjaria, A.S. Altekar, R.S. Sharma, V.P. Varma, A.K. Sen, B.K. Sarkar, D.N. Dutta, C. Drekmeier, J. Spellman etc. A complete list of works on ancient Indian polity in which Manu's *rājadharma* has been critically interpreted from various viewpoints is given in the sixth chapter of this volume which deals with the political conceptualizations in the *Manusmṛti.* Similarly Manu's views on society and economy, religion and philosophy, customs and rituals have been critically examined, interpreted and evaluated in many works. These along with their contents have been referred to under different chapters in the present work.

Studies and researches on the *Manusmṛti,* including publications of new critical editions and fresh translations, did not cease to continue in the post-Kane period. A. Jha's *Essentials of Mānavadharmaśāstra* (1950) is a general treatment of Manu in an historical perspective. N.V.Banerjee's *Studies in the Dharmaśāstra of Manu* (1980) also belongs to the category in which the historical analyses and interpretations predominate. Among works dealing with the special aspects of the *Manusmṛti* pertaining both to form and content, mention may be made of M.D. Paradkar's *Similes in the Manusmṛti* (1960), R.M. Das's *Women in Manu and His Seven Commentaries* (1962). C. Tiwari's *Śūdras in Manu* (1963), M. Achyuthan's, *Educational Practices in Manu, Pāṇini and Kauṭilya* (1975), R.S. Vaidyanatha Ayyar's *Manu's Land and Trade Laws* (1876), R.N. Sharma's *Ancient India according to Manu* (1980), etc. These titles are self-explanatory in which Manu's views on different aspects of social, economic and cultural life have been carefully collected and examined in the light of other textual and allied evidences. Other works such as R.S. Betai's *A Reconstruction of the Original Interpretation of the Manusmṛti* (1970), M.V. Patwardhan's *Manusmṛti: The Ideal Democratic Republic of Manu* (1968) and *Manuvāda or the Hindu Socialistic Democracy* (1973), N.N. Banerjee's *Manu and Modern Times* (1975) etc., have an

idealistic perspective. There are also a few comparative studies such as J.P. Suda's *Manu, Marx and Gandhi* (1967), K.R.R. Sastry's *Manu and Tiruvalluvar, A Comparative Study* (1973), T.M. Manickam's *Dharma according to Manu and Moses* (1977) and so forth. Other works are mentioned in the bibliography.

A few new editions of the *Manusmṛti* should also be mentioned in this connection. K. Motwani brought out a new edition of the text in 1959 under the title *Manu Dharma Śāstra.* Jayantakrishna Harikrishna Dave published a critical edition of the *Manusmṛti* (1972) in five volumes with the commentaries of Medhātithi, Sarvajñanārāyaṇa, Kulluka, Rāghavānanda, Nandana, Rāmacandra, Maṇirāma, Govindarāja and Bharuci. This project was sponsored by the Bharatiya Vidya Bhawan. In Mandlik's edition, as we have seen above, there were six commentaries, namely, those of Medhātithi, Sarvajñanārāyaṇa, Kulluka, Raghavānanda, Nandana and Rāmacandra. In his third volume Mandlik edited the commentary of Govindarāja. Two other editions of the *Manusmṛti* also deserve mention, one by L. Sternbach (1974) and the other by N. Kurundakara (1983). A Russian translation of the *Manusmṛti* made by F.F. Il'in came out from Moscow in 1960. It should be mentioned in this connection that the first Russian translation of the *Manusmṛti* was made by S.D. Elamanovich which came out from St. Petersburg in 1913. J.D.M. Derrett's *Manuśāstra-vivaraṇa* (1975) is a translation of the text in two volumes containing as well Bhāruci's commentary (on Books 6-12). According to Derrett, the *Manusmṛti* is 'one of the world's premier compositions in ancient law, more valuable in every sense than Hammurabi and able to hold its own comparison to the covenant and priestly codes of Moses'.

The latest important publication is *The Laws of Manu* (1991) by Wendy Doniger (O'Flaherty) and Brian K. Smith. It is a translation of the text with an introduction and notes. The introductory portion is divided into three parts. The first part attempts to situate the text in Indian religious and social history and delineate its sources and its subsequent impact. It

also seeks to demonstrate the historical origin of a tension between what may be regarded as mutually contradictory world- views in the work. This part deals with the importance of the *Manusmṛti*, the history of the text in Europe, with special reference to the British view point and Neitzsche's extraordinary interpretation, the Vedic background, revaluation of all values and the authority of the Veda on Manu. The second part deals with the structure and meaning of the text emphasising on the coherence of Manu's law in extremity, contradictions and the dichotomy of idea and reality. The third part of the introduction explains the approach to the text taken in this new translation, an approach based on the assumption that the text presents a coherent sequence of logically integrated thoughts. It says that there are two major problems with Bühler's translation. It is unreadable in part because English was not the native language of Bühler, in part because he was using an impossible system of transliteration, and in part because in his laudable desire to be accurate he wrote 'brutal translatorese'. Moreover, Bühler often translated the commentaries as part of the text. His frequent and highly technical footnotes confused the readers rather than to enlighten them. That is why the present translation is designed both to make the text accessible to a wide, generally educated audience and to offer to more specialised scholars new interpretations of many difficult verses. In Wendy Doniger's own language,

> The beauty of Manu's aphorisms lies in their transparency; the later commentators make them opaque. The beauty of the original text is its openness, the commentaries close it forever. It is this open possibility that I hoped to preserve in this translation. For it is the privilege of orientalist ... to reopen a text that the native commentaries have closed. If we are to give credit to the text itself for being rational and coherent it is our right, as well as our duty, to find out our own rationality and coherence in it. And sometimes we

achieve this over the deadbodies of the commentators who, as was *their* right and duty, found their own rationality and coherence in it, different from our own and, I think, often different from that of the text (*intro*, LXXI).

We have thus had a stock-taking of the major works on the *Manusmṛti*. In conclusion it may be said that the main purpose of the author of *Manusmṛti* was to lay down the infrastructure of an all-embracing Indianness which later became synonymous with Hinduism and the Hindu way of life. It evidently went to his credit to formulate the process through which the whole of this vast subcontinent comprising numerous ethnic, linguistic and religious communities with varying degrees of material, mental and intellectual attainment could come under an organised pronational framework without losing their ethnic and cultural identity. This was possible through the formulation of various institutions - religious, social, political, economic and legal - which were given for the first time a wider theoretical prespective in the *Manusmṛti* and subsequently elaborated by the authors of the Dharma and Artha Śāstras. As V. Raghavan has rightly observed: "If Pāṇini has determined the nature of Sanskrit for all time, Manu has determined Hindu conduct for all time."[48] The role of *Manusmṛti* is thus unique in Indian history covering all its aspects because this particular text has simultaneously served the twofold functions of a receiver and a transmitter. In other words it is a culmination of all the earlier traditions which it had received and the traditions thus conserved and conceptualized in it became the guiding principles of what was subsequently known as the Indian way of life.

NOTES

1. It was published by the East India Company under the title *A Code of Gentoo Law*. A German translation of it appeared from Hamburg in 1778.
2. Actually it was done in 1792 but was published in 1794 shortly after

his demise. Prior to Jones, Charles Wilkins attempted to translate the *Manusmṛti* but after some initial endeavour he abandoned the idea of translating Manu. A German translation of Sir William's rendering was made by Huttner which was published from Weimer in 1797. The preparation of a revised text of Sir William's translation was begun in 1840 at Calcutta but the work was continued only down to iii. 33. Sir G.C. Haughton's edition of Sir William Jones' translation was reprinted at Madras in 1863 and by Grady at London in 1869.

3. Jones also equated Manu with other first borns of different ancient mythologies. According to him there is a strong resemblance between Manu with his Divine Bull (Dharma) and the Mneues of Egypt with his companion Apis. Manu's brother is Yama, the guardian of the dead. In the same way, the Greeks made Minos, the judge of the other world, thus attributing him to Yama's function. Jones also referred to the Deluge legend with Manu as the saviour, parallels of which are found in other mythologies.
4. *Institute of Hindu Laws or the Ordinance of Manu,* Calcutta 1794. Goldstücker termed Sir William Jones' translation, "excellent", in his *Literary Remains,* Vol. I.
5. Both quotations are form P. Percival's Introduction to Haughton's *Mānavadharmaśāstra,* Madras, 1863. This work, as stated above, is a revised edition of Sir William's earlier translation the *Manusmṛti.*
6. *English works of Raja Rammohan Roy* : Ed. by J.C. Ghosh, Two Vols. Calcutta, 1887. A collection of his Bengali writings with a few selected English works. Ed. by A.K. Ghosh, was published from Calcutta in 1973.
7. *Indische Studien,* Vol. I, Berlin 1849, pp. 69, 143, 243-44.
8. *Original Sanskrit Texts,* Vol. I, London 1858, pp. 35-42, 161, 238.
9. *History of Ancient Sanskrit Literature,* London 1859, pp. 132ff.
10. The *Śrauta, Gṛhya* and *Śulva* sūtras of the Mānava school and the *Kāṭhaka Gṛhyasūtra,* which is related to the *Mānava Gṛhyasūtra* come under the *Maitrāyanī Saṃhitā.* The *Mānava Gṛhyasūtra* and *Mānava Śrautasūtra* were edited by F. Knauer which were published from St. Petersburg in 1897 and 1900. On *Mānava Gṛhyasūtra* see also P.V. Bradke in *ZDMG,* XXXVI, pp. 417-77.
11. Jolly in *SBE,* VII, pp. XXVI-XXVII; P.V. Bradke in *ZDMG,* XXXVI, pp. 417-77, cf. Johanntgen, *Über das Gesetzbuch des Manu,* Berlin, 1863, pp. 76ff.
12. *Indian Wisdom,* London 1875, pp. 203-291.
13. Reference has already been made to the fact that Sir William Jones, impressed by the Hindu belief in its antiquity proposed to ascribe the *Manusmṛti* to the age of Moses, about the year 1280 B.C. Elphinstone placed it at 1900 B.C. Eggelling (*Encyclopeadia Britannica* - 11th Ed. XXIV, p. 175) thought it impossible to date the text because accord-

ing to him, some of its passages belonged to the remotest antiquity while others were late and no particular standard of judgement could be fixed on this question. Schlegal confidently asserted it not to be later than 1000 B.C. Johanntgen put 350 B.C. as the latest date possible. According to Weber the earliest date is the middle of the 2nd century B.C. the latest the end of the 1st century A.D. Arguing from its metrical form, Max Müller (*India*, London 1883, pp. 91, 366) assigned it to a date around A.D. 300, while the researches of Bühler and Jolly (cf. *Infra*) placed it within two preceding centuries. Macdonell (*Sanskrit Literature*, London, 1900, p. 428) holds that *Manusmṛti* cannot be later than A.D. 200. This date has been suggested by P.V. Kane (Cf. *Infra*).

14. *The Ordinances of Manu*, London 1884.
15. *Oriental and Linguistic Studies*, Vol. I, p. 72.
16. Whitney, *Sanskrit Grammar*, xviii.
17. Cf. *Ibid.* p. 424ff.
18. Burnell, *Op. Cit.* p. xxxvii.
19. e.g. *The Mutual Relations of the Four Castes according to the Mānava Dharmaśāstra*, 1881; "Professed quotations from Manu found in the *Mahābhārata*" in *Journal of the American Oriental Society*, Vol. XI. pp. 239-275; etc.
20. *The Laws of Manu* in *SBE*, Oxford, 1886.
21. Manu II. 10.
22. Manu XII. 111
23. Manu III. 232.
24. Manu III. 185.
25. Cf. Manu III. 16-19, VI. 21; VIII 140 etc.
26. IV. 5-8.
27. See Kātyāyana's *Vārttika* 39 on Pāṇini I. 2.64 and Patañjali's remark thereon (Keilhorn, *Mahābhāṣya* Vol. I, p. 242).
28. This view was first expressed by Bühler in his lectures on the Hindu Law delivered in the Vienna University in 1881-82 and was accepted by J. Jolly in *Tagore Law Lectures* (delivered in 1883), Calcutta 1885, pp. 41f.
29. *Proceedings of the American Oriental Society*, Oct. 1883, p. XIX.
30. *The Mayukha and Yājñavalkya, Introduction to Yājñavalkya* Bombay 1880, p. XLVII.
31. Jolly, *Tagore Lectures*, p. 57.
32. Mandlik, *The Vyavahāra Mayukha and Yājñavalkya*, XLVII; Jolly. *Tagore Lectures*, p. 44.
33. *J.A.O.S.* XI. pp. 239ff; cf. His *The Great Epic of India*, New York 1901.
34. *History of Indian Literature*, Eng. trans. by J. Mann and Th. Zachariae, Second ed., London 1882, p. 279.
35. Mandlik, *Op. cit*, p. XLVII.

36. *Recht und Sitte*, Eng. trans. by R.K. Ghosh under the title *Hindu Law and Custom*, Calcutta 1928.
37. M.N. Dutt, *Hindu Religious Codes*, Vol. V. Calcutta 1908.
38. Second ed., Madras 1932-34.
39. Dhananjay Keer, *Dr. Ambedkar: Life and Mission*, Third ed., New Delhi 1981, p. 81.
40. *Manusmṛti*, 5 Vols. University of Calcutta 1922-29.
41. *Indian Historical Quarterly*, 1927, pp. 808-13.
42. *Manu Dharmaśāstra: A Sociological and Historical Study*, Madras, 1958.
43. Published posthumously in 1968 on account of his birth centenary by the Jadavpur University.
44. Radhakumud Mookerjee Lectures in the Lucknow University 1946.
45. *History of Dharmaśāstra*, 5 vols. Pune, 1930-62.
46. IV. 5-8.
47. II. 3; XI. 67.
48. *The Cultural Heritage of India*, Vol. II, Calcutta 1962, p. 335.

Chapter II

The Manu Mythology

Dara Shuko's identification of Manu with Adam may not be historically correct but in a mythological perspective it is not devoid of significance. In ancient mythologies the First Born is regarded as a divine incarnation, the progenitor of the human race, the founder of material sciences and propounder of a special ethical way of life.[1] In the Jewish, Christian and Islamic traditions Adam was not merely the first human being; at the same time he was the 'chosen person' of God who created him to serve His own designs. He was therefore far more than an average human being. Even Christ is described as an incarnation of Adam. Naturally he has been the subject of an extensive mythology. The same happened in the case of Manu, who was conceived not only as the First Born but also was assigned to perform certain divinely ordained functions. He was also the progenitor of mankind, often a Creator-God equated with Prajāpati, a sage chosen by the Supreme Being to propagate laws for the human races, the mental born son of Brahmā, the revealer of religion, the institutor of Yajñas, the legal and moral representative of different aeons in his various incarnations, the principal agent of the Second Creation which took place after the flood, counsel of the gods in their troubles, the moral guardian, the symbolic upholder of the universe and so forth.

The development of a Manu mythology began to take place in hoary antiquity. It is in the *Ṛgveda* that we come across for the first time, the incipient stages of this mythology. The antiquity of Manu and the heritage associated with his name are both attested by the *Ṛgveda* where we find the main ideas

that Indian tradition has always connected with him. Manu in the *Ṛgveda* has no claim of historical reality.[2] In the *Ṛgveda* the word Manu or Manus is often used in the sense of Man. The concept of the origin of mankind is somewhat fluctuating in the Vedas but it is generally believed that the human race has been descended from a first man. He is Manu, the son of Vivasvat; and is often called Manu Vivasvat.[3] In the *Ṛgveda,* the *Ṛsis* often speak of Manu 'as father'[4] without expressly saying 'of whom'. But in another place the sage speaks of Manu as 'our father'[5] (*Yāni Manurāvṛṇitā pitā naḥ*). The word Manu in several cases and in compound words like 'Manu-jāta', 'Manuprītasaḥ' and 'Manur hita' occur hundreds of times. In the *Ṛgveda* the prayer is: 'O Gods! May you protect us, help us, speak in our favour, may you not lead us far from ancestral path of Manu.'[6] He was the first sacrificer.[7] Elsewhere in the *Ṛgveda* Manu is described as *pitā* who obtained prosperity through sacrifice. In another verse he is referred to as 'our father' who chose the pure remedies of the Maruts,[8] prepared hymns as portals of access to the Gods[9] and the protecting father who is the same as sacrifice.[10] In another verse[11] the paternal or ancestral path of Manu is spoken of. His sacrifice is an archetype of subsequent sacrificial system which was referred to several times, with the adverbs 'Manusvat' 'like that of Manu'.[12]

As ịn the preceding passages Manu is spoken of as the progenitor of the worshippers so also in some passages his descendents are spoken of. Thus it is said that Agni abides among the offsprings of Manu.[13] Elsewhere Agni is invoked together with other gods in connection with the children of Manu.[14] Reference has also been made to the people (*viś*) of Manu.[15] From these, it appears that the authors of the hymns regàrded Manu as the progenitor of their race. They also looked upon him as the First person by whom the sacrificial fire has been kindled and as the institutor of the ceremonials of worship. The connection of Manu with the sacrificial fire is attesed by a few verses of the *Ṛgveda.*[16] In the *Ṛgveda* the poet

says 'O Agni : Manu established you as a light for the people.[17] The gods are often referred to as those to whom he offered sacrifices.[18] Worshppers made Agni the accomplisher of sacrifice, as Manu did.[19] When Manu kindled the fire he presented his first offspring with the seven priests of gods. The worshippers also did the same.[20] Like Manu they invoked Agni who was kindled by Manu.[21] Manu is also spoken of as the conqueror of Viśiśipra.[22] The Aśvins are said to have instituted sacrifice for Manu[23] and Soma is described as flowing for Manu who is the upholder of life.[24] The worshippers offer Soma as Manu did.[25] Manu is said to have kindled fire and offered oblations to the Ādityas for securing protection of mankind.[26] There are other passages which also speak of Manu as the first who kindled sacrificial fire.[27] In one passage of the *Ṛgveda* the adorable invoker is described as bringing Indra being projected by Manu.[28]

There is a class of passages in which Manu is mentioned in a comparative term. In these verses various deities have been invoked with a complementary phrase, "as was done by Manu".[29] There are also several passages in which Manu has been described as being the object of special favour of intervention on the part of some of the Gods.[30] There is also a reference to the sky being displayed to Manu.[31] Viṣṇu is referred to as measuring the terrestrial regions three times for Manu.[32] Elsewhere Viṣṇu is said to have strode over the earth, bestowing it on Manu for an abode.[33] Again there are some passages in the *Ṛgveda* in which it is doubtful whether Manu and Manus denote an individual or stand for 'man' in general.[34] At least there are some passages in which the latter implication is more pronounced.[35]

Among the other allusions to Manu in the *Ṛgveda* it is said that Kāvya Uṣaṇa is said to have established Agni for Manu.[36] Indra is spoken of as the shatterer of many cities (of the Asuras) and the killer of the Dasyus and as bringing prosperity to Manu as the lord of heaven.[37] Nābhānediṣṭha is referred to as *ayam Nābha*[38] and Sāvarṇa or Sāvarṇī is said to be same as

Manu.[39] In many of the verses of the *Ṛgveda* in which the word Manu occurs, commentators and translators often hold that the word Manu stands for Manuṣya and not merely for Manu, an individual sage. As for example a prayer is made to the Aśvins to come with help as they did in the past age (*purā*) in the case of Sayu, Atri and Manu.[40] Similarly reference is made to his sacrifices with Aṅgiras and Yayāti,[41] Bhṛgu and Aṅgiras,[42] Atharvan and Dadyāñc,[43] Atri and Kāṇva, in past ages (Pūrvathā).[44] The Gods,[45] Mātarisvan,[46] and other agents[47] are said to have given Agni to Manu or to have instituted him as a sacirificer for Manu. The Ṛṣis of a few *suktas*[48] of the eighth *maṇḍala* are said in the Anukramaṇī to be Manu Vaivasvata, and Manu is mentioned in some of these verses in which it is told that thirty three gods are said to have been offered worship by Manu.[49] Indra is said to have drunk Soma beside Manu Vivasvat[50] or Manu Sāmvarṇi[51] and to have drunk the Soma of Manus, three lakes, to strengthen himself for Vṛtra fight.[52] Soma is said to have been brought to Manu by a divine bird.[53]

In the *Atharvaveda*[54] Manu Vaivasvata is spoken of as the calf of the cow Virāj. There it is also said that *devairdattam manunā sākaṃ etad vādhūyaṃ vāsaḥ.*[55] In the same text Manu is mentioned in connection with the healing herbs. "Without fastening they (the protection plants) held fast; thus it has been arranged by Manu."[56] In connection with love charms it is said: "I envelope thee in my garment that was produced by Manu, that thou shalt be mine alone, shalt not even discourse to other women."[57]The flood legend and Manu's boat are also foreshadowed in the *Atharvaveda.*[58]

In the *Taittirīya Saṃhitā*[59] and the *Tāṇḍa Mahā Brāhmaṇa*[60] it is said that whatever Manu said is medicine. In the *Chāndogya Brāhmaṇa* we also find *Manurvai yatkimcid avadat tadbheṣajam bheṣajatāyāḥ.* The *Taittirīya Saṃhitā* connects Manu with Iḍā in connection with a sacrifice. There it is said that at the instance of Mitra and Varuṇa, Manu called upon Iḍā in the form of a cow. Butter was pressed from the feet of the latter and so she

has been described as Mānavī. Manu made a *pākayajña* with the assistance of Iḍā who was drawn by the gods in the front direction and by the Asuras in the back direction.[61] In other verses of the *Taittirīya Saṃhitā,*[62] Manu is described as the performer of religious ceremonies of morning, midday and evening, as one who kindles Agni and bears the oblation of the gods. He has been compared with Indra. As Indra is among gods, so Manu is among men. The *Taittirīya Saṃhitā*[63] also says that mankind is Manu's. In this text we have the story of Manu dividing his wealth among his sons and of the exclusion of his son Nābhānediṣṭha.[64] In another passage[65] it is said that Indra was sacrificing for Manu with his wife and by her Manu prospered.

The *Kāṭhaka Saṃhitā*[66] refers to the flood legend in connection with Manu which has been elaborated in the *Śatapatha Brāhmaṇa*[67] in which Manu is called Vaivasvata and Sāvarṇī. Yama is also a son of Vivasvat and the first of the mortals. Manu is a doubtlet of Yama, an ancestor of the human race. But Manu is regarded as the first of men living on earth, while Yama, as the first man who died became king of the dead in other world. Hence Manu Vaivasvata is described as the ruler of men and Yama Vaivasvata, the ruler of Manes. In the V*ājasaneyi Saṃhitā* (XXXVII. 12) the earth is described as the mare of Manu. Its implication may be found in the *Śatapatha Brāhmaṇa (X*IV. 1.3.5) in which it is said that once the earth carried Manu assuming the form of a horse. In the *Śatapatha Brāhmaṇa*[68] Manu is called Prajāpati, the lord of creatures. It relates a legend according to which Manu had a bull into which a voice urging for the slaying of the Asuras had entered. The Asuras thereupon sacrificed the bull, and when it had been slaughtered the voice departed out of it and entered into Manu's wife Mānavī. Then they sacrificed Mānavī and the voice departed out of her entered into the sacrifice and sacrificial vessels. The Asuras were unable to stamp it out.[69] This story also recurs in the *Taittirīya Brāhmaṇa*[70] in which it is stated that an Asura-slaying voice had entered into the sacrifi-

cial implements of the devout believer and sacrificer Manu. The Asuras when heard the sacrificial implements sounding were overcome. The *Kāṭhaka Brāhmaṇa*[71] says that Manu had platters. The Asuras took them from him and smashed them in the forest. The bull of Manu licked the platters. When the Asuras heard its low they were destroyed. Then the two priests of the Asuras known as Tṛṣtra and Vārutri approached Manu and wanted to make sacrifice for him with the bull and with his wife, but Indra disclosed the identity of the two Asura priests and they fled. He threw after them the water which was there for consecration, as the result of which the heads of the two Asura priests were cut off. Indra released Manu's wife through whom all creatures were sprang from Manu.

In the *Taittrīya Brāhmaṇa*[72] Iḍā is described as the daughter of Manu who placed the *gārhapatya* fire and through the *gārhapatya* she produced for him offspring and cattle. In the *Kāṭhaka Brāhmaṇa*[73] Iḍā is said to have promised to Manu that she would so place Agni for him that man could be born among the gods. The story how Nābhānediṣṭha was disinherited by Manu has been given in the *Ṭaittrīya Saṃhitā*[74] in which it is said that Manu divided his property among his sons but disinherited his son Nābhānediṣṭha who was living as a Brahmacārin. When questioned by Nābhānediṣṭha Manu said that he did not disinherit him and asked him to help the Aṅgirases who were performing a sacrifice to reach heaven, in cosequence of which he would earn wealth from them. This was done accordingly and when he received the cattle, Rudra came on the spot and demanded them as his own. Thereupon Rudra took a share of sacrifice and did not injure the cattle. The *Aitareya Brāhmaṇa*[75] gives a different version of this story. Here it is said that the brothers of Nābhānediṣṭha disinherited him saying that they had given him their father - the judge and divider - as his share. Then Nābhānediṣṭha went to Manu who sent him to the Aṅgirases who were then performing a sacrifice in order to secure heaven. Nābhānediṣṭha helped them with the recitation of two *Ṛgvedic hymns* (x. 61-62) on the sixth day

and received from them a provision of one thousand. As he was collecting the thousand, a man in a dark clothing appeared before him and demanded the sum. Nābhānediṣṭha came to Manu and informed him the situation. Manu said that the amount really belonged to the man in the dark clothing but he would return it back to him. Then Nābhānediṣṭha told the man what was said to him by Manu. The man is dark clothing returned the thousand saying that he had sopken the truth. This Nābhānediṣṭha hymn is concluded by a statement that a thousand fall to his lot who knows the heavenly world on the sixth day. The implication of these two versions of the Nābhānediṣṭha myth is not very clear. The *Taittirīya Saṃhitā* account has an important aspect which indicates that the property divided was movable property like cattle. In the *Aitareya Brāhmaṇa* version, the sons are said to have made the division, leaving Nābhānediṣṭha to the care of their father. Does this suggest that the sons were legally owners with their father?

Yāska explains Manu to be the son of Vivasvat,[76] the Sun (Āditya) and Sāvarṇa, the substitute of Sāraṇya,[77] counting him among the divine beings of the celestial region.[78] In the *Nirukta* there is a discussion about the rights of sons and daughters. One of the views was that the children of both sexes take their father's wealth and a ṛk and a *śloka* are cited in support of that position. The *śloka* refers to the opinion of Manu Svāyambhūva. In the *Chāndogya Upaniṣad* it is said that the advice received by Manu from Prajāpati was circulated by him among the people (III. 11.4). The *Śatapatha Brāhmaṇa* says that human beings are all subjects of Manu (X.4.3.3.).

The well known legend describing how Manu was saved in a ship from a deluge which swept away all other creatures by a fish (in the post-Vedic mythology an Avatāra of Viṣṇu) is described in the *Śatapatha Brāhmaṇa.*[79] The legend is as follows: One morning while Manu was washing, a fish came into his hands and told him about an impending flood from which it would rescue him. Manu kept it in a jar, then in a pit and

when it had outgrown this, took it to the sea. Then the fish swam to the ship which was made previously and Manu fastened the cable of the ship to its horn. By this Manu reached the Northern mountain and fastened the ship to a tree. Manu descended as the water abated. Now the flood had swept away all the creaturs, Manu was left alone. Desirous of offspring he performed a sacrifice and in a year a woman was produced. Mitra and Varuṇa met her and wanted to know her identity. She introduced herself as the daughter of Manu since she was generated by him. Manu begot offspring on this woman who came to be known as Iḍā. The myth of the deluge occurs in *Avesta* also. It may be of Indo-European origin though generally regarded as borrowed from a Semitic source.[80] The story of Noah's Ark, as found in the *Genesis* V-X may be recalled in this connection. In the Semitic tradition Noah, the patriarch, the second Manu is our sense, tenth in descent after Adam, made an ark at God's command which saved his family and specimens of every animal from the flood sent by God to destroy the world. His sons, Shem, Ham and Japheth were regarded as ancestors of the races of mankind. In the epic of Gilgamesh, Pir Napishtim, the progenitor of the race of Gilgamesh, was instructed by the God Ea to build a ship and store there the seeds of life to protect himself from the impending deluge. The flood created such a havoc that the gods were even frightened. They were shivering in cold. The goddess Ishtar was screaming. After many days the flood subsided, Pir Napishtim descended on a hill. His descendants populated the world once again. The flood legned also recur in the *Mahābhārata* and Purāṇas as we shall see later.

Fragments of Manu mythology are found in the *Mahābhārata* in which various ancestries have been attributed to Manu. He is referred to as the father of the human race, often as one of the seven or twenty one Prajāpatis.[81] He is said to have been issued from the primordial egg[82] and described as the son of Brahmā.[83] In the *Mahābhārata* Manu is frequently mentioned in connection with various gods. He communicated

the Cākṣusī to Soma.[84] Indra, the king of the gods, performed a sacrifice on the bank of Vindusaras where Manu is said to have stayed with Brahmā, Rudra and other gods.[85] Manu came near the river Sarasvatī for the investiture of Skanda.[86] Sometimes Manu is identified with Śiva and is regarded as the progenitor of the Ikṣvāku line.[87] Manu is described as having an abode of his own. If one goes to the Kanyā -samvedya pilgrimage with a restrained mind and temperance in the food and drink one can attain this abode.[88] Cākṣuṣa Manu is described in the *Mahābhārata* as having a son called Variṣṭha while Prācetasa Manu is mentioned in connection with *rājadharma.* Svārociṣa Manu is said to have learnt the religion of Nārāyaṇa from Brahman.[89] Sāvarṇa is mentioned in connection with seven heavenly sages.[90] Svāyambhūva Manu is also described as a Prajāpati who held discourses with the Siddhas regarding liberation.[91] He is counted among eight Prakṛitis.[92] Brahmā appointed Manu as the lord of the people.[93] Vaivasvata Manu is the son of Vivasvat, grandson of Kaśyapa and brother of Yama. He is associated with the flood legend. He was given a sword by the Lokapālas for the protection of creatures. The names of his sons have been found in the *Mahābhārata.* Vaivasvata Manu begot sixty sons: the name of his ten sons are the following: Veṇa, Dhṛṣṇu, Naraṣyanta, Nābhāga, Ikṣvāku, Kāruṣa, Śaryāti, Ilā, Pṛsadhra and Nābhāgāriṣṭa. The rest perished querrelling with one another.[94] Vaivasvata Manu is the father of Ilā.[95] The name of the son of Svārociṣa Manu is Śaṅkhapada who learnt religion from his father.[96] Regarding Cāksuṣa Manu the great epic only refers to his son Variṣṭha.[97]

Thus, besides one unspecified Manu the *Mahābhārata* mentions six Manus, namely, Cākṣuṣa, Prācetasa, Svārociṣa, Sāvarṇa, Svāyambhūva and Vaivasvata. There is also the concept of Prajāpti Manu (Manu sprung from Prajāpati or Brahmā, or Manu, equated with Prajāpati or Brahmā, or Manu, the creator) whose epithets correspond to a great extent to the descriptive appellations of Manu found in the Vedic texts. In the *Bhagavadgītā* (X. 6) it is said that the Manus are four in

number. But the concept of seven Manus eventually gained a better ground. Later the number seven was doubled. According to the evidence of the *Manusmṛti,* the supreme lord divided himself in two parts, male and female and produced Virāj. From Virāj was produced Manu who was not only the creative principle who brought into existence the ten great sages, such as Mārici etc., but also composed the sacred laws and taught them (I.32-36, 58). "Six other high-minded very powerful Manus who belong to the race of this Manu, the descendant of the self-existent (Svāyambhūva) and who have severally produced created beings, are Svārociṣa, Auttami, Tāmasa, Raivata, Cākṣuṣa, possessing great lusture, and the son of Vivasvat." (I.61-62).

The Purāṇas contain glimpses of a mythology associated with these seven or fourteen Manus. According to the *Viṣṇu Purāṇa,* from the primordial egg originated Brahmā who was none other than Hiraṇyagarbha. From his right thumb originated Dakṣa whose daughter was Aditi, the mother of the sun. Manu sprang from the sun. The Lord appointed the self-created Manu, who formerly sprang from Brahmā's self and resembled Brahmā himself, to rule over the creatures. The self-created Manu went by the designations of Deva and Yama.[98] He took Śatarūpā as his wife. The *Viṣṇu Purāṇa* gives a detailed list of the descendants of Manu. There it is said that being desirous of having offspring Manu celebrated a sacrifice in honour of Mitra and Varuṇa.[99] Manu Svāyambhūva, the first Manu, had two heroic and pious sons, Priyavrata and Uttānapada.[100] In every Manvantara Manu, the seven *Ṛṣis,* the king of the gods and sons of Manu rule over the earth. Manu's sons such as Citrasena, Vicitra and others are destined to be the kings of the earth. The sons of Bhautya Manu are Uru, Gabhira, Bradhna and others.[101] The sons of Dharma Sāvarnī are Savarga, Sarvadharma, Devanika and others. The Manus and their sons are possessed of wealth and powers, ever abiding by the way of rightenousness of heroism and hence serving as the fountain-head of the maintenance of the

cosmos.[102] Ikṣvāku was born of Manu's nostril as he was sneezing.[103] The theory that in every Manvantara Manu and his sons rule over the earth is popularised by the Purāṇas.

The *Bhāgavata Purāṇa*[104] mentions that the sages, Manus, gods as well as powerful sons of Manu along with the Prajāpatis (Gods presiding over the creations) are all parts of Hari only. Manu is the power of his comprehension. At the time of the Manvantaras for maintaining the continuity of Manu's race, he maintains his unchallenged rule in ten quarters. In the Manu-eras the supreme Lord retains his s*attvaguṇa* and protects the universe by incarnating as Manus. The self-possessed Brahmā gave up his body in human form to the Manus. In most Purāṇas Manu is said to have been the father of nine valliant sons, besides the eldest, who is represented to have had a dual personality as the male Ilā and the female Ilā. Of these sons only four are important as being the originators of important lines. Ikṣvāku and his son Vikukṣi founded the Aikṣvāka or the solar line. From Dhṛṣṭa, Śaryāti and Kāruṣa came into existence the Dhārṣṭakas, Śāryātas and Kāruṣas respectively. From Ilā as the female, who married Budha was born Pururavas, the originator of the Aila or lunar dynasty. From the Ailas sprang various dynasties such as the Kānyakubjas, Yādavas, Turvasus, Druhyus, Ānavas, Pañcālas, Bārhadrathas, Cedis, etc.

According to the *Mārkaṇḍeya Purāṇa*[105] there are fourteen Manus presiding over different aeons.[106] At first there was Manu Svāyambhūva, then Svārociṣa, Auttama or Auttami, Tāmasa, Raivata and Cākṣuṣa. These six Manus have passed and Vaivasvata is the Manu now. The five Sāvarṇas, Raucya and Bhautya are yet to come.[107] It is said that Brahmā created Manu Svāyambhūva and his wife Śatarūpā. They had two sons, Priyavrata and Utānapada and also two daughters. Ruci married one daughter Ṛddhi and begot Yajña and Dakṣiṇā. The other daughter Prasuti was married to Dakṣa and brought forth 24 daughters.[108] The descendants of Svāyambhūva and his son Priyavrata peopled the whole world and got the seven island-continents divided amongst them - Agnidhra got Jambudvīpa,

Medhātithi Plakṣadvīpa, Vapuṣmat Śālmalīdvīpa, Jyotiṣmat Kuśadvīpa, Dyutimat Krauñcadvīpa, Bhavya Śākadvīpa and Savana Puṣkaradvīpa.[109] Svāyambhūva received a weapon capable of piercing the heart of an enemy from Rudra and gifted it to Vasiṣṭha.[110] This legend occurs in the *Mahābhārata* also as we have seen above. King Uttama is said to belong to the race of Svāyambhūva,[111] and so also king Durgama whose son became Raivata Manu.[112]

Regarding the second Manu Svārociṣa, the *Mārkaṇḍeya Purāṇa* says that he was the son of the Apsaras Varūthiṇi and Gandharva Kali. Because he shone with his own lusture like the sun he was famed by the appropriate name Sva-rocis. He saved the Vidyādhara Indīvara from a curse and married his daughter Manoramā. He also married two other Vidyādhara girls - Vibhāvarī and Kalāvatī - and lived in pleasure with his wives. Once he overheared the conversations of two birds and also the remarks of a deer about him and understood that by following a life of pleasure he was not doing justice to himself. He settled his three sons in three separate kingdoms - Vijaya in Kāmarūpa on the east, Merundanda in Nandavati on the north and Prabhava in Tāla on the south. Then again he fell in love with the goddess of a forest and had by her a son Dyutimat who also became a Manu. He was again astonished by a conversation between two ducks and gave himself up to a religious life.[113]

Auttama Manu was the son of king Uttama by a Nāga princess. He was called Auttama because he was born in an excellent family and at an excellent time. He had excellent limbs as well. By the innate splendour of the austerities of Auttama his seven sons beame the seven great *Ṛṣis* in his period.[114] The next Manu Tāmasa was the son of king Svarāṣṭra who was driven from his kingdom by enemies and became an ascetic in a forest. There he met his deceased queen in the shape of a doe and begot a son by her who became the Manu Tāmasa.[115] The fifth Manu Raivata was the son of king Durgama who visited the hermitage of the sage Pramuca and married

Revatī, the adopted daughter of the sage. Manu Raivata was possessed of all rightousness, unconquered by mankind, who understood the meaning of every sacred book, knew the Vedas, the sciences and the books of practical arts.[116] The sixth Manu Cākṣuṣa was taken by a witch from his parents when he was an infant and was changed for the son of king Vikrānta. He was brought up as a prince and on reaching boyhood he revealed the fraud, abandoned his princely state and became an ascetic.[117] The seventh Manu, Vaivasvata, was the son of the sun and Saṃjñā. His brother was Yama. The eighth Manu would be Sāvarṇi, also the son of the sun by Shadow-Saṃjñā (Chāyā).[118] The succeeding Manus, from the ninth to the twelfth would be kṇown as Sāvarṇa.[119] The thirteenth Manu would be known as Raucya born of an Apsaras by a Prajāpati Ruci.[120] The fourteenth Manu, Bhautya would be the son of the sage Bhūti by the grace of Agni.[121]

In the *Matsya Purāṇa,* Manu has been brought in a mundane level and is basically represented as an enquirer who approached Viṣṇu in his fish-incarnation with questions pertaining to life and universe. This Manu is the precursor of the lawgiver Manu. But a Manu mythology is also there. In fact the *Matsya Purāṇa* begins with the flood legend in consequence of which Manu had the chance of talking directly with the Supreme Being who imparted to him all forms of knowledge in connection with gods, men, animate and inanimate beings.[122] The *Matsya Purāṇa* describes the origin of Vaivasvata and Sāvarṇi Manus respectively from Samjña and Chāyā, the consorts of the sun. It also refers to the ten powerful sons of Vaivasvata Manu.[123] The eldest was Ilā who was born of the performance of the putreṣṭi sacrifice. His brothers were Ikṣvāku, Kuśanābha, Ariṣṭa, Dhṛṣṭa, Nariṣyanta, Kuruṣa, Saryāti, Prisadhra, and Nābhāga who were all valiant and illustrious. Manu, after anointing his son Ilā, and putting the reins of the government into his hands, went to practise asceticism in the forest called Mahendravana.[124]

Mention of Manu's sons is found in the *Mārkaṇḍeya Purāṇa*

in which it is said that the gods, the seven Ṛṣis and Indra, Manu and the kings, his sons - all are created with Manu and pass to dissolution with him in regular order.[125] Manu Svāyambhūva had ten sons equal to himself by whom the whole earth comprising seven continents with their mountains and oceans were peopled.[126] According to the *Harivaṃśa*, Svāyambhūva Manu had ten sons viz., Kaśyapa, Cyavana, Bṛhaspati and others. The sons of Svārociṣa Manu were Sukṛti, Aya, Nabha, Jyoti, etc. The sons of Auttami Manu were Madhu, Mahādeva, Suci, Urja, etc. The name of the sons of Vaivasvata Manu were the Rudras, Vasus, Ādityas, Aśvins and Ikṣvākus. The sons of Sāvarṇi Manu would be Ārya, Dhṛṣṇu, Dhṛtiman, etc. Among other Sāvarṇis, the names of the sons of Dakṣasāvarṇi would be Sūta, Uttamauja, Śatānika, Suvarcā and others. Rudra Sāvarṇi had nine sons.[127]

The *Harivaṃśa*[128] gives a list of six anterior Manus, the process of their creation, the duration of each Manvantaras and a description of the other Manus. The fourteen Manus are: Svāyambhūva, Svārociṣa, Auttami, Tāmasa, Raivata, Cākṣuṣa, Vaivasvata, Sāvarṇi, Bhautya, Raucya, Brahmāsāvarṇi, Rudrasāvarṇi, Merusāvarṇi and Dakṣasāvarṇi. The post-Vaivasvata list is in slight variance with those of the *Mārkaṇḍeya* and *Matsya* Purāṇas. Among them the period of the first six Manus is over. Vaivasvata Manu is present Manu and other seven Manus like Sāvarṇi will come next. Svāyambhūva Manu is the first Manu who had ten sons. In the Manvantara of Svārociṣa the deities like Tasitar were born. The deities of Auttami Manvantara were Bhānus. In the fourth Manvantara Tāmasa Manu appeared. The seven *Ṛṣis* of this Manvantara were Pṛthu, Agni, Dhātā and others. The Satyas were the deities in this Manvantara. Dyuti, Sutapa, Parantapa and others were the sons of Tāmasa Manu. Next came Raivata Manu whose sons were Dhṛtiman, Avyaya, Araṇya, Nirutsaka, etc. The sixth Manu was Vaivasvata. His sons were Rudras, Vasus, Ādityas, Aśvins, and Ikṣvākus. There were five Sāvarṇi Manus. The first Sāvarṇi is named as Vaivasvata Sāvarṇi for he is the son

of the sun. The other four Sāvarṇis were the sons of Brahmā. They practised religious austerities in the Sumeru and were called Meru Sāvarṇi. Their mother was Priyā, the daughter of Dakṣa; so they all were the grandsons of Dakṣa. Next two Manus, Raucya and Bhautya, were the sons of Prajāpati Ruci. The latter was born in the womb of Bhauti and was namded as Bhautya. The Maharṣis of this Manvantras will be Rāma. Vedavyāsa, Aśvathāman, Kṛpācārya, Gālava etc. The sons of Sāvarṇi Manu will be Ārya, Dhṛṣṇu, Dhṛtiman and others. First Sāvarṇi is the ninth Manu. The second Sāvarṇi will come in the tenth Manvantara. He is Dakṣa-Sāvarṇi. Sūta, Uttamauja, Śatānīka, Suvarca and others will be the sons of Dakṣa Sāvarṇi. The third Sāvarṇi will appear in the eleventh Manvantara. Next will come Rudra Sāvarṇi who will have nine sons. The fourth Sāvarṇi will belong in the twelfth Manvantara. The thirteenth Manu is Rucya and the fourteenth Manu is Bhautya. After the Bhautya Manu a *kalpa* is over.

According to the *Vāyu Purāṇa*[129] the social norms which were established by Brahmā fell into abeyance and these were revived by Manu Svāyambhūva who was the first king of the earth having his capital on the bank of the Sarasvatī. The second Manu Svārociṣa was the son of his daughter Aditi. Svāyambhūva's son Priyavrata was the first of the Kṣatriyas. Three of his sons - Uttama, Tāmasa and Raivata - became respectively the third, fourth and fifth Manus. Svāyambhūva Manu's second son Uttānapada had three sons - Dhruva, Kīrtivat and Uttama. Cākṣuṣa Manu belonged to the line of Dhruva in whose line also belonged the wicked king Veṇa who was deposed by his subjects and his son Pṛthu from whom the earth received its name. Fifth in descent from Pṛthu was Dakṣa whose daughter's grandson, Manu Vaivasvata, saved humanity from the deluge which occurred at his time.

The *Mārkaṇḍeya Purāṇa* is in fact a study of the fourteen Manvantaras in which the gods, demi-gods, sages, personalities and kings pertaining to each Manvantara have been furnished along with the myths and legends clustering around them.

The ninth chapter of the *Matsya Purāṇa* is, however, a brief summary of all the Manu-eras in which the names of the sons of each Manu, the group of Devas (normally consisting of seven) and that of the sages have been furnished.

The *Viṣṇu Purāṇa* gives a description of a Manvantara. One day of Brahmā comprises four and ten reigns of the Manus. The chronology is: The seven saints, the celestials, Śakra, Manu and his sons - kings all of them - are created at the same time and likewise destroyed at the same time. A little over seventy one four-*yugas* constitute a Manvantara - the period of Manu as well as the gods.[130] Svāyambhūva Manu was the first Manu by whom the earth was peopled and he was the lord of the first Manvantara in the *kalpa* of Varāha.[131] There were twelve well known celestials, in a former Manvantara, named the Tuṣitas, who on the approch of the present Manvantara and at the end of the reign of Manu Cākṣuṣa assembled and said to one another that they would enter the womb of Aditi and be born in the next Manvantara. At the end of the reign of Manu Cākṣuṣa were born the sons of Kaśyapa and the sons of Marīci by Aditi, the daughter of Dakṣa. Those who in the reign of Manu Cākṣuṣa were Tuṣitas are called the twelve Ādityas in the Manvantara of the Vaivasvata.[132] In every *kṛta* age the presiding Manu becomes the legislator and during the Manvantaras the celestials of the various classes receive sacrifice. In every Manvantara, the Manu, the seven *Ṛṣis,* the king of the gods and the sons of Manu rule over the earth. Manu's sons become the powerful kings of the earth. In the thirteenth period Raucya is destined to be the Manu and in the fourteenth Bhautya. The son of Chāyā, who is also called a Manu, is Sāvarṇi on account of his belonging to the same caste as his elder brother, the Manu Vaivasvata. In the era when Sāvarṇi shall be the Manu the orders of the celestials will be Sutapas, Amitābhas and Mukhyas each consisting of twenty one divinities. In the eleventh period Dharma Sāvarṇi will be the Manu and the leading celestials will be Vihaṅgamas, Kāmagamas, and Nirmānaratis, each consisting of thirty; Vṛṣa will be their

king. The seven *Ṛṣis* will be Niścara, Agnitejas and others. Savargas, Sarvadharmas, Devanikas and others - the kings of earth - will be the sons of Manu. At the end of every four *yugas* the Vedas disappear. And the seven sages descending on the earth again establish them. During the Manvantara the celestials of various classes receive sacrifices. And those born in the race of the Manus lord over the earth for that period. In every Manavatavtra, the Manu, the seven *Ṛṣis,* the king of the gods and sons of Manu rule over the earth.[133]

A close study of the Purāṇas reveals that there is a gradation among various Manus. The *Mārkaṇḍeya Purāṇa,* as we have seen, connects seven Manus with seven island-continents, viz., the *dvīpas* known as Krauñca, Plakṣa, Śālmali, Kuśa, Jambu, Śāka and Puṣkara. Each of these seven islands is presided over by a Manu. The theosophists offer an interesting though highly speculative interpretation of this association. According to them these seven Manus may be called Race Manus and they are guided by a Globe Manu who presides over all the seven island-continents and under whose guidance the work of creation, preservation and destruction continues. According to Madam Blavatsky.

> in man, as in nature, according to cis-Himalayan esoteric philosophy which is that of the cosmogony of the Original Manu, it is the septenary division that is intended in nature herself.[134]

Each Manu has a double form, Root-Manu and Seed-Manu, and hence the total number of Manus are fourteen. Bhagvan Das explains this in the following way:

> The Manus are of different grades. Every Round has a Root-Manu at its beginning, from whom all laws proceed, and a Seed-Manu at its end, in whom all results are embodied. Hence each Round has two Manus, and is therefore a Manvantara 'between two Manus'. On each

> Globe, through which the evolutionary wave passess - of these there are seven in a Round - there is a minor Manu for each Root-Race.[135]

Manu is sometimes referred to as a king in the *Mahābhārata*. The injunctions of Manu regarding the *rājadharma* and other matters as well as topics like Manu-Bṛhaspati-Saṃvāda, as found in the *Mahābhārata* will be treated in the next chapter. In one passage of the *Mahābhārata* it is stated that Manu and other kings had not obtained such prosperity as Yudhiṣṭhira had by his Rājasūya.[136] Nala, the king of Niṣadha country has been compared with king Manu,[137] Nārada told Yudhiṣṭhira that he became everywhere as famous as Manu and other kings.[138] The *Mahābhārata* also refers in the pilgrimage of king Manu and his associates.[139] The kings like Manu came to see the encounter between the Kauravas and Arjuna.[140] Arjuna while disclosing Yudhiṣṭhira's identification to Virāta told that Yudhiṣṭhira looks after the well being of his subjects like king Manu.[141] Brahmā appointed Manu as the lord of people while there was turmoil and disorder in the world. Manu was presented a sword by the Lokapālas and was told to protect the creatures with that sword which contained *dharma* within its womb, and to punish them with rebukes, fines and forfeitures, loss of limbs and even death for grave reasons. Manu received it through Kṣupa.[142] Reference to Manu as a mythical king is also found in the *Rāmāyaṇa.* Manu Vaivasvata or Sūryaputra, brother of Yama, was Prajāpati and Mānavendra or first king, who founded the race of Ikṣvāku, the first king and bearer of rod in the Kṛta age.[143] Manu established the city named Ayodhya in the bank of river Sarayu. The king of Ayodhya, Daśaratha was equated with Manu for his virtues. Rāma showed Sītā that city which king Manu has previously given to Ikṣvāku. Manu is said to have married ten daughters of Daksa.[144] His association with Sarasvatī has been mentioned.[145] The divine self-create Manu took to wife the female Śatarūpā.[146] Manu's daughter Āruṣi is described as the wife of Cyavana.[147] Kaśyapa, the son of

Marīci, begot upon Aditi, the daughter of Dakṣa, the Ādityas and Vivasvat also called Mārtāṇḍa. Saṃjñā, the daughter of Viśvakarman was the wife of this Mārtaṇḍa who bore him three children, the Manu Vaivasvat, Yama and goddess Yamī.[148] Manu is also regarded as a female, a daughter of Pradha and Kasyapa.[149]

The story of the Manu and the fish in connection with the flood legend, is found in the *Mahābhārata*.[150] Once, while Manu, the son of Vivasvat, was performing religious austerity in the bank of a river, a fish came to him and told him that it was afraid of the big fishes, who used to eat the small fishes like it in conformity with the law of nature. It asked Manu for protection and promised him to do a good turn in return. Manu kept the fish in a jar. When it became larger in shape, Manu put it into a big pond, then in the Ganges and at last took it to the sea. Then the fish told Manu about a coming deluge and advised him to construct a ship and to embark on it before the final destruction. Manu did the same. Then the fish appeared and Manu fastened the cable of the ship to its horn. After many years a peak in the Himalaya had been observed and the fish advised Manu to fasten that boat to that peak. The fish was Prajāpati Brahmā in disguise. By his grace, Vaivasvata Manu created the animate and inanimate beings of the universe.

The *Agni Purāṇa*[151] also mentions the Flood Legend. There it is said that at the end of the past *kalpa*, there was a universal dissolution, the instrumental cause of which was Brahmā. There the earth and men were submerged under the rising ocean. At that time Manu Vaivasvata practised hard penances for attaining objects of enjoyment and salvation. Once there arose from water a small fish who requested Manu not to throw it in the water. Hearing this Manu put it into a vessel. Increasing in size the fish again told him to provide it a bigger accommodation. Then Manu kept it into a water jar. When it had outgrown this Manu threw it into a tank by its request. Lastly when it assumed proportions according to its size Manu threw it into the ocean. Then it assumed a size extending over

a hundred thousand *yojanas*. Beholding such a wondrous fish Manu wanted to know his identity. Thus accosted by Manu the fish disclosed its identity that he incarnated himself for the protection of the Universe. He also foretold of a coming deluge. In the seventh day the ocean will surmerge the earth. Then a boat will approach Manu to take all the seeds of creation. He told him to bind the boat with a huge serpent. Having said this the fish disappeared. Manu awaited for the moment of the deluge. Then he got upon the boat. The fish had one horn of gold. He tied the boat to its horn. Thus the fish saved Manu and other creatures.

Glimpses of the flood mythology have been found in *Matsya Purāṇa* [152] where it is stated that in ancient times Vaivasvata Manu, the first king of the solar dynasty after making over his kingdom to his son, devoted himself to rigid asceticism. After a period of million years of continued asceticism, Lord Brahmā being pleased with him, told him to ask for a boon. Having been thus addressed by Brahmā, Manu prayed to bestow on him sufficient power for the protection of the whole creation movable and immovable, when the hour of *pralaya* will come. Brahmā granted his prayer and disappeared. One day when Manu was making a libation of water to the manes and his deceased ancestors a carp fell into his hands. On seeing that tiny fish Manu wanted to preserve it and put it into a water jar. That fish eventually grew into the form of a large fish and cried for deliverance. Manu took it out and deposited it in a well. Water on the well also proved insufficient. Then he accommodated it into a tank. In the tank again the fish grew a *yojana* in length and again appealed to him to help it go out of the tank. Then Manu put the fish in the Ganges and this also proved inadequate. It was then placed in the vast expanse of the ocean. Seeing all these Manu became surprised and wanted to know its identity. Then the fish, who was no other than Viṣṇu, foretold him of a catastrophy that would happen in the form of a great deluge. He asked Manu to take charge of a boat and help the distressed at the time of the impending danger. By rescuing the afflicted from such an

aweful misfortune, Manu was destined to be rendering a great paternal service to creation. On hearing such words from Viṣṇu, Manu begged of him to reveal to him the exact time of destruction which was likely to come. He also entreated the Lord to point out to him the means of saving the creation from such a distress and to let him know when he would again be fortunate enough to meet him face to face. The fish replied that there would be no rain for hundred years: then there would be a famine in which all inferior beings would be starved to death. He also foretold that everthing would be destroyed, only the sun, the moon, himself. Brahmā, Manu, the sacred river Narmadā, sage Mārkaṇḍeya, the sacred Vedas, the Purāṇas, the god Śiva and various sciences would be saved and the reign of the Cākṣuṣa Manu would terminate with the coming dissolution. At the commencement of dissolution Viṣṇu appeared again in the form of horned fish. At the same time Śesa, the serpent king appeared before the king Vaivasvata Manu in the shape of a rope. After fastening the boat to the horn of the fish, by means of the rope, Manu entreated the lord to relate to him how the dissolution and the creation of the universe took place, how the generation of mankind came into being, the meaning of Manvantara, the history of eminent men, the expanse of the universe, the way of charity, the path of duty, the precepts of Śrāddha, the division of Varṇa and Āśrama, the ways of sacrificial rites, the greatness of the devas etc. In answer to his question Matsya narrated the story of the second creation by Svayambhū after the period of the great dissolution.

The *Bhāgavata Purāṇa*[153] also narrates the flood legend. At the end of a *yuga*, Bhagavat Viṣṇu was found by Vaivasvata Manu as a fish who was the support of the earth (or who held the earth like a boat) and hence was the refuge of all kinds of living beings. He collected the Vedas which fell down from the mouth of the lord in the waters and joyfully sported in the terrible water (of the deluge.)

To sum up in the Vedic, Epic and Puranic literature we come across fragmented accounts pertaining to one or more

characters having the appellation Manu. This name of the supposed divine progenitor of all beings may be derived from the root *man* which means 'to think' or 'to rationalize' (and especially, according to the Indian tradition, 'to think upon and understand the Vedas) and the word *mānava,* meaning 'men' in particular and 'mankind' in general is its secondary derivative. This conceptualization was endowed with numerous attributes and epithets and associated with a host of gods and goddesses, divine, semi-divine and mundane beings as also with abstract principles like time, space, law, virtue and so forth. Though in the *Ṛgveda* he is a simply the first man, father of the race and its guide in all matters, sacrificial and other, he is associated in various capacities with gods like Indra, Agni, Mātarisvan, Soma, Yama and others, with individuals like Aṅgiras, Yayāti, Bhṛgu, Atharvan, Dadhyañc, Atri, Kānva, Kāvya Usana, etc., with Asuras and demons, with various sacrifices and sacrifial utensils, with a number of symbolic intricacies and legendary phenomena such as the flood legend appearing in the Brāhmaṇa literature and amplified in later epico-puranic texts. The process of multiplying the number of Manus was also on the move. In the Vedas the names of Vaivasvta and Sāvarṇi Manu occur several times. In the Epic and the Purāṇas Manu is also described as the father of human race, a Prajāpati issuing from the primordial egg, a divine being associated with various deities and rituals, a teacher of *dharma* and also a law-giver. Apart from the generic Manu the *Mahābhārata* mentions Cākṣuṣa, Prācetasa, Sāvarṇa, Svarociṣa, Svāyambhūva and Vaivasvata Manu. The Purāṇas mentions fourteen Manus, each presiding over a fabulous span of time as the supreme ruler and law-giver and regarded as a kind of Indian Adam or Noah.

NOTES

1. The appellation 'Manu' or 'Manus' is often used in the sense of 'Man' in the Vedic texts. The word primarily denotes 'man' *par excellence* or the 'representative man' and 'father of the human race'

(cf. Goth. *manna*, Germ *mannus*, mentioned by Tacitus as the mythical ancestor of the West Germans, *mann, man*, Ang. Sax. *man*, Eng. *man*), See Monier William's '*A Sanskrit English Dictionery*', Oxford, 1899, p.184.

2. *Rv.* I. 80.16; II. 33.13; VIII. 63.1; X. 100.5.
3. *Rv.* III. 34.4; III. 57.4; X. 130.8 cf. Sāyana's Com. on *Rv.* X. 63.7; also see VIII. 52.2; IX. 113.8; X. 14.1, 5; X. 58.1; X. 164.2.
4. *Rv.* 1.80.16; I. 114.2; VIII. 63.1.
5. *Rv.* II. 33.13.
6. *Rv.* VIII. 30.3.
7. *Rv.* X. 63.7.
8. *Rv.* II. 33.13. It is to be observed that while in the two preceeding passages Manu is styled merely 'Father Manu' he is here called 'our father Manu' (*Manu pitānaḥ*).
9. *Rv.* VIII. 52.1
10. *Rv.* X. 100.5
11. *Rv.* VIII. 30.3
12. *Rv.* I. 76.5, etc.
13. *Rv.* I. 68.4
14. *Rv.* III. 3.6
15. *Rv.* IV. 37.1; VIII. 23.13.
16. *Rv.* I. 36.19; I. 76.5
17. *Rv.* I. 36.19
18. *Rv.* V. 35.15; VIII. 30.2; X. 36.10; X. 65.14
19. *Rv.* I. 44.11
20. *Rv.* V. 21.11.
21. *Rv.* VII. 2.3
22. *Rv.* V. 45.6
23. *Rv.* VIII. 10.2
24. *Rv.* IX. 96.12
25. *Rv.* IV. 37.3
26. *Rv.* X. 63.7; X. 69.3
27. *Rv.* I. 14.11; VI. 16.9; VIII. 19.21.
28. *Rv.* VIII 34.8
29. *Rv.* I. 44.11; V. 21.1; VII. 2.3; VIII. 27.9; VIII. 43.13 etc.
30. *Rv.* I. 112.16; VII. 91.1; VIII. 15.5
31. *Rv.* I. 31.4
32. *Rv.* VI. 49.13
33. *Rv.* VII. 104
34. *Rv.* I. 130.5; V. 2.12; VIII. 47.4; VIII. 18.22; X. 91.9
35. *Rv.* I. 117.11; I. 130.8; I. 175.3; II. 20.6-7; VI. 21.11; VIII. 37.5-6.
36. *Rv.* VIII. 23.14
37. *Rv.* VIII. 98.6
38. *Rv.* X. 62.4

39. *Rv.* X. 62.1
40. *Rv.* I. 112.10
41. *Rv.* I. 31.17
42. *Rv.* VIII. 43.13
43. *Rv.* I. 80.10.
44. *Rv.* I. 139.9
45. *Rv.* I. 36.10
46. *Rv.* I. 128.2
47. *Rv.* X. 46.9
48. *Rv.* VIII. 27.31
49. *Rv.* VIII. 27.4; VIII. 27.14; VIII. 30.2
50. *Vāl.* IV.1
51. *Val.* III. 1
52. *Rv.* V. 29.7.
53. *Rv.* IV. 26.4
54. *Av.* VIII. 10.24
55. *Av.* XIV.2.48
56. *Av.* III. 9.2; Bloomfield's trans. in *S.B.E.*
57. *Av.* VII. 37.1. Bloomfield. p.36
58. *Av.* XIX.39.7-8. SBE. XLII. p.67
59. II. 2.10.2 *Yadvai kiṃ ca Manuradvadattadbheṣajam.*
60. XXIII. 16.17 *Manuvai yaṃkti Cavadattadbheṣajam.*
61. II. 6.7.1; I. 7.1.3
62. II. 5.9.1; VI. 2.5.2f; VII. 5.15.3
63. II. 1.9.4-5; *Tait Saṃ.* II. I. 5-6 *Mānavyo hi prajāḥ.*
64. II. 1.9.4-5.
65. VI. 6.6.1; also see III. 1.9.4; V.4.10.5.
66. XI. 2
67. I. 8.1.1-10; XIII. 4.3ff.
68. VI. 6.1.19
69. I. 1.4.14ff.
70. III. 2.5.9
71. II. 30.1
72. I. 1.4.4
73. VIII. 4
74. III. 1.9.4.
75. V.14
76. *Nir.* XII. 10
77. Cf. *Rv.* X. 17.2
78. *Nir.* XII. 34
79. I. 8.1; *S.B.E.*, XII. 216. Trans, by J. Eggeling; For other trans. See. Max Müller, *History of the Sanskrit Literature*, 1869, p. 425; J. Muir, *Original Sanskrit Texts*, Vol. I, 2nd Ed. 1873. p. 181ff.
80. Windner, *Die iranische Flutsage*, Festgruss an Roth 213-6; R. Andree,

Das Flutsagen; N.K. Sanders, *Gilgamesh*, Pelican.

81. *Mbh* XII. 321-33.
82. I. 1. 27-30
83. *Paitāmaha Manor devastasyaputra Prajāpatiḥ* I. 66.16 (Cal. ed., but in the critical ed. I. 60.16 it is *munir* instead of *manor.*).
84. I. 158.50
85. VI. 7.43.
86. IX. 44.10
87. XIII. 2.5; XIII. 14-20; XIII. 17.34.
88. III. 82.117
89. XII. 34.9, 51; XII. 336.33; XII. 349. 37
90. XIII. 18.48; XII. 25.30.31.
91. XII. 37.3
92. XII. 327.29
93. XII. 67. 21ff
94. I. 70. 11ff; cf. XIII. 137.19; XII. 343.26; XII. 350.42-55.
95. I. 90.7
96. XII. 349.51; XII. 149.37.
97. XIII. 18.20. *Variṣṭho nāmo Cākṣuṣaya Manoḥ sūtaḥ*
98. I. 7; IV. 1. Eng. trans. M.N. Dutta, Varanasi, 1912, pp. 237ff.
99. IV. 1
100. I. 11
101. III. 2
102. I. 7
103. IV. 2
104. I. 3.27-30; II. 1.36; II. 7.20; III. 11.26; III. 20.50; etc. Eng. trans. G.V. Tagara, Delhi 1976, pp. 29ff.
105. Eng. trans. F.E. Pargiter, Bib. Ind., Calcutta, 1904.
106. XLVI. 32-33.
107. LIII. 6-8
108. L. 13-21.
109. LXIII. 11-19
110. LXIII. 24-25
111. LXIX. 55
112. LXXV. 66.69
113. LXIII-LXVII
114. LXIX-LXXIII
115. LXXIV
116. LXXV
117. LXXVI
118. LXXVII-LXXX
119. XCIV
120. XCV-XCIX
121. C. 1-45

122. *Matsya.* Chs. I-VIII
123. Ibid. ch. XI
124. XI. 40.42
125. *Mārkaṇḍeya,* XLVI. 33
126. *Ibid.* LIII. 9
127. *Khila Harivaṃśa,* I. 7-9. Ed.D.Chanda, Beng. trans., Calcutta, 1389 B.8, pp. 17-24.
128. *Ibid.*
129. VIII. 160-67; XXI. 28; LVII. 39-41.
130. *Viṣṇu* I. 3
131. *Ibid.* II. 1
132. *Ibid.* I. 13
133. *Ibid.* III. 2
134. *Secret Doctrine,* Adyar ed., IV. p. 145
135. *Science of Social Organisation,* I. p. 92.
136. *Mbh.* II. 49.21
137. *Mbh.* III. 50.4. *Sākṣād iva Manoh svayam*
138. *Mbh.* III. 83.110.
139. *Mbh.* III. 90.10.
140. *Mbh.* IV. 51.10
141. See Cr. Ed. of *Mbh.,* Vol. V. p. 281. note no. 1128.
142. *Mbh.* XII. 67.8ff; XII. 122.39
143. *Rām.* I. 5.6
144. *Mbh.* XII. 343.57
145. *Mbh.* V. 117.14
146. *Viṣṇu,* 1.7
147. *Mbh.* I. 66.46; *Āruṣī tu Manoḥ kanyā*
148. *Viṣṇu.* II. 2
149. *Mbh.* I. 59.44.
150. *Mbh.* II. 185
151. *Agni.* II. 3-15
152. *Matsya.* Chs. I-II.
153. *Bhāgavata* II. 7.12

Chapter III

The Historical Manu

Whether or not the *Manusmṛti* is a metrical restatement of a hypothetical *Mānavadharmasūtra* is a question which, as we have seen above, can never be satisfactorily resolved. But the tradition of Manu as the first-born and the first lawgiver has persisted in India through the ages. In the Indian mythological tradition, there happen to be numerous ages, each of which has a Manu as its lawgiver. Evidently this coinage of the name of Manu is concerned with Mānava or mankind in general. In this sense a Mānava school may also indicate - as against the technical formulations of the scholars referred to above - a set of institutes meant for the mankind in general, transmitted orally or otherwise from an obscure point of hoary antiquity. Whether or not the present version of the *Manusmṛti* is a narration of the teachings of a traditionally accepted ominiscient Manu by Bhṛgu or someone (*mānavam śāstram bhṛguṃ proktam*)[1] is not very relevant to us, but the fact remains that the well known collection of laws and precepts known as the *Manusmṛti*, which is the oldest and most sacred Sanskrit work after the Vedas, was composed by an individual who used the hallowed name of Manu for its universal acceptance. We should distinguish this historical Manu and also the Mānava tradition of ancient institutes associated with him (not in the sense of a supposed pre-existing but non-existent *Mānavadharmasūtra*) from the tradition of the mythical Manus we have recorded in the preceding chapter. It should also be stated in this connection that the metrical *Manusmṛti* must have earlier versions which were recast several times before it assumed it present form.

In the *Taittirīya Saṃhitā*[2] and the *Tāṇḍyā-mahā Brāhmaṇa*[3] it is said whatever Manu said is medicine. The *Taittirīya Saṃhitā*[4] also says that mankind is Manu's (*Mānavyo hi prajāḥ*). In the *Nirukta*[5] there is a discussion about the rights of sons and daughters. One of the views propounded there is that children of both sexes take their father's wealth and a *ṛk* and *śloka* are cited in support of that position. The *śloka* refers to the opinion of Manu Svāyambhūva. It is noteworthy that the *śloka* concerned is opposed to *ṛk* which means that the *śloka* is not *śruti* but is *smṛti*. So before Yāska wrote there were texts of the *Smṛti* type, may be in the verse, in which Manu was spoken of as a lawgiver. Gautama refers to the name of Manu as the only teacher of Dharma,[6] who is cited for the proposition that there is no expiation for the three sins of *brahmahatyā*, drinking wine and violation of the bed of *guru*. Haradatta says that in the extant *Manusmṛti* the same propositions are laid down about *brahmahatyā* and *surāpāna* (in Manu XI. 89 and 146 respectively), but that as to violation of *gurutalpa* a passage from the *Manusmṛti* has to be searched out (i.e., such a passage is not found there). In spite of what Haradatta says there are verses in the extant *Manusmṛti* (XI. 104 -105) which say that death is the expiation for violation of the Guru's bed. The relation between *Vasiṣtha Dharmasūtra* and the *Manusmṛti* is most important. At least 61 verses of the extant *Manusmṛti* are identical with Vasiṣṭha's. Of these some expressly mention the quotation as 'Mānavam' or 'Mānavam ślokam' or use the word 'Udāharanti' about seventeen times, leaving no doubt as to whether they are quotations.[7] There are two places in *Vasiṣṭha Dharmasūtra* where the name of Manu occurs (*Vasiṣṭha* XII.16 and XIX. 37). The latter is cited as a Mānava śloka, because this is not found in our Manu. Besides these two, there are about forty verses that are common to the *Vasiṣṭha Dharmasūtra* and the *Manusmṛti* and about a dozen verses which though not strictly identical, are more or less similar. There are several prose *sūtras* of *Vasiṣṭha* which correspond to the verses of Manu almost word for word. The hypothesis that commends

itself to us is that the *Vasiṣṭha* contains borrowings from the *Manusmṛti* or its purer ancient original. Āpastamba connects Manu with the promulgation of Śrāddhas.[8]

The Śānti and Anuśāsana *parvans* of the *Mahābhārata* in numerous places speak of Manu, sometimes as Manu simply, sometimes as Svāyambhūva Manu and also as Prācetasa Manu. In the Śānti parvan it is stated that Svāyambhūva Manu insisted on non-violence, truthfulness, equity in distribution, kindness, restraint, politeness, steadiness and raising offspring on one's own wife as the principal ideals of life.[9] Prācetasa Manu has been referred to in connection with Rājadharma,[10] in which it is said that the teacher who does not protect, the wife who does not speak soothing words, the cowherd who prefers to travel within the village and the barber who prefers to resort to the forest should be abandoned like a broken boat in the sea. Elsewhere in the same *parvan* it is stated, how the Supreme Being composed a hundred thousand *śloka*s on *dharma*, how Manu Svāyambhūva promulgated those *dharmas* and how Uśanas and Bṛhaspati composed *śāstras* based on the works on Manu Svāyambhūva.[11]

We have already had the occasion to refer to mythical Manus, their achievements and affiliations mentioned in the *Mahābhārata*, but there are many passages which refer to various Manus in connection with legal and moral questions and these Manus belong to the historical tradition. Though the passages pertaining to the moral and legal problems have been variously attributed to Prācetasa, Svāyambhūva or other Manus, the authors had in their minds, the single historical Manu of hoary antiquity whose views were recast and versified in various ages. In the *Mahābhārata* Manu is supposed to hold that the king is like God to the men and is equal to ten Śrotriyas (*manuṣyānāṃ ca yo dhātā rājā rājyakaraḥ punaḥ / daśa śrotriyasama rājā ityevaṃ Manuravravṛt)*[12]. Yudhiṣṭhira is being charged by Bhīma for following the doctrine of Manu mechanically.[13] Bhīsma while giving advice to Yudhiṣṭhira about Rājadharma mentions that according to Manu the duty of a Kṣatriya is to go

for a war whenever he is called for it.[14] The following diktats have been attributed to Manu in the *Mahābhārata.* According to Manu fire springs from water, Kṣatriyas from Brāhmaṇa, iron from stone, but the all-penetrating power of these three has no effect on that whence they are produced.[15] Manu says that those who pay reverence to the Brāhmaṇas attain the heaven[16] (Brahmaloka). Previously Manu has fixed the law that no one will rule over others even in the time of distress.[17] According to Manu intelligence is the basis of success. He also tells that, a person who is wealthy, has a desire for money and does not listen to one's secret-words, becomes successful by his intelligence.[18] Manu says that the king who protects both the beloved and unbeloved people by providing proper punishment (Daṇḍa) is equal to Dharma.[19] Manu says that the man who is absorbed in the water by reciting the *aghamarṣaṇa* hymn becomes free from all sins like the man who has taken his bath after the Aśvamadha sacrifice. People adore him and everyone is pleased with him.[20] There is a along discourse between Manu and Bṛhaspati in which Manu gives him sermons on the causes of creation, effects of knowledge, the cosmic principles, efficacy of Yajña, knowledge of *brahman,* constituents of *brahman,* role of consciousness, the qualities and the sense organs and the *summum bonum* of life.[21] In the Anuśāsana Parvan, Bhīṣma, while discussing about marriage refers to Manu. He also mentions that Manu does not applaud the practice of a girl living with a person whom she does not like.[22] Manu has said that a gift of drink is the best of all gifts and therefore should a man cause wells and tanks and lakes to be excavated.[23] Manu has said that a person who is the giver of water earns regions of inexhaustible bliss in the other world.[24] Conversant with every duty, Manu himself has said that he who, observant of proper restraints, earns inexhaustible merit upon the recipient.[25] Manu has said that if a *śrāddha* is performed with a copious measure of sesame, such *śrāddha* becomes inexhaustible.[26]

All these injunctions attributed to Manu in the *Mahābhārata*

undoubtedly refer to those promulgated by an historical Manu whose views were prescribed in tradition. Apart from these, there are Manu-passages in the *Mahābhārata*, which are in common to those of the extant *Manusmṛti*. These pertain to cosmology, the concepts of *nimeṣa, kāṣṭhā, kalā, muhūrta*, day and night of men and gods, duration of night and day of *brahman*, the ages with preceding and following twilights, position of *dharma* in the four ages, the sets of duty ascribed to mankind at different ages, the creation, sound as the quality of ether, touch as the quality of air, colour as the quality of light, taste as the quality of water, smell as the quality of earth, each succeeding element acquiring the quality of the preceding one, the great elements combining together with their functions, spontaneous adoption of the course of action of the Lord in each succeeding creation, the dispositions with which the abstract qualities are created, and so forth.[27]

The relation between the *Manusmṛti* and the *Arthaśāstra*[28] of Kauṭilya has been a matter of great concern among the scholars. At the outset it should be stated that there is a characteristic difference between the two works. While the *Manusmṛti* insists on Dharma (spiritual and moral good) as the principal aim of life and treats Artha (material good or well-being) and Kāma (pleasures of senses) as inferior and calls upon all to give up Artha and Kāma that are opposed to Dharma,[29] the *Arthaśāstra*, which is meant exclusively for the benefit of rulers (*narendrārthe*) emphatically states that Artha alone is supreme because Dharma and Kāma depend upon Artha.[30] Though Manu and Kauṭilya deal with many matters that are common to both, the principles and emphasis are different and hence the *Arthaśāstra* may be called as a treatise parallel to *Manusmṛti*.

In the *Arthaśāstra* the name of Manu and Mānava school occur several times. There are no less than 40 statements in the *Arthaśāstra* which are same as those of Manu. What is more significant is that the *Arthaśāstra* contains a few verses from the *Manusmṛti* itself. For example the verse *saṃvatsareṇa patati*

etc., found in *Arthaśāstra* IV. 7. is same as the verse found in Manu XI. 181.[31] Similarly, the verse *nāsya guhyaṃ pare* etc., found in *Arthaśāstra* I.15 has its parallel in Manu VII. 105. A half-verse in *Arthaśāstra* III. 14 (*anahitāgniḥ śatagur-ayajvā ca sahasraguḥ*) is found in Manu XI. 14. The first two lines in *Arthaśāstra* III.7 have almost the same idea and words as Manu VIII. 332. But it will be wrong to suggest that Kauṭilya borrowed all these from the extant *Manusmṛti.* It is difficult to say whether the present form of the *Manusmṛti* is earlier than the *Arthaśāstra* of Kauṭilya because the language of the latter is more archaic than that of the former. While Kauṭilya following the Sūtra style, prefers prose to verse, and uses words, some of which are obsolete and a few against the rule of Pāṇini, the extant form of *Manusmṛti* is in verse with simpler phrases and in accordance with the rules of Pāṇini. According to Shamasastry[32] what still more strikingly proves the priority of the *Arthaśāstra* to the *Manusmṛti* as now extant, is the marked difference between the states of societies presented in them, though as regards the views both the texts have a common heritage. There are many fundamental points on which Manu and Kauṭilya differ.

Secondly we shall have to take into account the fact that we have no specific historical information in regard to the date of composition of both the texts. While it is now generally agreed that the text of the present *Manusmṛti* was formulated some time between 200 B.C. and A.D. 200 (undoubtedly a vast span of time), there is a divergence of opinion among the scholars in regard to the date of the composition of the *Arthaśāstra* of Kauṭilya. There are three principal groups of writers on the question of the age of the *Arthaśāstra.* First come those who hold that the *Arthaśāstra* is a genuine work of Cāṇakya or Kauṭilya, the minister of Cāndragupta Maurya (321-287 B.C.) Among the exponents of this view mention may be made of Jacobi, Shamasastry, Fleet, Breloer, Meyer, Jayaswal, Ganapati Sastri, D.R. Bhandarkar, N.N. Law, Sten Konow and several others. The second group of scholars assigns the *Arthaśāstra* to about A.D. 300 and the principal representatives of this group

are Jolly, Keith, Winternitz etc. There is a third group of scholars such as B.M. Barua, E.H. Johnston and a few others who do not accept either 300 B.C. or A.D. 300 as the date of the *Arthaśāstra* but put it at different dates between 300 B.C. and A.D. 300. If the first date be accepted as the date of the composition of the *Arthaśāstra* in that case it must be an earlier production than the extant *Manusmṛti*; in the case of the second date of the *Arthaśāstra*, the extant *Manusmṛti* is the earlier one; and in the case of the third date of the *Arthaśāstra* both the work belong almost to the same age.

It is against this background that we are to explain the references to Manu and the Mānava school as found in the *Arthaśāstra* of Kauṭilya, besides the common verses, statements and expressions which have simultaneous occurence in both the texts. No doubt can be raised on the fact that the traditional Manu mythology was known to Kauṭilya as it was known to many other ancient authors belonging to different disciplines. His acquaintance with the Manu mythology is revealed in the following statement occurring in the Arthaśāstra:

> People suffering from anarchy, as illustrated by the proverbial tendency ρf a large fish swallowing a small one (*mātsyanyābhibhūtaḥ prajāḥ*) first elected Manu, the Vaivasvata, to be their king; and allotted one-sixth of the grains grown and one-tenth of the merchandise as sovereign dues.[33]

But his references to Mānava or the school of Manu lead us to a difficult position. In the beginning of the treatise Kauṭilya categorically states the views of the Mānava school in the determination of the end of sciences. Elsewhere he refers to the views of the school of Manu on the assembly of ministers, the punishment for the loss of revenue, false witness and seizure of property:

> The school of Manu holds that there are only three sciences: the triple Vedas, Vārtā and the science of govern-

ment, inasmuch as the science of Ānvikṣikī is nothing but a special branch of the Vedas.[34]

The school of Manu says that the assembly of ministers (*mantripariṣad*) shall be made to consist of twelve members.[35]

The school of Manu holds that a fine equal to the loss of revenue and multiplied by the serial number of the circumstances of the guilt just narrated in order shall be imposd upon him.[36]

False witnesses, say the followers of Manu, shall be fined ten times the amount which, no matter whether it is true or false, they cause to be lost.[37]

The school of Manu holds that the fine for the direct seizure of precious stones and superior or inferior raw materials shall be equal to their value.[38]

Now the question is: whence did Kauṭilya get the views of the school of Manu? Most Western scholars thought that the source of Kauṭilya was not the extant *Manusmṛti* but the *Manāvadharmasūtra* which was later versified in the from of *Manusmṛti.* Indian writers who did extensive work on *Manusmṛti* like M.M. Ganganath Jha do not subscribe to the theory of the existence of a *Mānavadharmasūtra.* According to Kane, from the references to Svāyambhūva Manu and Prācetasa Manu contained in the *Mahābhārata* it appears that there were two works in verse on (*dharma* and polity) attributed to these two or there was one work containing both. These were subsequently recast as the *Manusmṛti.* These earlier versions were taken into account by Kauṭilya.[39] The *Manusmṛti* itself admits more than one redaction of the text and the *Nāradā-smṛti* states that the original text by Manu was successively condensed by Nārada Mārkaṇḍeya and Sumati.

The *Nītisāra* of Kāmandakī[40] which deals with the theories of social order, authority and obligation of the temporal ruler, theories of state structure and organs of government, principles and policies of government, inter-state relations, functions of envoys, ambassadors and spies, application of various

political expedients, varieties of battle arrays, attitude towards morality and so forth in 20 *sargas* and 36 *prakaraṇas* is almost a summary of Kauṭilya's *Arthaśāstra.* Kāmandakī openly calls Kauṭilya or Cāṇakya or Viṣṇugupta his *guru* and the text itself bears the testimony of Kauṭilya's all embracing influence. According to Jayaswal, the *Nītisāra* was composed in the second half of the Gupta period[41] while according to R.N. Saletore it was not earlier than A.D.700.[42] One should presume that the author of the *Nītisāra* must have been acquainted with the contents of the *Manusmṛti,* but the reality is that all his references to Manu and Mānava school are adopted from the *Arthaśāstra* of Kauṭilya. Kāmandakī did not care to check up with the extant *Manusmṛti* what he had written on Manu or the Mānava school. He simply copied from Kauṭilya. In the *Nītisāra* the Mānava school is mentioned in connection with the division of knowledge essential for the preservation and development of the state and society (*loka saṃsthiti)* in which Kāmandakī says that according to the school of Manu, Trayī, Vārtā and Daṇḍanīti are three branches of knowledge, Ānvikṣikī being a special branch of the Trayī (*trayo vārtā daṇḍanītiriti vidyā hi Mānavāḥ)*; in connection with *maṇḍalayoni* or the nave of interstatal circle in which the school of Manu compute five constituent elements of *mantrī* and others (*prakṛtis,* operative organs) for the sovereigns; in connection with *vigrahavikalpa* or kinds of hostilities in which two are recognised by the school of Manu viz., *kulaja* or that which is inherited from forefathers (continuing for generations, *sahaja* or natural enemy) and *aparādhaja* (caused by wrongs and transgression); and in connection with the council of ministers which should, according to Manu, be composed of twelve persons.[43] In the last case instead of the Mānava school the individual name of Manu has been mentioned.

In the Pali canon there is no text of the Dharmaśāstra type. The *Vinaya Piṭaka* deals with the disciplinary rules for the monks. Still there are some stray evidences which suggest that the *Manusmṛti* was known to the Buddhists. In *Dhammapada*

(X. 131) the following is stated: "He who, seeking his own happiness punishes or kills beings and also longs for happiness will not find happiness after death."[44] The verse is a direct adaptation of Manu (V. 45) which says:

> Yo' hiṃsakāni bhūtāni hinastyātmasukhecchayā
> sa jivaṃśca mṛtaścaiva na kvacit sukhamedhate

It is, however, a fact that in the Pali canon the name of Manu is not directly mentioned. It is only in the Cylonese *Cullavaṃsa* [45] that the name of Manu occurs as a lawgiver. A king has been praised in the *Mahāvaṃsa* for giving judgement according to Manu.[46] In the *Vajrasuci* of Aśvaghosa several verses are quoted as from the *Mānavadharma* which occur in the extant *Manusmṛti.* Buddhism in India was a monastic ideology and that is why its exponents did not prepare any special code for its lay adherents who were allowed to follow the existing codified and customery laws. But outside India, especially in the South-East Asian countries where Buddhism went as an organised religion and also with a civilizing mission, codes were to be prepared for guiding the social life of the converts, and it is most interesting to observe that in the Buddhist countries such codes were named *Mānava-dhammasattham* after Manu. And these codes were formulated on the basis of the extant *Manusmṛti* with regional modifications. In the concluding section of this chapter we shall deal with the codes of the South-East Asian countries bearing the name of Manu.

The Jain authors directly or indirectly were influenced by Manu.[47] This influence is greatly observed in the Jain form of marriages and in the Jain caste system. The author of the *Trivarṇikācāra*[48] echoes Manu III. 21 while describing the eight forms of marriages.

> Brāhma daivastathā cārṣaḥ prājāpatyastathāsuraḥ
> Gāndharvo rākṣaścaiva paiśācascaṣṭamo' dharmaḥ

In the voice of Manu the Jain texts state that a woman when a child must be kept under the control of her father, when married under her husband and when a widow under her son; thus a woman is never allowed to live independently.[49] The *Vyavahāra Bhāṣya*[50] says:

Jāya pitivvasā nārī dattā nārī pativvasā
Vihavā puttavasā nārī nāsthi nārī sayaṃvasā

Malliṣenasuri in his commentary on Hemacandra's *Anyayogavyavacchedika* has quoted certain verses from the *Manusmṛti* without mentioning the name. Some such verses are:

> (The ancestors are satisfied for) two months with fish, three months with the meat of gazelles, four with mutton, and five indeed with flesh of birds (com. on verse 11; Manu III. 268).
>
> He also during a hundred years annually offers a horse-sacrifice, and he who entirely abstains from meat, obtain the same reward for their meritorious conduct (com. on verse 23; Manu V. 53).
>
> There is no sin in eating meat, in (drinking) spirituous liquor, and in carnal intercourse, for that is the natural way of created beings, but abstention brings great rewards (com. on verse 23; Manu V. 56).[51]

The aforesaid commentary contains a few more verses from Manu. The influence of Manu is also found in such Jain texts as the *Bhadrabāhusaṃhitā,* Amitagati's *Vardhamānanīti,* Hemacāndra's *Arhannīti* etc. Influence of Manu is also detected in the Jain enumeration of mixed-castes. This is best demostrated in the *Ācārāṅga Niryukti,* composed about the sixth century A.D. in which mixed-castes like the Ambaṣthas, Ugras, Niṣādas, Āyogavas, Māgadhas, Sūtas, Kṣatrkas, Vaidehas, Cāṇḍālas and their hybrids such as the Svapākas, Vainavas,

Pukkasas, Kukkurakas, etc., are described almost in accordance with what is found in the *Manusmṛti*.[52]

In the *Rāmāyaṇa* there are verses cited from Manu which occur in the extant *Manusmṛti*, besides other stray references to Manu under diverse contexts.[53] The *Mahābhāṣya* of Patañjali[54] contains a verse which is the same as Manu II. 120. The *Pratimānāṭaka* of Bhāsa speaks of *Mānavīyadharmaśāstra* and *Prācetasaśrāddhakalpa*.[55] Śūdraka's *Mṛcchakaṭika*[56] refers to the ordinance of Manu that a Brāhmaṇa sinner should not be sentenced to death, but he should be banished. A Manu mythology was known to Kālidāsa and in many places of his *Raghuvaṃśa* Manu is described as an ideal king whose rule of law persists through all ages.

> Just as among the Vedas the *praṇava* is the quintessence and most respected so also the source of all royal dynasties and universally respected by the wise is Manu Vaivasvata.[57]
>
> Just as the moon emerged from the *kṣīra* ocean so also in the pure lineage of Manu appeared a moon-like Dilīpa.[58]
>
> Just as the wheels of a chariot run by an efficient driver do not go out of the track created out of the wheelmark of a foregoing chariot, so also during his rule there was no deviation from the system continuing from the time of Manu.[59]

Elsewhere in the *Raghuvaṃśa*[60] the greatness of Manu is highly extolled. But Kālidāsa's Manu is an idealised figure and has little to do with the law-giver Manu. The latter aspect was not unknown to Kālidāsa, but in his poetic imagination the mythical Manu was more suitable. From an historical point of view, however, the extant *Manusmṛti* was quite popular since the third century A.D. When the author of the *Pañcatantra* refers to the Dharmaśāstra of Manu etc.,[61] the extant *Manusmṛti* is meant. It is pertinent to note that the text of the *Manusmṛti* has been the same, with very few exceptions, from the sixth

century onwards, as the quotaions in the *Tantravārtika* and the Śaṅkarabhāṣya on the *Vedāntasūtra* show.

Kumārila's *Tantravārtika* stands in the special relation to the *Manusmṛti*. He places Manu at the head of all Smṛtis, even higher than the Dharmasūtra of Gautama. He cites numerous quotations from the first chapter of *Manusmṛti* to the last. A few examples may be cited. After finishing the discourse of the importance of the Veda, consisting of *vidhis, arthavādas, mantras* and *nāmadheyas*, Kumarila starts his discourse on the Smṛtis and mentions *Manusmṛti* as the foremost among them. The *Tantravārtika* says that the authors of the Smṛtis are generally prepared to accept as authoritative the usages of the countries, castes and families that are not opposed to the Vedas and quotes Manu II.6 in this connection.[62] Śabara, the commentator on Jaimini's Sūtras, who must be placed earlier than A.D. 500, refers to Manu as the law-giver (*Manvādipraṇī-tavidhi-vidhānadharma*) and quotes a verse as a Smṛti passages which is practically the same as Manu VIII. 416. Śaṅkarācārya in his commentary on *Vedāntasūtra* and other works has quoted the *Manusmṛti* very frequently. He looks upon the *Manusmṛti* as one of the authorities on which Bādarāyana has relied.[63] In his commentary on the *Bṛhadāraṇyaka Upaniṣad* Śaṅkara quotes Manu dozens of times and calls the *Manusmṛti* Mānavam.[64] In his commentary on the Vedānta Sūtras he quotes Manu I.5,21, I.27, II.87, X.4.126, XII. 91, 105-06 etc.[65] The references also testify that he had before him the extant *Manusmṛti*.

It is, however, on the Smṛtis and the Purāṇas that the influence of the *Manusmṛti* is all-embracing and far-reaching. All the Smṛti texts are mostly based on Manu. The *Yājñavalkya Smṛti*, which according to Kane was composed about the third century A.D., treats of almost all subjects that we find in Manu. As Kane has aptly pointed out, the correspondence of Yājñavalkya's words with the text of Manu is in most cases very close so much so that one cannot help feeling that Yājñavalkya had *Manusmṛti* before him and purposely made an attempt to abridge the somewhat loose expressions of Manu.[66] In fact

Yājñavalkya has condensed 2700 verses of Manu in a little over than 1000 verses. He has often compressed two verses of Manu into one.[67] Though Yājñavalkya has based his text solely on Manu, as a creative law-giver he has elaborated or shortened some of Manu's topics, excluded certain portions (e.g., the first chapter on cosmology) and incorporated a few new features. The *Nāradasmṛti*[68] in its introductory tells about the successive abridgements of the original work of Manu by Nārada, Mārkaṇḍeya and Sumati Bhārgava. There are about 50 verses that are common to Manu and Nārada. But it is interesting to note that, besides those passages which are found in the extant *Manusmṛti*,[69] there are verses in the name of Manu which are not found there or found with variations. This is indicative of the fact that Nārada had a version of Manu before him which was somewhat different from our Manu.

The *Parāśarasmṛti* must have been an ancient one as Yājñavalka[70] mentions Parāśara among the ancient authorities, but the extant *Smṛti* belongs to a later period. The *Parāśarasmṛti* frequently quotes the views of Manu as 'Manurabrabid'. Numerous verses in the *Parāśarasmṛti* are word for word the same as those of the *Manusmṛti*. The Smṛti of Bṛhaspati which was composed before A.D. 500, says that Manu occupies a pre-eminent position because it correctly represents the sense of the Veda and that a Smṛti which is in conflict with Manu should not be esteemed. In numerous places it pointedly refers to the present text of the *Manusmṛti*. The complete Smṛti of Bṛhaspati has not been discovered.[71] Bṛhaspati, like Parāśara and Nārada, had regarded Manu as the supreme authority, but on some points especially in the case of the widow's right to succeed to her deceased husband's estate, he departs from Manu. The Smṛti of Kātyāyana who formed a tirumvirate with Nārada and Bṛhaspati has not also been completely recovered.[72] One interesting fact in the verses of Kātyāyana is that they refer at least to a score of times to the views of Bhrgu and that some of the verses ascribed to Bhṛgu are found in the extant *Manusmṛti*. Other Smṛtis and digests

also consider Manu as their sole authority and incorporate many a Manu-verse in their bodies, though they often show signs of departure from Manu on certain points. This is amply illustrated in Viśvarūpa's commentary on Yājñavalkya which quotes over 200 verses of the *Manusmṛti* either wholly or in part from all the twelve chapters.

The teachings of the law-books were popularised by the Purāṇas in which the authoritativeness of Manu in all temporal, ethical and spiritual matters is confirmed. In fact the deification of Manu and the creation of a Manu mythology are mostly due to the efforts of the Puranic authors who thought it prudent to raise Manu in a supramundane level so that these ordinances might be obeyed by the masses as expressions of divine will. For example, in the *Matsya Purāṇa*[73] it stated that after the great deluge Manu, seated on the boat, asked the Lord Nārāyaṇa who was in the form of the fish, about the origin and end of the universe, the laws of gift and Śrāddha, the division of castes, etc. Having received the proper knowledge in regard to all these, Manu asked Matsya (Nārāyaṇa in the form of fish) about the creation of the universe by Brahmā, advisability of the marriage relation between the Sagotras and their children and a lot of questions on *dharma.* Manu thus learnt from the lord the history of different divine and human dynastics, containing a variety of interesting anecdotes, procedure of the ceremony of Śrāddha, the account of general auspicious ceremonies, greatness of the Pitṛs, greatness of Yoga, various vows, rules about tanks, the process of consecrating a tree, various ways of worship by married women, the method of bathing in solar and lunar eclipses, gift and charity, places of pilgrimage, penance, duties of each Yuga, duties of a king, the state policies, punishments, removal of dangers, propitiation of the Grahas, house-building and architecture, various forms of gifts and so forth.

Though in the extant *Manusmṛti* itself a divine origin of the ordinances of Manu is claimed, this idea was popularised by the Purāṇas through interesting anecdotes, but the emphasis

of the Purāṇas was more on the religious and ritualistic aspects than on *vyavahāra* or purely legal topics. The Puranic topics mostly pertain to the rites, daily worship, impurities, duties of the four stages of life, taboos in relation to food, rules regarding the four castes, gifts, purification of objects, *gotras* and *pravaras*, practices to be given up in the Kali age, the nature of the Kali age, actions and their effects and rewards, morals, sins of greater and lesser degrees, building and consecration of temples, idols etc., hells, sacraments, rites of peace-making, penances and expiation, funeral rites, duties of women, places of pilgrimage, performances of various days, works of public utility, marriage, vows and so forth.[74] Most Purāṇas, from the view point of their Smṛti contents, are concerned with Chapters III-VI and IX-XII of the *Manusmṛti*. The Purāṇas do not show much interest in *vyavahāra* or the legal topics. These are only described in the *Agni Purāṇa*[75] which deals with the institution of law suits, debts and their repayment, the citing of witnesses in a legal matter, the partition of properties, the settlements of boundary disputes and the punishments for abusing the deformed and for singing lampoons. In the *Skanda Purāṇa*[76] eight ordeals are described. In much the same way the *rājadharma* or the science of polity did not attract the attention of most Puranic authors. An exposition of the duties and conduct of a king is found in the *Mārkaṇḍeya Purāṇa*[77] and a few glimpses of them in the *Kālikā Purāṇa.*[78] The *Matsya Purāṇa*[79] also deals with some aspects of the science of polity. It is only in the *Agni Purāṇa*[80] that the science of polity has been treated in greater details under the following sections: the duties of a king; the duties of the servants of a king; the sites and construction of forts; the systems of administration; the duties of a king in the female apartment; the duties of a king towards the royal princes; the acts of a man through the innate forces of his nature, the code of criminal law; the occasion of an expedition; the nature and significance of dreams; the auspicious signs for an expedition; birds unfolding the good or evil fate; portents indicating danger to a beseigning army; the

conditions of journey; the nature of penalties; the daily duties of a king; the duties preceding the day of march; the prayer to Indra; the royal duties; the seven factor of government; the balance of power and how to treat with the neighbouring kings; the utility of diplomacy; and the arragement of the various divisions of the army.

Now about the epigraphic references to Manu. Four kinds of inscriptions are to be mentioned in this connection. The first comprises those inscriptions in which the person of Manu occurs as a legendary ruler with proverbial wisdom, used for the purpose of comparison with the king issuing the inscription concerned. The second comprises those inscriptions which refer directly or indirectly to the *Manusmṛti* or its author. The third comprises a class of land grants at the end of which laudatory or imprecatory verses ascribed to Manu (and sometimes other lawgivers such as Vyāsa) occur. The fourth comprises those inscriptions in which the name of Manu does not directly occur but his views and terminology pertaining to statecraft and legal procedure have reflection.

Regarding the inscriptions of the first category we may refer to the Haraha inscription of Īśānavarman[81] the Maukhari king of Kanauj, who flourished in the middle of the sixth century. It speaks of the king as one

> whose name was worthy of being praised and
> whose lovely excellent fame filled the world,
> while he remained for the perpetuation of
> the moral laws in the world on the path
> of virtue and discrimination like Manu.

In the Pulibumra plates of the Eastern Cālukya king Jayasiṃha I (A.D. 632-663) occur the words *Bṛhaspatiriva nayajño, Manuriva vinayajñaḥ, Yudhiṣṭhiraiva dharmaparāyaṇaḥ*[82] which is suggestive of the fact that the said king had the knowledge of diplomacy like Bṛhaspati, wisdom like Manu and steadfastness in law and conduct like Yudhiṣṭhira. The

inscriptions of the Maitrakas of Valabhi belong to the second category. A grant of Dhruvasena of the Valabhi year 207 (AD 525-26) qualifies the king as *Mānavādī-praṇitā -vidhi-vidhāna-dharma.*[83] The Palitana plates of Siṃhadeva of the year 255 of the Valabhi era (AD 574) of Sāmanta Mahārāja Siṃhāditya speaks of Varāhadāsa (father of the ruling chief) as one "whose intellect was purified by plunging into the waters of the several Smṛtis composed by Manu and others."[84] Some inscriptions like the Palitana plates of Dharasena II or the Wale plate of Guhasena speak of the Smṛtis in general.[85] Dadda V, a ruler of the seventh century, said to have mastered the precepts of Manu.[86] An inscription of the twelfth century refers to a Cālukya king who 'walks on the path of Manu'[87]. A much later grant of Cāhamāna Ratnapāla (AD 1119-20) refers to the law book of Bhṛgu which is probably same as that of Manu.[88]

Inscriptions of the third category, as we have stated above, are the land grants in which there are laudatory and imprecatory verses ascribed the Manu or other law-givers. In most cases these verses occur at the end of the grants extolling the virtues the donor earns by his gift or the evil consequences he has to suffer in the case of any deception. These are conventional verses and the writers were not critically concerned about their exact sources. Thus a verse ascribed to Manu may not be found in the *Manusmṛti*, but may be found elsewhere. It may also be reversed; a verse ascribed to a different law-giver may be found in Manu's text. Again, there are cases in which the verse quoted in the inscription is actually found in the text of Manu or of any law-giver whose name is specifically mentioned. The Banaras copper plate of Govindacandra of Kanauj[89] thus refers to Manu IV. 235 which states the following:

> Both he who respectfully receives (a gift) and he who respectfully bestows it, go to heaven; in the contrary case (they both fall) in hell.[90]

The concluding section of a grant of Kadamba

Kṛṣṇavarman[91] says *Atra Manu gītā ślokā bhavanti* (here are the following verses sung by Manu), and thereafter follow four benedictive and imprecatory verses. The Ramanathan plates of Indravarman[92] also quote similar laudatory and imprecatory verses and ascribe them to Manu and Vyāsa. Such customary verses ascribed to Manu are found in many land grants. Inscriptions of the fourth category in which Manu is not mentioned by name but his views on the duties and responsibilities of the ruler, ministers and officials, state policy, various topics of law, judicial procedure, etc., occur are numerous inscriptions.[93]

The *Manusmṛti* exercised a great influence in the development of law in many countries of South East Asia. It is well - known that the island of Java once received along with Indian culture also the Indian law and that from that time onwards it was maintained as the prevailing system of law in the neighbouring island of Bali. As early as in 1849 Friederich provided interesting information regarding the laws of ancient Java and Bali where Manu has been accorded a very high position as an ancient king and law-giver.[94] That the reception of Indian law in Java must have been accomplished long before the tenth century A.D. is proved by a copper-plate discovered there bearing the date Saka 849 which contains a verdict of the court (*jayapatra*) composed quite in agreement with the rules laid down by the Indian jurists.[95] The treatise of Manu is referred to with great reverence in literary works like *Bhomakāvya, Ṛṣiśāsana, Pratyastibhuvana, Puruṣadasanta* etc. The Javanese law books such as the *Kuṭāra-Mānava, Svarajambu* etc., are solely based on *Manusmṛti.* Among the Indonesian law-books the *Kuṭārā-Mānava* has a special position. In the *Śivaśāsana*[96] the importance of *Kuṭāra-Mānava* as a Dharmaśāstra is highly extolled. The text of the *Kuṭāra-Mānava* was first edited and published by Jonker[97] in 1885 who tried to trace its Indian source with reference to the tradition of Prabhu (lord) Manu, the originator of the system of law, and of a *Mānavadharmaśāstra* and cited parallel passages not only

from the *Manusmṛti* but from Yājñavalkya, Nārada, Bṛhaspati and other law-givers.[98] The importance of *Kuṭāra-Mānava* is attested by the fact that it occurs as the name of an authoritative text in the Bendesari inscription of the fourteenth century. In the Trawlan inscription of A.D. 1358 occurs the phrase *Kuṭāramanavādi-śāstrā-vivacana-tātparya.*[99] The *Kuṭāra-Mānava* contains two legal texts - *Kuṭāraśāstra* and *Mānavaśāstra* - one supplementing the other. The text itself echoes the Indian tradition of Bhṛgu's recasting of the *Manusmṛti.* Here it is stated that the *Mānavaśāstra* was introduced by king Manu who was as great as Viṣṇu and the Kuṭāraśāstra is its recast made by Bhṛgu and preached by Paraśurāma. The name, *Kuṭāra* was probably after the axe (*kuṭhāra*) by which Paraśurāma was characterised. According to H.B. Sarkar[100] a critical study in different chapters of the *Kuṭāra-Mānava* reveals that the portions of Manu's original which have been adopted in this work are arranged from the view-point of their contents basically following the plan of the *Manusmṛti* itself. From this what transpires is that the author had a profound knowledge in Sanskrit, or he depended on some Javanese translation of the *Manusmṛti.* Among the works of the latter category was the *Svarajambu* and it was probably used by the author of the *Kuṭāra-Mānava.* The eighth and nineth chapters of the *Manusmṛti* were especially used in this work. Though the author drew heavily from the *Manusmṛti,* he did not ignore other Smṛtis.[101]

It is not difficult to understand why the law book of Manu could retain its value outside India in countries where Indian civilization had brought Brahmanical traditions. In such countries it was natural that the native rulers, whose education did not differ from that of the Indian princes were inspired by the precepts of Manu and other Indian law-givers to render justice. So it is not surprising that the local laws were constituted there within Hindu or Indian frame as may be seen in Java and may be conjectured, through epigraphy, in Champa and in ancient Cambodia. Sanskrit inscriptions from these regions

are very much suggestive in this regard. For example, we have an inscription from Cambodia in which occur verses, one of which is identical with Manu II. 136 and the other is a summary of Manu III. 77-80.[102] The introduction of Buddhism in these regions did not change the situation. The right path preached by the Buddha was meant for individual salvation. The Buddha or his disciples had never contemplated to bring a revolutionary change in the social order. The Buddhist canonical books contain rules forming a code but only for the use of the Saṃgha, the community of monks and nuns. The lay converts, the Upāsakas, were permitted to live in the condition and social environment in which they were previously living. Accordingly, after their conversion they were subject to the same legal rules as before, the rules of their government, caste, corporation, village or family. But the situation was somewhat different in those countries outside India proper where Buddhism had necessarily to play the role of educator, played in India by Brahmanism. The Buddhist immigrants and local converts could not remain unconcerned with the administration of justice, social codes and personal laws. It seemed natural enough that they had looked for their models in India. This accounts for the emergence of the *Dhammasattham* (Dharmaśāstra) literature. Among the Indian texts forming the substrata of this *Dhammasattham* literature, foremost was the *Manusmṛti*. Though its ritualistic and typically Brahmanical aspects were tailored, the authors of the *Dhammasattham* literature found other portions of the *Manusmṛti*, especially its laws pertaining to statecraft, occupations, property relations, civil and criminal codes, judicial procedure etc., quite valid and useful for their purpose. Such a tailoring is found in the Siamese version of the *Manusmṛti*[103] which was composed about A.D. 1614. Moreover, the hallowed name of Manu was sufficient to give these works a stamp of authoritativeness.

Rev. Father Sangermano, who lived as a missionary at Ava and Rangoon from 1783 to 1807, wrote a book on Burma, which was published in 1843 after his death.[104] This work

contained an "extract out of the Burmese law book called "Damasat" (*Dhammasattham*). In 1847, Richardson edited the *Damathat or the Laws of Menoo* (Dharmaśāstra or the Laws of Manu) in Burmese and English and in 1850 R. Rost wrote about the *Manusāra* composed in Pali and about its relation with the *Manusmṛti*. These studies eventually became of great importance when by the act of 1875 the Buddhist law was officially prescribed for the Buddhists in Burma. Colonel H. Brown, the Commissioner of Pegu, had extracts from four *Dhammasatthas* edited by Moung Tetto in 1875-77. In 1881 A. Führer copied six palmleaf manuscripts of the *Manusāra* and in 1882 published a summary of their contents collected in 1134 verses along with parallel passages from the *Manusmṛti* and later Indian law-books. Fresh research on the Burmese law was undertaken by Sir John Jardin, the British Commissioner for the administration of justice in Burma who discussed a series of legal questions of Burma in his eight *Notes on Burmese Law (1882)* and also persuaded Dr. E. Forchhammer, a German archaeologist appointed by the British Government in 1881 as the head of the Archaeological service of Burma, to do inquiry on the origin and history of the Burmese law. Forchhammer, whose work was published in 1885, tried to prove that the Burmese law-books which mostly bear the title *Manudharmmasattham* (Manudharmaśāstram) came to the Burmese through the Mons or the Talaings who were superior to them in culture.[105]

According to Forchhammer, the Mons or Talaings of Rāmaññadeśa, a people who constitute today a very small ethnic element in the population of Burma and Siam, played in the past a very important role in these countries as a vehicle of Indian civilization. It is through the efforts of this gifted people that the Buddhists of Burma and Thailand were provided with treatises in Pali similar to Sanskrit Dharmaśāstras. The first reference we find to a *Dhammastthạm* is in a Burmese tradition, according to which a Mon priest named Sāriputta, at the request to the king Narapatizithu of Pagan composed in

1174 a code based on a *Manudharmmasattham.* The code was called *Dhammavilāsa* after the title bestowed by the king to its author. The second oldest *Dhammasasttham* ascribed to king Wagaru or Wareru of Martaban (1281-1306) was edited and translated into English by Forchhammer[106] in 1892 which contains the Pali text besides an interlinear Burmese version. This Wareru Code is a Mon translation of a Pali *Manudhammasattham.* This Mon version was in its turn translated into Burmese in the second half of the sixteenth century and according to J.S. Furnivall[107] revised in AD 1637. Therefore we get our information of the original Pali source only through two or three successive translations made at dates very different from one another. The work is very short, only 39 pages in English translation. Beginning with traditional Buddhist formula of the adoration of the Three Jewels, followed by an introduction stating the legend of its origin, it enumerates the eighteen topics of law corresponding broadly to the eighteen topics of the *Manusmṛti.*

Forchhammer has carefully compared the legal rules in the Wagaru Code with those of Manu, Yājñavalkya, Nārada, Kātyāyana and others and came to the conclusion that "there are indeed very few passages in the Wagaru which are not clearly and distinctly Hindu law as contained in Manu and other ancient codes."[108] This is, however, a little exaggeration, though it cannot be denied that the Wagaru Code has drawn much from the *Manusmṛti.*[109] But there are many points of departure as well. Forchhammer himself says that "the Wagaru mentions neither Brahma, nor the Vedas, nor the sacrificial fire, nor any point denoting influence of the Brāhmaṇas and of civil and religious institutions peculiar to Brahmanical India."[110] It is also interesting to note that the Buddhist elements, apart from the prayer to the Three Jewels, are also entirely absent. As regards the origin of the *Manudhammasattham* on which the Wagaru Code is based Forchhammer assumes that the Wagaru code is a remnant of Buddhist civil codes which emanated from a Buddhist Mānava school in India. According

to him these came from Kanchipuram and Srilanka to Burma, and were composed between the seventh and nineth century. This ingenious theory was accepted by Julius Jolly.[111] But according to R. Lingat[112] this theory is extremely weak and seems most unlikely. A Buddhist Mānava school is nothing but a figment of imagination. If the original codes in Pali were composed between the seventh and nineth century, they could not be overlooked by the great commentators on Pali canonical and non-canonical works. The Wagaru code was simply a Mon code, written by the Mons for the use of Mons. This is attested by the facts that according to this code marriage may be dissolved very easily; remarriage of women is allowed unreservedly and without any prejudice being shown against it; and property relations between husband and wife are governed by rules entirely different from Hindu law. Only those portions from Manu are taken which are basically secular and universal in contents. The *Vyavahāra,* that part of the Brahmanical codes which deals especially with the disposal of law-suits, is substantially a technical handbook unrelated to the Brahmanical speculations about Dharma, and it is from this part of the *Manusmṛti* alone that the authors of the Wagaru code had borrowed materials.

NOTES

1. In the *Manusmṛti,* Manu is supposed to speak in his own person, as far as i.60. After that Bhṛgu is the speaker and the closing verse of the whole code (XII.126) describes it as "inunciated by Bhṛgu, while in XI.244 Prajāpati or Brahmā himself is declared to have created it by the power of austerity.
2. *Taitt Saṃ;* II.2.10.2 *Yadvai kiṃ ca manuravadattadbheṣajam.*
3. *Tāṇḍya* XXIII.16.17 *Manuvai Yatkimcāvadattadbheṣajam bheṣajatāyai.*
4. *Taitt, Saṃ* II.1.5.6
5. *Nirukta* III *aviśeṣeṇa mithunāḥ putrā dāyādā iti: tadetadṛkślokābhyāmuktam: aṅgādaṅgātsaṃbhavasi hṛdayādadhijāyase; ātmā vai putranāmāsi sa jīva śaradaḥ śataṃ; iti; aviśeṣeṇa putrāṇāṃ dāyo bhavati dharmataḥ; mithunānāṃ visargādau manuḥ svāyambhūvobravit.*
6. *Gautama dharmasūtra* XXI.7

7. As against the view of Bühler and others, Jha and Kane say that here '*Mānavam*' does not mean *Mānavadharmasūtra*. That is gratuitous assumption. Kumārila (650 -700 A.D.) quotes the extant *Manusmṛti* as Mānavam on *P.M.S.* I.3.2. (p.167 of Anan.ed.); *tathā ca mānavepya-bhihitaṃ pratyakṣaṃ anumānaṃ ca.*
8. *Āpastamba Dharmasūtra* II. 7 16.1
9. *Mbh.* XII. 21.12
10. *Mbh.* XII. 57.43 *Prācetasena Manunā ślokau cemau udāhṛtau Rājadharmeṣu.*
11. *Mbh.* XII. 386. 38-46 *Ṛṣinuvāca tān sarvānadṛśyaḥ puruṣottamaḥ; kṛtam śatasahasraṃ hi ślokānāmidamuttamam; lokatantrasya kṛtsnasya yasmāddharmaḥ pravartate...Tasmāt pravakṣate dharmān Manuḥ svāyaṃbhūvaḥ svayam...svāyaṃbūveṣu dharmeṣu śāstre cauśanase kṛte; Bṛhaspatimate caiva lokeṣu praticārite.*
12. This verse does not occur in the critical Edition as belonging to the main body of the epic. See F.N. 26/402 under I.37, Critical Edition Vol. I. p.180. In Calcutta and Kumbhakonam editions it occurs in I. 41.
13. *Mbh.* XIII. 36. 20.
14. *Mbh.* XII. 55.17
15. *Mbh.* XII. 56.23-24.
16. *Mbh.* XII. 79.29.
17. *Mbh.* XII. 89.15
18. *Mbh.* XII. 113.17.
19. *Mbh.* XII. 121. 9-10.
20. *Mbh.* XII. 148.26
21. *Mbh.* XII. 194-199
22. *Mbh.* XII. 44.17.22
23. *Mbh.* XIII. 64.3
24. *Mbh.* XIII. 66.19
25. *Mbh.* XIII. 67.30.
26. *Mbh.* XIII. 88.4
27. *Mbh.* II. 233, 4-8, 12, 16-17:
XII. 232. 12-32; Manu. I. 18, 28-29, 64-78, 81-86.
28. First published in 1909 by R. Shamasastry; Eng. trans. by him in 1915 with an introductory note by Fleet and a big preface by Shamasastry himself dealing with its authenticity and age; its revised editions were published in 1919, 1924 and 1951; Jolly and Schmidit's edition with an English introduction, notes and a Sanskrit commentary was published in 1923. M.M. Ganapati Sastri published the *Arthaśāstra* with his own commentary called *Śrīmūla* in 1924 in three parts. R.P. Kangle (1960ff.) edited the text prepared from all available mss. materials with glossary, Eng. trans., explanatory notes and study in historical outline (3 vols. Bombay). J. J. Mayer made a German

translation (Leipzig 1925-26) and V.I. Kalyanov in Russian (Lenengrad 1959). It has also been translated in four South Indian languages, in Hindi and Gujarati as also in Marathi (by Karandikar and Hivargaonkar 1927-29) and Bengali (by R.G. Basak 1951).

29. Manu IV. 176
30. Kauṭilya I.7
31. It is also found in *Mbh.* XII. 165. 37: *Baudh. Dh. S.* II. 1.62 f.
32. *Kauṭilya's Arthaśāstra* Mysorc 1967. Pref.
33. Kauṭilya I. 13; Shamsasastry's trans. pp. 22-23.
34. I. 2; *Ibid.* p. 5.
35. I. 15; Ibid p. 28.
36. II. i. *Ibid.* p. 63.
37. III. 11. *Ibid.* p. 203.
38. III. 17. *Ibid.* p. 219.
39. *History of Dharmaśāstra*, Vol. I. Poone 1968, p. 208.
40. A revised edition of R.L. Mitra's *Kāmandakīya Nītisāra* (Bib. Ind. Calcutta. 1861) has been done by S.K. Mitra in 1982. Apart from this, we may refer to the edition published in the Trivandrum Sanskrit Series (No.12, 1912); the text printed by the Anandasrama Sanskrit Series (Poona 1952); Eng. trans. by M.N. Dutt (Calcutta 1896); and *Nītisāra di Kāmandkī* by C. Formichi.
41. *JBORS*, XVIII, p. 37
42. *Ancient Indian Political Thought and Institutions*, p. 9.
43. *Kāmandakī*, II. 3, VIII. 24; X.19; XII. 48.
44. *SBE.* London 1898, Vol. X. Max Müller's Trans. p. 36.
45. *PTS.* ed. 1925-29 by W.Geiger LXXX. p. 55; LXXXIII. 6: LXXXIV. 2; XCVI. 26.
46. Jolly, *Hindu Law and Custom*, p. 94; cf. *Mahāvaṃsa* LXXX. 9; LXXXIV. 1-2; XC. 56; XCVI. 27.
47. See C.R. Jain, *Jain Law*, Madras 1926: J.L. Jaini. *The Jain Law*, Arrah 1916; V.A. Sangave, *Jain Community. A Social Survey*, Bombay 1959.
48. XI. 70
49. J.C. Jain, *Life in Ancient India as depicted in Jaina Canon.* Bombay 1947, p. 152.
50. III. 233; cf. Manu IX. 3.
51. Bühler's trans. *SBE.* XXV. pp. 124, 177.
52. *Ācārāṅga Niryukti* 20-27; cf. Manu X. 6-56.
53. In *Rām.* IV. 18. 30-32 two verses are quoted as 'sung by Manu' which correspond to *Manusmṛti* VIII. 318 and 316 respectively.
54. Vol. II. p. 58.
55. Ed. Ganapati Sastri, TSS, 42, Trivandrum 1915, p. 99; cf. A.D. Pusalkar, *Bhāsa: A Sudy,* Delhi 1968, pp. 65, 357 n.
56. IX. 39
57. *Raghu* I. 11.

58. *Ibid.* I. 12.
59. *Ibid.* I. 17.
60. II. 4; II. 33; IV. 7; IX. 3.
61. Tato dharmaśāstrāṇi Manvādīni, arthaśāstrāṇi Cāṇakyādīni, Kāmaśāstrāṇi Vātsyāyanādīni.
62. *JBBRAS,* 1925, 98-100.
63. On this *Sūtra smaranti ca* (*V.S.*, III. 1.14) Sankara adds *Manuvyāsaprabhṛtaya śiṣṭaḥ.*
64. On I. 4.17.
65. On *V.S.* I.3, 28; IV. 2.6; III.4.38, I. 3.36; II. 1 and 11.
66. Kane, *HD.* I. p. 430.
67. e.g., Manu II. 243, 247, 248 are equal to *Yāj* I. 49. *Manu,* III. 46-48, 50 equate *Yāj* I. 79 and so forth.
68. There are two versions of Narada, the smaller version was translated by J. Jolly in 1876. The text of the longer version was also edited (Bib. Ind. 1885) and translated (*SBE.* Vol. 33) by him.
69. Manu IV. 87; VIII. 12-14, 18-19; 64, 72, 89, 93, 98-99, 113, 140-41, 143, 148-149, 186-87, 189, 191, 224-25, 232-33, 235, 267-69, 281-84; IX. 3.47, 216, 357-58.
70. *Yāj* I. 4.
71. Führer collected 84 verses ascribed to Bṛhaspati in the legal treaties to Aparārka and others and published them with German translation and notes in 1879. Jolly collected 711 verses of Bṛhaspati and published their translation in *SBE.* Vol. 33.
72. 973 verses of Kātyāyana were collected and translated into English by P.V. Kane in 1933. Additional 121 verses were collected and published by K.V. Rangaswami Aiyangar in *Kane Felicitation Vol.* pp. 7-17.
73. Chs. II-IV.
74. *Brahma* XX, XIII, XVI-XVII, CVIII-CIX, CXIII-CXV, CXXII-CXXIII, *Garuḍa* XLV-LII, CVIII-CXXXVII; CCXIII, CCXXII-CCXIII; *Kūrma* (Uttara) I-XXVI; *Mārkaṇḍeya* XII-XV, XXVI-XXVII, XXXI-XXXII; *Matsya* XVI-XXII, LIV-C, CLXXIX-CCVI, CCXVI-CCXXVII, CCLXXIV- CCLXXXIX; *Vāyu* XVI, XVIII; *Agni* XXXVIII-CVI, CLV-CLVII, CXVII, CCLXIII, CCCLXXI; *Varāha* XII-XIV; XCVIII-CXI; CLXXXVII- CLXXXVIII; *Viṣṇu* I. 6; III. 9-16 etc.
75. Chs. CCLIII-CCLVIII
76. *Skanda* I (Kumārikā), 44.
77. Chs. XXVII-XXVIII, Pargiter's Tr. pp. 145-48.
78. Ch. LXXXVII.
79. Chs. CCXVI-CCXXVII, CCXL.
80. Chs. CCXX-CCXLII.
81. *Ep. Ind.* XIV. pp. 110-20.
82. *Ibid,* XV. p. 256.
83. *Ind. Ant.* II. p. 205.

84. *Ep. Ind.* XI, pp. 16-20.
85. *Ibid.* pp. 80-82.
86. *Ind. Ant.* XVII. p. 198; cf. VIII. pp. 97, 303; IX. p. 48.
87. *Ep. Carnatica* V. pp. 23. 151.
88. *Ep. Ind.* XI. pp. 304-13.
89. *Ibid.* II. p. 360.
90. Bühler's trans. of Manu IV. 235.
91. *Ep. Ind.* VI. 18.
92. *Ibid.*, XII. p. 135.
93. *Ibid.*, III, pp. 80-81, 322; IV. pp. 288, 346; VI. pp. 178, 217-18, 349; IX. pp. 95, 326; *CII*, III, pp. 147, 168, 182; *Ep. Carnatica* IV, pp. 60, 62; VII. pp. 50, 58, 59, 89, 146, IX. pp. 39, 73, 85; X. p. 78; XI, pp. 13, 41, 45; XII. p.115.
94. 'Voorloopig Verslag' in the *Transactions of the Batavian Society*, Vol. XXII an translated into English by Logan in *Journal of the Indian Archipelago*, Vol. III, pp. 243 ff., and again in JRAS, N.S. Vols. IX and X.
95. Jolly, *Hindu Law and Custom*, p. 94
96. In the *Ṛṣiśāsana* it is stated that Manu was the first king who intorduced the *Śivaśāsana.*
97. E.C.G. Jonker, *Een Oud-Javaansch Wetboek Vergeleken met Indische rechtbronnen*, Leiden 1885.
98. *Ibid.*, pp. 11, 19, 175, 231 etc.
99. Published by H.B. Sarkar in *Indian Culture*, Vol. II.
100. *Dvīpamaya Bhārater Prācīn Sāhitya*, in Bengali, Calcutta 1970, p. 156.
101. R.C. Majumdar, 'Hindu Law in Java and Bali' in *S. Krishnaswamy Aiyangar Presentation Volume*, pp. 445-61.
102. A. Bergaigne, *Inscriptions Sanscrites et du Cambodge*, p. 423.
103. Its extracts were first published by Low in 1847 in *Journal of the Indian Archipelago*, Vol. I.
104. *A Description of the Burmese Empire*, Rome 1843, Second ed. by J. Jardine, Rangoon, 1885.
105. *The Jardine Prize: An Essay to the Sources and Development of Burmese Law*, Rangoon 1885.
106. *King Wagaru's Manudhammasattham*, Rangoon 1892.
107. J.S. Furnivall, 'Manu in Burma' in *Journal of the Burmese Research Society*, Vol. XXX(ii), 1940, pp. 351 ff.
108. *The Jardine Prize*, p. 58.
109. Cf. Furnivall, *op.cit.*, pp. 351 ff.
110. Forchhammer, *op.cit.*, p. 58.
111. *Hindu Law and Custom*, pp. 92-93.
112. 'The Buddhist Manu' in *ABORI*, Vol. XXX, p. 284-97.

Chapter IV

Manu and the Vedic Tradition

The *Manusmṛti* is regarded as the earliest text of the Dharmaśāstra category. The term Dharmaśāstra is generally applicable to the metrical codes, otherwise known as Smṛti. The term Smṛti indicates that these codes were authorities on the basis of Śruti which were considered as a revelation (*pratyakṣa*) from which remembrance (*smṛti)* arose. Most of the Smṛtis do not pretend to be anything more than the compositions of ordinary mortals based on the teachings of the Vedas. But the *Manusmṛti* is regarded as an exception. It claims to have a divine origin and to be the epitome of all the Vedic knowledge and the upholder of the Vedic tradition. The whole first chapter of the *Manusmṛti* is devoted to the purpose of showing the mighty scope of the book and of setting forth its divine character as well as the manner in which it was revealed to the mankind. In fact, the entire spirit of the *Manusmṛti* conforms so profoundly with the various aspects of the Vedic tradition that Śaṅkara and Kumārila did not hesitate to regard it as authoritative as the Vedas. While refuting the doctrine of the Sāṅkhyas, Śaṅkara says that it contradicts not only the Vedas but also the doctrine of Manu which reflects the purest Vedic spirit. According to Śaṅkara, Manu (XII. 81) implictly blames the doctrine of Kapila for its dualism. Kapila is not mentioned in the Śruti, but Manu, the champion of absolute non-dualism who holds that apart from the One Self there is no second, is mentioned therein and we have a Śruti passage (*Taitt. Sam.* II. 2.10.2) which proclaims the excellence of Manu, viz., 'whatever Manu says is medicine'[1]. Quoting Manu XII. 105-06 Śaṅkara says that according to Manu, per-

ception, inference and Śāstra, (testimony), the three branches of valid knowledge, are to be taken into account by one desiring clarity in regard to the right thinking. He who applies reasoning is not contradicted by the Veda and the doctrine of law (Smṛti).[2]

Regarding the relation between the Veda (Śruti) and the Dharmaśāstra, the following is said by Manu:

> But by Śruti (revelation) is meant the Veda and by Smṛti (tradition) the institutes of the sacred law: those two must not be called into question in any matter since from those two the sacred law shone forth ... the Veda, the sacred tradition, the customs of virtuous men, and one's own pleasure, they declare to be visibly the fourfold means of defining the sacred law. The knowledge of the sacred law is prescribed for those who are not given to the acquisition of wealth and to the gratification of their desire; to those who seek the knowledge of the sacred law, the supreme authority, is the revelation (Śruti) . . . But when two sacred texts (Śruti) are conflicting, both are held to be law; for both are pronounced by the wise (to be) valid law.[3]

In this connection the following comment of Kumārila, deserves special mention.

> Inasmuch as these Smṛtis have emanated from human authors and are not eternal, like the Veda, their authority cannot be self-sufficient. The Smṛtis of Manu and others are depended upon the memory of their authors, and memory depends for its authority on the truthfulness of the source; consequently the authority of not a single Smṛti can be held to be self sufficient, like that of the Veda; and yet inasmuch as we find them accepted as authoritative by an unbroken line of respectable persons learned in the Veda, we cannot reject them as absolutely untrustworthy. Hence it is that there arises a doubt as to their untrustworthy character.[4]

According to the *Mīmāṃsāsūtra*[5] when a *smṛti* conflicts with *śruti* it has no authority, where it does not conflict, there is presumption of corroborative *śruti*. According to the *Āpastamba Dharmasūtra*[6] in case of a conflict what is laid down in the *śruti* is more authoritative. According to the *Gautama Dharmasūtra*[7] when there is a conflict between two equally authoritative texts there is option.

Elsewhere Manu has clarified the fourfold means of defining the sacred law.

> The whole Veda is the (first) source of the sacred law, next the tradition and the virtuous conduct of those who know the (Veda further), also the customs of holy men and (finally) self-satisfaction.[8]

These four are the Śruti or Veda, Smṛti, Sadācāra and Ātmanastuṣṭi. The word Veda or śruti stands for the Saṃhitās along with their respective Brāhmaṇas. In the next verse Manu makes his position more clear.

> Whatever law has been ordained for any (person) by Manu that has been fully declared in the Veda: for that (sage was) omniscient (II. 7).

Most commentators on Manu categorically hold that, the term Veda referred to by Manu denotes the Vedic texts. Apart from the commentators, among the earlier authorities, Jaimini[9] emphatically declares that the Vedic injunction is the only trustworthy source of our knowledge of Dharma, i.e., of what is right, what is conducive to good, temporal and spiritual. In the Dharmasūtra of Baudhāyana[10] it is stated that Dharma has been enjoined in each Veda. The second source of knowledge consists of the Smṛtis. The third is what proceeds from the cultured persons who are free from jealousy and selfishness, fairly well off, free from avarice, haughtiness, greed, delusion and anger. Those persons are *cultured*, who have studied the Vedas, along with their supplements and who are versed in the

art of making deductions from them; those are persons from whom, the direct knowledge of Śruti can be derived. In the *Gautama Dharmasūtra*[11] we come across the same approach in which it is said that, Veda is the source of Dharma, the Smṛti and Śīla of persons learned in the Veda.

From an historical point of view, two significant points may be deducted from what we have discussed above. The first point is that Manu's defining of the sacred law in terms of the fourfold categories of the Veda, the Smṛti, Ācāra and Ātmanastuṣṭi was accepted in principle by other authorities including the authors of the Mīmāṃsā and Dharmasūtra tradition. While the terms Śruti and Smṛti are self-explanatory, the inclusion of the concepts of Ācāra and Ātmanastuṣṭi in the category of the Vedic knowledge are innovatory. And what could have been the cause of including these two categories within the purview of Vedic knowledge? Was it a fact that Manu wanted to reinterpret the Vedas in the line of some new-fangled principles which were influencing the life and morals of the people belonging to his age? To be more precise, was it due to counteract the Buddhist influence? According to Medhātithi Sadācāra means *sādhūnāmācārah*, 'practice of good men' and it has also to be construed with *Vedavidām*, "learned in the Veda" and the two qualifications 'goodness' and 'Vedic learning' come under 'culture'. When in regard to any action there are no Vedic or Smṛti declarations available, but cultured people are found to do it as "Dharma"—something *right*—then that action is to be regarded as enjoined by the Vedas. This clearly suggests that Manu has broadened the scope of the Veda besides the dimensions of the Vedic texts proper and incorporated within it extra Vedic knowledge pertaining mostly to the existing ethical approaches of his time. It is also interesting to note that the commentators have accepted the typically Buddhist term Śīla in their interpretation of Ācāra. Medhātithi on Manu (II.6) takes the two terms Śīla and Smṛti as inter-related—the two together standing for "conscientious re-collections". He also suggests another explanation of Śīla by

which it pertains to all acts, the meaning being that whatever one does one should do with the mind, free from all "love and hate". Among other commentators, Kulluka explains Śīla as standing for the 'devotion to Brahman'. According to Sarvañja Nārāyaṇa in cases where neither Vedic nor Smṛti texts are available one's duty can be determined on the basis of the Sila of a large number of persons learned in the Veda. Nandana defines it as 'that excellent quality of the soul which makes a man respected among the wise as defined in the *Mahābhārata.*'

Ātmanastuṣṭi is otherwise called *svasya priyam,* that is self-satisfaction. This 'self-satisfaction' is explained by Medhātithi as meant to be of those only who are 'learned in the Veda and good' (*vedavidām sādhūnām*), the idea of this being that the 'source of Dharma' is based upon the trustworthy character of the persons concerned. When the 'learned and good' feels satisfied regarding the righteousness of a certain action that action must be accepted as right. Another explanation offered by Medhātithi is that 'whenever one is doing anything, he should keep his mind tranquil and calm, free from love and hate. This self satisfaction pertains to all act'.[12] Kulluka however holds that self-satisfaction is the authority only in regard to the choice of alternatives. Kumārila holds that trustworthiness belongs to the self-satisfaction of such persons as have their minds steeped in the moral grandeur of the Vedas. One point is however clear from these interpretations. This self-satisfaction pertains to those who are 'learned in the Veda' and 'good'. There cannot be any invariable concommitance between 'some form of learning' and 'goodness'. By the latter moral qualities are extolled, which have been regarded as authoritative as the Vedas.

That Manu tried to give a new orientation to the Vedas, in accordance with the changing demands of time is attested by the fact that he was not very much interested in the Vedic rituals. He has not openly condemned the Vedic rituals and used very guarded language to express his dislike for them. He believes that the rituals are performed with the deliberate

purpose of securing some reward. In the Dharmasūtra of Āpastamba[13] it is categorically stated that one should not do his duties with the view to attain wordly ends. This finds confirmation in the following words of Manu.

> To act solely from a desire of rewards is not laudable, yet an exemption from that desire (is not) to be found 'in this (world); for on that desire is grounded the study of the Veda and the performance of the actions prescribed by the Veda. The desire for rewards, indeed has its root in the conception that an act can yield them and in consequence of that conception sacrifices are performed. Vows and the laws prescribing restrains are all stated to be kept through the idea that they will bear fruit. Not a single act here appears ever to be done by a man free from desire; for whatever man does, it is the result of the impulse of desire.[14]

Here Manu is in striking agreement with the views thus propounded in the *Bhagavadgītā*:

> The states of mind of those who have no firm understanding are many-branched and endless. The state of mind consisting in firm understanding regarding steady contemplation does not belong to those, O son of Pṛthā, who are strongly attached to worldly pleasures and power and whose minds are drawn away by that flowery talk which is full of the ordinances of specific acts for the attainment of those pleasure and that power, and which promises, birth as the fruit of acts—(that flowery talk) which those unwise ones utter, who are enamoured of Vedic words who say there is nothing else, who are full of desires, and whose goal is heaven ... that sacrifice is good (*sāttvika*) which being prescribed in (scripture) ordinances is performed by persons not wishing for the fruit of it, and after determining in their mind that the sacrifice must needs be

performed. But when a sacrifice is performed, O highest of the descendants of Bharats, with an expectation of fruit from it and for the purpose of ostentation, know that sacrifice to be passionate (*rājasika*). They call that sacrifice dark (*tāmasika*) which is against the ordinances (of scripture), in which no food is dealt out, which is devoid of *mantras*, devoid of *dakṣinā* presents and which is without faith.[15]

According to the *Bhagavadgītā*, sacrifices, duly performed may be capable of taking people to heaven for transient pleasures (IX. 20-21) and even yielding enjoyments on earth (III. 10-12). Since attachment to pleasures and enjoyment distracts the mind and takes away concentration, valuable for attaining immortality, ritual sacrifices are decried (II. 42-46). The chief contribution of the *Bhagavadgītā* is to give an entirely new connotation to the old term Yajña and to use it generally in the sense of detached action. The same may be said of Manu's interpretation of Vedic ritualism.

All these seem to suggest that Manu made a departure from the ritualistic tradition of the Vedic age. The anti-ritualistic stand was probably due to the influence of Buddhism, Jainism and similar other thought-movements. But this does not mean that he was sympathetic to the new fangled thought-movements, which flourished in India since the 6th century B.C. He categorically states that the sacred law has been revealed from two basic sources — the Śruti and the Smṛti — and "every twice-born men, who relying on the institutes of dialectic treats with contempt these two basic sources of the law must be cast out by the virtuous as an atheist and a scorner of the Veda".[16] The term used by Manu in this connection is *Hetuśāstrāśrayato* Medātithi explains it as "relying upon the argumentative science of the Bauddhas, Cārvākas, etc., while according to Kulluka and Nārāyaṇa, it means "relying on methods of reasoning directed against the Veda".[17] Elsewhere Manu says that, the Hetuka is not fit to be honoured.[18] The

Hetuvādins have been described by Manu as *Nāstiko Vedanindakaḥ.* This has been explained in a latter work called *Parāśaramādhava*[19] in which we read: "The detracting of the Veda is of three kinds. The first is that which consists in seeking to prove the untrustworthy character of the Veda by means of auguments culled from Baudha, Jaina and other treatises; this has been described by Yajñavalkya as being equal in heinousness to the murdering of a Brāhmaṇa. The second consists in neglecting the acts laid down in the Veda through one's tendency to wranglings and disputations; it is this that is referred to by Manu under II. 11, who further regards it as equal in heinousness to the drinking of wine. The third consists in lack of due faith—the acts laid down being done only through fear of popular odium and not through any faith in them; this has been mentioned among minor sins.[20]

That Manu was indeed conversant with the Vedic texts is attested by so many references to the four categories of the Vedic literature found scattered all over the text. The *Ṛgveda* has been mentioned eleven times in the *Manusmṛti*[21] and passages from it are quoted at fourteen places.[22] The *Sāmaveda* likewise is mentioned six times[23] and *Yajurveda* five times.[24] The *Atharvaveda* has been referred to only once with reference to its original names, the Atharvan and the Angiras.[25] The Upaniṣads are mentioned either in the name of Upaniṣad or in that of the science of Rahasya.[26] The Brāhmaṇa literature was also perfectly known to Manu which has been called by him also as Mantraśāstra.[27] In fact Manu has quoted from a variety of Vedic sources. For example, in II. 181 which also occurs in the *Taittirīya Āraṇyaka*[28] such phrases as *punarmāmitrindriyam* occur frequently in later Vedic works. Manu V. 86 refers to the *pavamānī* verses addressed to Sūrya.[29] The verses XI. 262 ff. extolling the recital of the Vedas find close parallels in the Dharmasūtras.[30]

Notwithstanding frequent references to the Vedas and Vedic rites, Manu's inclination was towards the essence of the teachings of the Vedas, not towards following the Vedic observances in a mechanical way. This essence of the Veda, he

understood in terms of *ātmajñāna* or knowledge of the Self. In his own words:

> If you ask whether among all these virtuous actions which one should be declared more efficacious than the rest of securing supreme happiness to man, the answer is that the knowledge of the Soul is stated to be the most excellent among all of them. It is the first of all sciences because immortality is gained through it.[31]

According to Medhātithi, Govindarāja, Kulluka and Nandana, the term *ātmajñānam* used by Manu means "the knowledge of the supreme soul as taught in the Upaniṣads". Nārāyaṇa, however, says that, it denotes knowledge obtained from concentration and meditation. According to Manu, there are six ways for the attainment of supreme bliss which are studying the Vedas, practising austerities, the acquisition of true knowledge, the subjugation of the organs, abstention from doing injury and serving the preceptor.[32] Medhātithi interpretes Manu XII. 83 in a different way. He makes a distinction between the acts taught in the Vedas and the six kinds of actions mentioned above and attaches greater importance to the former. He proposes two explanations for the expression *karmavaidikam* of Manu. According to him, the acts taught in the Veda may either be the Śrauta rites, 'such as the Jyotiṣṭoma' or those called in subsequent verses as '*nivṛtta*', that is the 'rites performed as a matter of duty without a desire for rewards'. Nandana and Govindarāja accept this explanation. But Nārāyaṇa, adopts Medhātithi's second explanation according to which *karmavaidikam* means "the knowledge of the Supreme Soul". The same also is the view of Kulluka who holds that the performance of *nivṛtta karma* leads to final liberation. According to Kulluka's explanation, the *vaidikam karma* means *paramātmopāsanā* or the worship of the Supreme Soul and he quotes the *Bṛhadāraṇyaka Upaniṣad* IV. 4.22 in support of his view.

In fact a critical study of the first and twelfth chapters of

Manu leads us to conclude that Manu had a greater preference to the realization of the concepts of the identity of Brahman and Ātman as enumerated in the Upaniṣads as the *summum bonum* of the Vedic knowledge. In his own words:

> The acts prescribed by the Veda are of two kinds, such as procure an increase of happiness and cause a continuation of mundane existence (*pravṛtta)* and such as ensure supreme bliss and cause a cessation of mundane existence (*nivṛtta*).[33] Acts which secure the fulfilment of wishes in the world or in the next are called *pravṛtta;* but acts performed without any desire for a reward, preceeded by the acquisition of true knowledge are declared to be *nivṛtta.*[34] He who sedulously performs acts leading to future births (*pravṛtta*) becomes equal to the gods; but he who is intent on the performance of those causing the cessation of existance (*nivṛtta*) indeed pass beyond the reach of five elements.[35] He who sacrifices to the Self alone, equally recognizing the Self becomes independent like an autocrat and self luminous.[36]

The last verse of the aforesaid quotation is indeed suggestive of Manu's own philosophical standpoint. The verse quoted above strikingly resembles many of the Upaniṣadic verses in which it is said that he who sacrifices to the Self alone, who connects himself with the nature of the all-comprehensive One, in other words, identifies his individual Self with the cosmic Self, attains true knowledge of liberation.[37] Likewise in the *Āpastamba Dharmasūtra*[38] it is said that he shines in heaven who is wise and recognizes all creatures in the Self who pondering thereon does not become bewildered and who recognizes Self in everything. This shows that the ritualistic tradition of the Vedas has been given a diminishing importance by Manu and in its place the knowledge of the Self has been given greater prominence. In fact, in the next verse Manu is even more categorical in which he says:

> After giving up even the above mentioned sacrificial rite, a Brāhmaṇa should exert himself in acquiring the knowledge of the Soul, in extinguishing his passions and in studying the Veda.[39]

Despite Manu's insistence on *ātmajñāna* as the *summum bonum* of the Vedas, he has preferred to put on record the general rules relating to the Vedic Yajñas. He has also referred to some specific Yajñas as especially efficacious. In the third chapter, he has given detailed descriptions of the functional aspects of the *Yajñas.*[40] He has enumerated the common sacrifices to be performed daily,[41] sacrificial rules relating to the house-holders and the hermits,[42] reason for performing sacrifices,[43] eligibility of persons for performing sacrifices,[44] materials needed for performing sacrifices,[45] persons initiated for sacrifices,[46] punishment for forsaking resolved sacrifices,[47] sacrifical fees, their payment and distribution,[48] sacrificing for oneself and for others[49] and cases in which sacrifices are forbidden.[50] Among specific sacrifices he mentions Agnihotra which is kindling, maintenance and worship of fire employed to attain manifold ends.[51] Oblations thrown into fire are supposed to reach the sun that sends rain which produces crops, the sustenance of all beings. Jaimini[52] holds that since it is obligatory it may be undertaken even by those who are not able to perform every detail of it in its entirety. The same is also the view of Manu who agrees with Śabara that there is no particular time fixed for kindling the sacred fires.[53] The Agniṣṭoma sacrifice has been counted by Manu as belonging to the category of Śrauta sacrifice.[54] It is one of the seven forms of Soma sacrifices and an integral part of the Jyotiṣṭoma, so much so that the two are considered to be identical. It is so called because in it Agni is praised and the last chant is addressed to Agni. It is to be performed every year in spring on the day of the new moon or the full moon.[55]

Manu prescribes Aśvamedha, Gosava, Agnistut, Abhijit, Sarvajit, Viśvajit and Trivṛt sacrifices for the removal of the

grave sin of Brāhmaṇa murder.[56] Agnistut is a Vedic sacrifice to be performed by one who has committed murder unintentionally. It is a form of *ekāha.*[57] Gosava is also a Soma sacrifice. One who desires *svārājya* (sovereignty) may perform it. *Āpastamba Śrautasūtra*[58] says that in Gosava the sacrificer should follow *paśuvrata* (act like cattle) for a year. Abhijit is also a Vedic sacrifice, belonging to the *ekāha* category which is performed as a penance of murdering a Brāhmaṇa. It follows the procedure of Soma sacrifice.[59] Viśvajit is also an *ekāha* (one day) sacrifice in which the sacrificer gives a thousand cows or all his wealth. According to Jaimini[60] in the Visvajit sacrifice the king can donate everything, but not land, since earth is common to all. Śabara in his commentary on this statement says that others have as much right over the earth as the king, and that the latter is entitled to a share of the crops produced from the earth, since he protects the people to whom the earth belongs. We shall subsequently see that Manu has totally endorsed this view.[61] Aśvamedha was originally a fertility-cum-agricultural ritual which later became transformed in a ceremonial for royal paramountcy. But Manu has prescribed this sacrifice as a means of expiation from all worldly sins.[62]

Among other sacrifices mentioned by Manu, Agnyādheya[63] is the first of the seven Haviryajñas and belongs to the nature of Iṣṭi.[64] Among the seasonal sacrifices Manu refers to the Darśapūrṇamāsa,[65] performed at the time of the new and full moon. Āgrayana,[66] the rite the offering of the first corn and Cāturmāsya,[67] the seasonal celebration lasting for a period of four months are observed with various austerities. He also refers to the Soma sacrifices[68] which is the most important Vedic sacrifice originally connected with the rites of pressing the Soma plants to extract wine (*savana*). There are three basic kinds of Soma sacrifices—Ekāha, Ahina and Sattra—all of which have been mentioned by Manu. Ekāha has only one day on which the Soma juice is extracted and libations made. We have already had the occasion to refer to the fact that all one-day sacrifices belong to this category. The Ahina[69] lasts from

two to twelve days. The Sattra[70] type lasts for more than twelve days, sometimes for a year or longer.

Notwithstanding Manu's enumeration of the Vedic rituals outlined above, he was less inclined to their efficacy as is significantly proved in his following observation:

> The four Pākayajñas and those sacrifices which are enjoined by the rules of the Veda are altogether not equal in value to a sixteenth part of the sacrifice consisting of muttered prayers.[71]

This strikingly resembles the *Bhagavadgītā*'s statement: "I am the single syllable (*Om*) among the words. Among sacrifices I am the *japa* sacrifice".[72] Manu's total agreement with this *Bhagavatgītā*-approach is endorsed by the following:

> All rites ordained in the Veda, burnt oblations and other sacrifices, pass away, but know that the syllable (*Om*) is imperishable. It is *brahman* and Prajāpati. An offering consisting of muttered prayers is ten times more efficacious than a sacrifice performed according to the rules of the Veda, a prayer which is inaudible to others surpasses it a hundred times, and the mental recitation of sacred texts a thousand times.[73]

The *Manusmṛti* itself exhibits different stages of the evolution of the religious beliefs and practices and Manu openly lays more emphasis on the Upaniṣadic concept of the identity of the *brahman* (the universal Self) and *ātman* (the individual Self) which later crystallized in the religious concept of a Supreme Being than on the personification of the natural phenomena in the form of deities as we come across in the *Ṛgveda* or their symbolic association with sacrifices as we find in the later Saṃhitās and Brāhmaṇas. Among the important Ṛgvedic deities mentioned in the *Manusmṛti* we come across Agni,[74] Indra,[75] Varuṇa,[76] Vāyu,[77] Mitra and other sun-gods,[78]

Soma[79], both in the form of plant and moon. Viṣṇu,[80] Yama,[81] Viśvedevāh (all-gods),[82] Aśvins[83], Bṛhaspati,[84] Dyāvāpṛthivī,[85] Maruts,[86] etc. It is interesting to note that the Ṛgvedic conceptions of these deities,their natural background and the degree and extent of anthropomorphism are completely absent in the *Manusmṛti.* Their names are only prescribed for the purpose of invocation in connections with sacrifices and domestic rituals. Indra, Soma, Agni, Sūrya, Vāyu, Kubera, Varuṇa and Yama are merely the guardian deities representing various directions to whom offerings should be made. Indra is described as having a world of his own whose incarnation is the mortal king.[87] Agni who is invoked with Soma, Yama, Viśvādevaḥ, Dhanvantari, Indra, Bṛhaspati and the Maruts retains some of his past glory owing to his association with the sacrificial cult. The two deities who maintain some glimpses of their Ṛgvedic past are Yama and Varuṇa. The former is the son of Vivasvat who is mentioned along with Agni and Soma in connection with funeral rites, *karma* and transmigration as also with *ātman* or individual Self.[88] He stimulates energy in the king along with Indra, Arka (sun), Varuṇa, Candra (moon), Agni and Pṛthivī and rules over both friends and foes. He is the chastiser of all evil-doers.[89] Varuṇa in the Ṛgveda is the mighty moral governor whose eyes notice everything and whose *pāśas* or fetters bind the sinners. Though later his position became lowered and he was reduced to an Indian counterpart of Neptune, Manu has insisted on his original Vedic character and described him as the Lord of punishment whose fetters are impossible to be avoided by the sinners. His anger may be subsided by offering prayers to him either singly or conjointly with Soma, Rudra, Aryaman and Mitra.

Besides the higher gods, Manu has not forgotten to refer to the deities conceived in the Vedas as *gaṇas* or tribes such as the Ādityas, Rudras, Vasus, etc.[90] Folk deities and spirits such as the Sādhyas, the Apsarases, the Gandharvas, etc., that have made their way into the Vedic texts are also mentioned.[91] Kubera the lord of the Gandharvas and Kaśyapa the

mythological ancestor of the gods have not been ignored.[92] But these deities, along with the higher ones whose exploits had attracted the imagination of the Vedic seers, have been treated with a diminishing importance in the *Manusmṛti.* Instead of the nature-gods of the past or the popular nature-spirits, Manu lays much more importance on the highly personalised deities who have made their appearance in the Brāhmaṇa literature. To this category belong such cosmogonic principles as Hiraṇyagarbha, Puruṣa, Prajāpati and so forth and Manu's insistence on these deified principles is obviously meant for providing the rationale or logical steps (which have been elaborated in the next chapter) for the establishment of the doctrine of *ātman* or *brahman* and to explain the earlier Vedic cults and conceptions in terms of this doctrine of the Self. In his own words:

> The Self alone is the multitude of the gods, the universe rests on the Self; for the Self produces the connection of these embodied (spirits) with actions.[93]
>
> Some call him Agni, others Manu, others Prajāpati (the lord of creatures) others Indra, others Prāṇa (the vital air) and again others the eternal *brahman.*[94]
>
> He pervades all created beings in the five forms and constantly makes them, by means of birth, growth and decay, revolve like the wheels of a chariot.[95]
>
> He who thus recognises the Self through the Self in all created bodies, becomes equal towards all, and enters the highest state, *brahman.*[96]

Thus, it is quite evident that despite Manu's handling of all the major topics as found in the Vedas and his delineation of all the Vedic ritualistic expressions his basic commitment is to the Upaniṣadic doctrine of Ātman or Brahman which he regards as the essence of the teachings of the Vedas. Though he is averse to the hererodox and professedly anti-Vedic

systems like Buddhism or Jainism he is wise enough to incorporate some aspects of their doctrines such as *śīla, sadācāra, ahiṃsā,* etc., within the purview of the teachings of the Vedas. For example, as regards the doctrine of *ahiṃsā,* Manu says that even teachings should be imparted to students in a non-violent way, without inflicting any corporal punishment, through sweet and gentle speech.[97] Elsewhere he says:

> He who injures innoxious beings from a wish to (give) himself pleasure, never finds happiness, neither living nor dead. He who does not seek to cause the sufferings of bonds and death to living creatures (but) desires the good of all (beings) obtains endless bliss. He who does not injure any (creatrue) attains without an effort what he thinks of, what he undertakes, and what he fixes his mind on. Meat can never be obtained without injury to living creatures, and injury to sentient being is detrimental to (the attainment of) heavenly bliss; let him therefore shun (the use of) meat. Having well considered the disgusting origin of flesh and the (cruelty of) fettering and slaying corporeal beings, let him entirely abstain from eating flesh.[98]
>
> By not injuring any creatures, by detaching the senses (from objects of enjoyment) by the rites prescribed in the Veda and by rigorously practising austerities (men) gain that state (liberation) even in this world.[99]
>
> Abstention from injuring (creatures), veracity, abstention from unlawfully appropriating (the goods of others), purity and control of organs, Manu has declared to be the summary of the law for the four castes.[100]

To sum up, the spirit of the *Manusmṛti* conforms so profoundly with the various aspects of the Vedic tradition that Śaṅkara and Kumārila did not hesitate to regard it as authoritative as the Vedas. According to Manu there are four means of defining the sacred law. These are Śruti or the Vedic texts,

Smṛti or the legal treatises composed under the influence of the Vedic tradition, Sadācāra or virtuous conduct and Ātmanasantuṣṭi or self-satisfaction. While the categories of Śruti and Smṛti are self-explanatory, the inclusion of the concepts of Sadācāra and Ātmanasantuṣṭi are thought-provoking from an historical point of view. Though according to the traditional commentators Sadācāra means the virtuous conduct of those who know the Veda further along with the customs of the holy men and Ātmanasantuṣṭi means 'the self-satisfaction of the virtuous which may be counted as law for cases not to be settled by any of the other authorities' or for cases where an option is permitted, it appears that these two concepts which basically insist on a person's individual sense of morality and judgement rather than of absolute dependence on codified and customary laws, were adopted by Manu from an alternative tradition—pertaining mostly to Buddhism and allied systems—in order to give a new interpretation of the Vedas in accordance with the changing demands of time. This is attested by the fact that Manu was not very much interested in the Vedic rituals. His views on rituals and sacrifices are in accordance with those expressed in the *Bhagavadgītā*. Manu's departure from the ritualistic tradition of the Vedas is probably due to the influence of Buddhism, Jainism and similar other thought-movements including the anti-ritualistic *bhakti*, and he does not hesitate to accept some of their key-concepts which are applicable to mankind in general. His *ahiṃsā satyamasteyam saucamindriyanigraha* (X.63) is nothing but a Sanskrit rendering of the teaching of Lord Mahāvīra.

But this does not mean that he has any soft corner for these heterodox systems. He vehemently criticizes their insistence on the untrustworthy character of the Vedas. That Manu was conversant with all branches of Vedic learning is very clear from the *Manusmṛti* itself. He mentioned the three Vedas and the *Atharvāṅgirasa*,[101] the Āraṇyakas,[102] the Vedāṅgas[103] and the Dharmaśāstras[104] and several authors such as Atri, Bhṛgu, Śaunaka and Vasiṣṭha.[105] His knowledge in the Upaniṣads is

revealed in numerous passages which also refer to the Ākhyānas, Itihāsas, Purāṇas and Khilas as well as the Vaikhānasamata.[106] That he knew some works opposed to the teachings of the Vedas—the writings of the Buddhists, Jaina and others—is indicated by his reference to *Vedabāhyā-smṛtayaḥ*, the heretics and their guilds, atheism and calumny of the Vedas, etc.[107] The incipient forms of the Sāṅkhya and Yoga were not also unknown to him.[108] But notwithstanding frequent references to the Vedas and Vedic rites his inclination is towards the essence of the teachings of the Vedas and not towards following the Vedic observances in a mechanical way. The term *ātmajñāna* used by Manu means, according to his commentators, the knowledge of the Self as taught in the Upaniṣads, the equation of the individual Self (*ātman*) with the cosmic Self (*brahman*). Though he prefers to put on record the general rules relating to the Vedic rituals and some specific sacrifices he says, almost in the same language of the *Bhagavadgītā*, that those sacrifices which are enjoined by the rules of the Veda are altogether not equal in value to a sixteenth part of muttered prayers. All the Vedic gods have been mentioned by Manu, but his emphasis on certain deified cosmic principles is meant to provide the rationale for the establishment of the identity of *ātman* and *brahman* and to explain the earlier Vedic cults and conceptions in terms of the doctrine of the Self. Though he is averse to the heterodox systems like Buddhism or Jainism he has incorporated some aspects of their doctrines within the purview of the teachings of the Vedas. His insistence on the doctrine of non-violence is by no means less vigorous than that of the Buddhist or Jains.

NOTES

1. On *Vedānta Sūtra* II.1.1.
2. On *Ibid.* II.I.11.
3. Manu II. 10.12-14. Bühler's Translation.
4. *Tantravārtika.* G.N. Jha's Translation. p. 105.
5. I. 3.3.

6. I. 30.9.
7. I. 6
8. Manu II. 6.
9. *Mīmāṃsāsūtra* I. 1-2.
10. I. 1.6.
11. I. 1. 1-2.
12. See, *Medhātithibhāṣya,* Translated into Bengali by Pandit Bhutnath Saptatirtha, Sanskrit College, Calcutta, 1361 B.S. p. 64ff.
13. I. 20. 1-2.
14. Manu II. 2-4, Bühler's Translation.
15. *Bhagavadgītā* II. 42-44, XVII. 11.13, K.T. Telang's Translation, *SBE* vol. VII. pp. 47-48, 118-19.
16. Manu II. 11.
17. According to Yājñavalkya, I. 2.27, the decring of the Veda should be regarded as equal to the killing of a Brāhmaṇa.
18. Manu IV. 30, But in XII. 111 Manu says that Hetuka is a person who must be a member of the Pariṣad.
19. *Prāyaścitta,* p. 424.
20. G.N. Jha, *Explanatory Notes,* p. 42. According to Hārīta VII. 21 that person is a Nāstika who decries what is said in the Veda, who does not discriminate between virtue and vice and who does not admit the existence of the other world.
21. Manu I. 23; II.158; III. 131; 142, 145; IV. 124. XI. 262-65, XII. 112.
22. Manu II. 181; V. 86; VII. 106; XI. 250-58, 260-61.
23. Manu I. 23, III. 145, IV. 123-24, XI. 263, XII. 112.
24. Manu I. 23; 1. 124; XI. 263, XI. 265, XII. 112
25. Manu XI. 33
26. Manu VI. 29; XI. 263.
27. Manu IV. 100
28. I. 30; cf. *Viṣṇu Smṛti* XXVIII. 51.
29. *Ṛv.* I. 50 1ff.
30. Cf. *Baudhāyana* III. 9. 5-21; IV. 5.29.
31. Manu XII. 83.
32. Manu XII. 85.
33. Manu XII. 88. Kulluka holds that by the expression "acts taught in the Vedas" is meant sacrifices like the Jyotiṣṭoma and the worship of images.
34. Manu XII. 89 Medhātithi explains "preceded by the acquisition of true knowledge (*jñānapūrvam*) as meaning "whereof knowledge is the chief part" (*jñānam ādyam mukhyaṃ yasya*).
35. Manu XII. 90. Kulluka remarks that the expression "becomes equal to the gods" gives only an instance of the rewards attainable by acts intended to have rewards. "Passing beyond the reach of five elements" means according to most commentators "obtaining final liberation".

36. Manu XII. 91.
37. Cf. *Īśā Upaniṣad* VI. *ātmānāṃ eva sarvadevatāmayatvana yojayete*, etc.
38. I. 23. 1
39. Manu XII. 92. The phrase, "above mentioned sacrificial rites" has been explained by Medhātithi and Kulluka as "*agnihotra* and the rest".
40. Manu III. 81-82.
41. Manu III. 70-74.
42. Manu III. 75-80, 93; IV. 21-24; VI. 5.
43. Manu III. 68-69.
44. Manu II. 171-72; IV. 205-6; XI. 36-40.
45. Manu XI. 11-15, 24, 26.
46. Manu I. 128; IV. 130-210; VII. 360.
47. Manu VII. 388.
48. Manu VII. 206-10. XI. 38-40.
49. Manu I. 88-90, X. 75-78.
50. Manu III. 65. 151-64; IX. 290, XI. 60-64.
51. Manu II. 15; IV. 10, 25; V. 167. VI. 9, XI. 42.
52. Jaimini VI. 3.1-10.
53. On Jaimini V; 4.16.
54. Manu II. 143.
55. For details see *Taitt. Sam.* 1. 2-4, III.1-3, VI. 1-6, VII. 1; *Taitt. Br.* I. 1-1, I. 4.1-6; I. 5-4, II.2.8; *Śat. Br.* III-IV, Ait. Br. 1-15; *Āp. Sr.* X-XIV; *Kat. Sr.* VII-XI. *Baudh. Sr.* VI-X; *Āśv. Sr.* IV-VI.
56. Manu XI. 75.
57. For details see *Taitt. Br.* II. 7.12; *Āśv.Sr.* IX.7.22-23.
58. XXII. 12-20; 13. 1-3.
59. Jaimini VI. 7.14; VIII. 1.16; *Āśv.Sr.* VIII. 5.13.
60. VI. 7.3.
61. Manu VIII. 39. IX. 44, etc.
62. Manu XI. 83.
63. Manu III. 143.
64. For details see *Taitt. Br.* I. 1; 2-10, I. 2.1: *Śat. Br.* II. 1-2; *Āśv. Sr.* II. 1.9ff., etc.
65. Manu IV. 25.
66. Manu IV. 24-25, vi. 10.
67. Manu IV. 26. VI. 10.
68. Manu IV. 26. XI. 7-10.
69. Manu XI. 198.
70. Manu V. 93.
71. Manu II. 86.
72. *Bhagavadgītā* X. 25.
73. Manu II. 84-85.

74. III. 86, 211; V. 96, VII. 4.7; VIII. 86; IX. 303, 310, 317-18; XI. 120, 122; XII. 121, 123.
75. III. 87; IV. 182; V. 95; VII. 4.7; VIII. 344, IX.303-04; XI. 122; XII. 121. 123.
76. III. 86. V. 96; VII. 4.7; VIII. 86; IX. 244-45, 303, 308.
77. V. 96; VII. 4.7; VIII. 86; IX. 303, 306; XI. 122.
78. III. 85; V. 96; VII. 4.7; VIII. 86; IX. 303; XII. 121.
79. III. 87. 158, 180, 211; IV. 231; V. 96; VII. 4.7; VIII. 86; IX. 129, 303, 306; X. 80; XI. 255; XII. 121.
80. XII. 121.
81. III. 87, 211; V. 96; VII. 4.7; VIII. 86, 92, 173; IX. 303, 307; XII. 17, 21-22.
82. III. 85-86; IV. 183; XI. 29.
83. IV. 231.
84. XI. 120, 122.
85. III. 86; IV. 183-84; VIII. 86.
86. III. 88; XI. 222.
87. IV. 122; V. 96; VII. 4, 7.
88. III. 211; VI. 21; VII. 86; VIII. 92.
89. IX. 303, 307, XII. 18, 20-21.
90. III. 284; XI. 222, 225.
91. III. 195; XII. 47, 49.
92. V. 96; VII. 4,7, 42; IX. 129.
93. XII. 119.
94. XII. 123.
95. XII. 134; cf. *Bhagavadgītā* XVIII. 61.
96. XII. 125.
97. II. 159: Ahiṃsā iva bhūtānāṃ kāryāṃ śreyo'nuśāsanaṁ
    Vāk caiva madhura ślakṣṇā prayojyā dharmani cchatā
98. V. 45-49.
99. VI. 75.
100. X. 63; cf. XI. 223; XII. 83.
101. I. 23; II. 158; III. 131, 142, 145; IV. 123-24; V. 86; VIII. 106; XI.33, 250-58; 262-65; XII. 192.
102. IV. 103.
103. II. 141; III. 185; IV. 98.
104. II. 10; III. 232; XI. 111.
105. III. 16; VIII. 140.
106. III. 232; IV. 1; IV. 83; IV. 94, etc.
107. IV. 30; IV. 61; IV. 163; XII. 95.
108. I. 14ff. VI. 70, 73.

Chapter V

Cosmological Conceptualizations

Cosmology is the philosophy of the universe. Cosmogony, ontology and teleology are related branches of cosmology dealing respectively with the questions concerning the origin, inner nature and purpose of the universe. Cosmography is the description of its general features. In the first chapter of the *Manusmṛti* we come across a compendium of the various cosmological ideas of the earlier periods. From these earlier ideas Manu had attempted to erect a framework of concepts and relations, in satisfaction of some emotional or intellectual drive, for the purpose of bringing descriptive order into the world as a whole and to bring uniformity among various theories of creation which were prevalent in his time. The cosmological projections of Manu, in which the earlier traditions are classified and given an orderly form, were readily accepted and elaborated by the Puranic authors.

The first work in which some aspects of Manu's cosmology were touched upon was published in 1823, and its author was John Marsh.[1] In 1887 H.W. Wallis published a work on Ṛgvedic cosmology in which discussions on certain aspects like the concept of the primordial waters as the primal element or that of the Golden Germ presupposed some of Manu's formulations.[2] Manu's world-view was dealt with in somewhat greater details in Roussel's work, published in 1893, in connection with the cosmological contents of the *Bhāgavata Purāṇa.*[3] The first work to deal exclusively with the contents of *Manusmṛti* pertaining to the cosmogonical theories was made in 1904 by Wilhelm Jahn.[4] Among subsequent works, one made by

Sampurnanand (1942) contains Manu's theories of creation within the framework of the Indian cosmogonical tradition as a whole.[5] The next work of importance is the fifth volume of Kane's *Magnum Opus* (1962) which contains a big chapter on cosmology.[6] Besides dealing with Manu's conception of the universe as described by him in terms of time, space, matter, etc., Kane has grouped his theories of creation into three categories: (i) The emergence of the universe from the fathomless waters, enveloped by darkness in the form of the Golden Egg through the irresistible power of the divine self-existent; (ii) emergence of the world as a result of union caused by the division of Brahmā's own body into two halves, male and female; and (iii) creation through the working of Brahmā's mind and of Ākāśa and other material elements. In N.N. Bhattacharyya's work on the history of Indian cosmogonical ideas (1971) it is said that the law-book of Manu serves to illustrate the hodgepodge state of views on cosmogony which prevailed before the time when the Purāṇas took their present form. A very brief account of Manu's creation theories is found therein.[7] R.F. Gombrich's articles 'Ancient Indian Cosmology' (1975) is also important for the understanding of Manu's cosmology.[8] S.S. Bhattacharjee (1978) has made a brief assessment of Manu and held that despite the want of details the *Manusmṛti* has to be admitted as the first work presenting the Hiraṇyagarbha theory of creation in its totality.[9]

Manu's cosmogony can be divided into few categories: those beginning with the material principles like earth, water, fire, air, etc.; those beginning with the abstract principles like chaos, time, night, desire, non-being, *ātman,* etc.; and those beginning with the divine principles like Prajāpati, Brahman, Viśvakarman, Puruṣa, etc. These categories again are not solely independent of one another. There are certain intermediary elements like the concept of the primeval waters, the world-egg floating on it, the Golden Germ or Hiraṇyagarbha and so on. Manu introduced a system of his own in order to reconcile conflicting views on the origin of the world by

associating some of them with secondary creations and by distinguishing their relative positions.

The *Ṛgveda* postulates only water as the primordial element from which others gradually evolved. In the Vedic literature, it is said that Hiraṇyagarbha or the Golden Germ is said to have arisen in the beginning from Great Waters, which contained the floating egg from which arose Viśvakarman, the craftsman who fashioned the earth. The concept of the primordial waters recurs in the mythology of the Brāhmaṇa literature which speaks of the waters as having produced after a year's fervour the Golden Egg from which sprang Prajāpati.[10] The conept of the universe being created from a Cosmic Egg is found in most mythologies of the world. That is why the champions of comparative mythology took up the subject with great interest. This approach in the field of Vedic mythology was initiated by Kühn and Max Müller and upheld by Macdonell, Bloomfield, Schroeder and Benveniste and later by Dumezil. But scholars like Muir, Bergaigne, Hillebrant, Oldenberg, Pischel and Geldner did not like to attach much important to it.[11] The comparative method in the context of the Cosmic Egg was revived by Sukumari Bhattacharji in her analysis of the Hiraṇyagarbha of the Indian tradition.[12]

Although Manu believed that the world came into existence through the agency of a Supreme Being, his approach was not towards a cosmogonic theory of the Biblical pattern in which Jahweh, the God of Israel,

> had measured the waters in the hollow of his hand and meted out heaven with the span and comprehended the dust of the earth, in a measure, and weighed the mountains in scales, and the hills in a balance.[13]

It was due to the fact that Manu had to accommodate the earlier mythological cosmogonies, widely differing ideas which were current in his time in his scheme. His views on the Primordial Waters and the Cosmic Egg may be summarised as

follows: The Universe existed in the shape of darkness, unseen by others, without any distinctive marks. Then the divine Self-existent (Svayambhū) dispelled the darkness, created the waters and placed his seed in them. That seed became a golden egg. In that egg the Self-existent was himself born as *brahman*. Also equated with Nārāyaṇa and the Puruṣa, this *brahman* resided in that golden egg during a whole year. Then he divided the egg in two halves, which formed heaven and earth, containing in the space between the eight points of horizon and the primordial waters.[14] So we have in this, three cosmogonic principles, viz. the Self-existent One—also known as *brahman*, Puruṣa and Nārāyaṇa—the Primeval Waters and the Cosmic Egg.

In the famous creation hymn of the *Ṛgveda*[15] the question is raised whether the fathomless waters existed before the formation of the world and the answer is given in affirmative. In the *Ṛgveda* waters are said to have given birth to Agni[16] and Savitṛ[17] and also connected with Aditi.[18] In the *Taittirīya Saṃhitā*[19] it is stated that in the beginning there was nothing but waters and Prajāpati as wind went over them or floated on a lotus leaf. In the *Bṛhadāraṇyaka Upaniṣad*[20] Gārgī opens a discussion with the philosopher Yājñavalkya by asking for an explanation of the popular theory that all this world is woven, warp and woof, on water. Likewise the *Chāndogya*[21] says "it is just water solidified that is this earth." In the *Kaṭha*[22] the following is stated: "He who was born of old from *tapas*, was born from the waters." Water as the primal element is also mentioned in other Upaniṣads.[23]

The Rgvedic conception of Golden Germ or Hiraṇyagarbha, emanating from the primeval waters, afterwards developed into that of World Egg of *brahman*. Full development of the conception of the World Egg theory is, however, to be found in post-Ṛgvedic literature. In the *Śatapatha Brāhmaṇa*[24] we have the following account:

In the beginning there was water, nothing but water. The

waters desired: 'How can we be reproduced?' So saying they toiled. . . . While they were performing austerity, a golden egg came into existence. . . . This golden egg floated about for the period of a year. From it in a year a male (Puruṣa) came into existence who was Prajāpati. . . . He divided this golden egg. . . . In a year he desired to speak. He uttered *bhūr* which became this earth; *bhuva* which became this firmament and *svar* which became that sky. . . . Desiring offspring he went on worshipping and toiling. He conceived progeny in himself; with his mouth he created the gods, etc.[25]

Another ancient account of the Cosmic Egg is found in the *Chāndogya Upaniṣad.*[26] It runs as follows:

> In the beginning there was non-existent. It became existent, it grew. It turned into an egg. The egg lay for the time of a year. The egg broke open. The two halves were one of silver, the other of gold. The silver one became this earth; the golden one the sky, the thick membrane (of the white) the mountains; the thin membrane (of the yolk) the mist with the clouds; the small veins, the rivers; the fluid was sea.[27]

In view of what we have exemplified above, it is abundantly clear that Manu has consistently used the ancient concepts of primordial waters and the cosmic egg in his scheme of cosmogonic evolution. The tradition of cosmic egg persisted in subsequent ages also and even it made way into the scientific works. The result of this compromise may be seen in the following abstract of the *Sūryasiddhānta.*[28]

> The Brahma-egg is hollow; within it is the universe consisting of earth, sky, etc., it has the form of a sphere, like a receptacle made of a pair of caldrons. A circle within the Brahma-egg is styled the orbit of the other; within that is the revolution of the asterisms; and likewise in order one

> below the other revolve Saturn, Jupiter, Mars, the Sun, Venus, Mercury and the Moon.[29]

According to Manu,[30] the waters are called *nārāḥ,* and as they were the first residence (*ayana*) of *brahman,* the latter was called Nārāyaṇa. An earlier reference to Nārāyaṇa is met with in the *Śatapatha Brāhmaṇa*[31] in which he is coupled with Puruṣa, pointing to such an identification. Basically a personification of the primordial waters, Nārāyaṇa was so much anthropomorphised that his original watery character was lost in the Nārāyaṇīya section of the *Mahābhārata,* though in the Purāṇas, the name Nārāyaṇa has been derived from water. It is interesting to note that according to the narrative of the *Mārkaṇḍeya Purāṇa*[32] whenViṣṇu, stretching Śeṣa out, wooed the sleep of contemplation at the end of a *kalpa,* the universe was converted into an absolute ocean.

The *Ṛgveda* postulates only water as primordial element or matter from which others gradually evolved. The idea of *māhābhūtas* or five material elements developed in later philosophy. Apart from water other material elements like earth, air, fire and space are first mentioned in different Upaniṣads.[33] The Cārvākas hold that the world is a spontaneous growth promoted by the chance-combination of material elements and no intervention of God is needed in creation. They believe in the doctrine of four elements—earth, water, fire and air—and omit the fifth which is space. The doctrine of five elements is recognised by most philosophical schools of India, especially by the Sāṅkhyas and the Vaiśeṣikas. The Sāṅkhya describes the five elements as evolutes of Prakṛti which come into existence when the equilibrium is disturbed owing to contact with Puruṣa. The Vaiśeṣikas insist on the capacity of an element to generate an effect, like water hardening into ice. Earth and water possess velocity (*vega*) and gravity (*gurutva*). The later is absent in fire and air. A substance of wider dimension can hold the object of limited dimension. The wider dimension is space or Ākāśa.[34]

Manu[35] says that the *māhābhūtas* or 'great elements' were produced from the divine self-existent. Elsewhere he says the following:

> That the great elements enter, together with their functions and the mind through its minute parts, the framer of all beings, the imperishable one.[36]
>
> Among them each succeeding element acquires the quality of the preceding one, and whatever place (in the sequence) each of them occupies even so many qualities it is declared to possess.[37]

The second verse quoted above, presupposes the ideas relating to substance (*dravya*) and quality (*guṇa)* of the philosophical tradition. For example according to the Nyāya Vaiśeṣika school of philosophy, the earth possesses the four qualities of smell, taste, colour and tangibility; water the three qualities of taste, colour and tangibility; light the two qualities of colour and tangibility; air the single quality of tangibility; and space the single quality of sound.[38] The basic quality of each element has been categorised in the *Manusmṛti* as follows:

> Mind, impelled by (*brahman's*) desire to create performs the work of creation by modifying itself; thence ether is produced; they declare that sound is the quality of the latter.
>
> But from ether, modifying itself, springs the pure, powerful wind, the vehicle of all perfumes; that is held to possess the quality of touch.
>
> Next from wind, modifying itself, proceeds the brilliant light, which illuminates and dispells darkness; that is declared to possess the quality of colour.
>
> And from light, modifying itself, (is produced) water, possessing the quality of taste; from water, earth which has the quality of smell; such is the creation in the beginning.[39]

While the Sāṅkhya traces the evolution of the *mahābhūtas* or gross elements to Prakṛti or primordial substance conceived as a Female Principle, Manu traces their emergence directly to the Supreme Being, the One variously equated with *brahman*, Puruṣa and other principles. Although the Sāṅkhya texts, as we find them in their present form, are later than Manu, scholars on the Sāṅkhya hold that there was an earlier form of this doctrine, the ingredients of which they had successfully traced from the earlier texts.

According to Belvalkar and Ranade:

> The original Sāṅkhya came indeed to be perverted in the *śvetāśvatara*, the epics and the *Bhagavadgītā* and later still in the theistic Yoga and the several sectarian and Vedānta coloured Purāṇas.[40]

In the Sāṅkhya there are two principles—entirely independent of each other—Prakṛti and Puruṣa. Prakṛti is characterised by the equilibrium of the three qualities of *sattva, rajas* and *tamas.* Puruṣa is characterised by passivity and indifference, but somehow comes to be influenced by the three qualities of Prakṛti. It is only the cooperation of the "blind Prakṛti and lame Puruṣa" that the creation starts out. The whole of the cosmos exists in a subtle form in Prakṛti, and creation is only the unmanifest becoming manifest, the *avyakta* becoming *vyakta.* When the equilibrium of Prakṛti is disturbed through the presence of Puruṣa, then from the former is developed *mahān* or *buddhi*, the thinking substance. Out of *mahān* emerges the principle of egoity (*ahaṃkāra),* which in its turn produces mind (*manas*), the five organs of sense (*buddhīndriya),* the five organs of action (*karmendriya*) and the five subtle elements (*tanmātra).* The last combining with one another form the five gross elements (*mahābhūtas).*[41] In the *Manusmṛti* these *tattvas* of the Sāṅkhya find expression.

From himself (*ātmanaḥ*) he also drew forth the mind

> (*manas*) which is both real and unreal; likewise from the mind egoism (*ahaṃkāra*), which possesses the function of self-consciousness (and as) lordly moreover the great one, the soul, and all (products) affected by the three qualities (*triguṇa, sattva, rajas* and *tamas*) and in their order the five organs which perceive the objects of sensation. But joining minute particles even of those six (*ahaṃkāra* and five *tanmāntras*) which possess measureless power with particles, of himself he created all beings. Because those six (kinds of minute particles) which form the creator's frame, enter those (creatures), therefore the wise call his form *śarīra* (the body).[42]

According to Bühler, the commentators offer different explanations of these difficult verses.

> According to Medhātithi, Govindarāja, Kulluka and Raghavānanda, they describe the production of the *tattvas*, the principles of Sāṅkhya system, the first three of which *mahat, ahaṃkāra* and *manas* have been placed in an inverted order; though Manu clearly states that the creator drew the *manas* which they take to mean the internal organ from the *ātman*, that he drew the *ahaṃkāra*, egoism, from the *manas*, and that he afterwards created *mahāntamātmānam*, 'the great one, the soul', yet they think that it must be understood that the *mahat* was produced first from it, the *ahaṃkāra*, and from the latter, the *manas*.[43]

Although Śaṅkarācārya considered the Sāṅkhya as opposed to the Vedas and contradictory to Manu's ideas[44] and although according to the historical point of view there are some non-Vedic elements in the Sāṅkhya,[45] the Vedic elements in it cannot, however, be ignored. The Sāṅkhya concept of Puruṣa is anomalous since it is passive, indifferent and inactive, though having a role in the affair of creation. Moreover, it is not one but many. Later commentators with Vedantic bias had

to make much labour to establish the oneness of Puruṣa and to equate it with *brahman* and to transform the primordial substance called Prakṛti into the illusory principles called Māyā. In the history of Indian philosophy attempts have been made time and again to reconcile the dualism of Sāṅkhya with the monism of Vedānta. The Sāṅkhya conception of Prakṛti as the material cause of the universe is incompatible with the Vedantic conception of *brahman*. And that is why greatest care is taken in the *Vedānta Sūtras* to refute the Sāṅkhya philosophy and there had always been a conscious attempt to revise the Sāṅkhya in the light of Vedānta. The beginning of such a process of associating the Sāṅkhya principles with early Vedantic monism finds expression in the cosmogonic passages of the *Manusmṛti*. Manu considered Puruṣa as a single divine creative principle and equated it with *brahman* and other creative principles.

Manu's conception of the Puruṣa[46] seems to have been directly based upon the Puruṣa-sukta of the *Ṛgveda*.[47] This is also attested by the fact that Manu repeats the same story of the formation of the four *Varṇas* as found in the Puruṣa-sukta. In the Puruṣa-sukta Puruṣa is described as having a thousand heads, a thousand eyes and a thousand feet and is equated with the universe. The gods offered up this Puruṣa as the victim for a sacrifice and from his limbs came into existence the *Varṇas*, the moon, the sun, Indra, Agni, Vāyu, atmosphere sky, earth the four quarters, etc. In the *Vājasaneyi Saṃhita*[48] Puruṣa is described as a resplendent principle pervading the universe. In the *Atharvaveda*[49] Puruṣa is conceived of as a man, the embodiment of the male principle of creation. In the Brāhmaṇa literature[50] Puruṣa is also conceived in the form of a human body and an agent of creation. But according to Manu[51]

> from that first cause which is indiscernible, eternal, and both real and unreal (*sat* and *asat*, existent and non-existent), was produced that Puruṣa who is famed in this world under the appellation of *brahman*.

Manu's identification of Puruṣa with *brahman* or *ātman* is attested also by the Upaniṣads[52] in which he is conceived as a person with sixteen parts and compounded with physical categories like earth, etc., psychological categories like mind, etc., moral categories like faith, etc., and ritualistic categories like sacrifice, etc. In the *Śvetāśvatara,*[53] Puruṣa is mentioned as the First Principle. In the *Chāndogya*[54] the space within the Puruṣa is equated with that within the heart. This conception of Puruṣa as a male principle of creation, somehow identified with *brahman* or *ātman* or with the supreme being of any sectarian cult, recurs in the Epico-Puranic tradition of India.

The word *brahman* occurs in the *Ṛgveda* in the sense of hymn, prayer, magic-formulae, priest, etc., but not as a cosmic principle. In the post-Ṛgvedic literature the concept of *brahman* became more prominent in which the ideas of Prajāpati and Puruṣa were grafted. In the *Atharvaveda,*[55] *brahman* is mentioned as the highest deity who sprang from toil and fervour. In the *Śatapatha Brāhmaṇa*[56] it is stated that 'verily in the beginning the universe was *brahman.* It created the gods and placed Agni in this terrestrial world, Vāyu in the atmosphere and Sūrya in the sky. The *Taittirīya Brāhmaṇa*[57] declares *brahman* to be the Self-existent, the first god, by whom the entire Universe is surrounded. In the Upaniṣads the concept of *brahman* has absorbed into itself all other cosmic conceptions and is described as the primal entity, incomprehensible, the supreme soul, the self-existent and the ultimate world-ground and is identified with Puruṣa, Prajāpati, Indra and all the gods as well as with the subtle and gross elements.[58] With the gradual enlargement and universalizing of the concept of *brahman,* not only everything associated with the world-ground was in some sense, a soul. This led to the equation of *brahman* with *ātman.* There are many passages in the Upaniṣads in which attempts are made to correspond parts of the bodily self with those of the world.[59] After this correspondence is made the next step with the development of abstract thought was probably to consider the world as really a soul (*ātman*)—a universal

soul (*brahman*) of which the individual is a miniature.

In the *Manusmṛti* there is a tendency to reach towards a single creative principle. In the *Śvetāśvatara Upaniṣad*[60] eight types of cosmogonical theories have been mentioned. These are Īśvara (God), Kāla (time), Svabhāva (inherent nature), Niyati (inevitability), Bhūta (elements), Yadṛcchā (chance), Yoni (female womb) and Puruṣa (the male principle)—each regarded as the first cause of the world.[61] Manu excluded Svabhāva, Niyati and Yadṛcchā and tried to bring a harmony among the other creative principles. The *Śvetāśvatara* directly traces the origin of the world to Īśvara, who is the supreme *brahman*, the material and efficient cause of the world, its protector and guide.

> Here the emphasis is not on *brahman*, the Absolute, whose complete perfection does not admit of any change or evolution, but on the personal Īśvara, omniscient and omnipotent, who is the manifested *brahman*.[62]

But though the cosmogony described by Manu was influenced by a kind of theism, it was not guided by the simplified approach as is found in the *Śvetaśvatara*. Sukumari Bhattacharji suggests that the Vedic deities and their subsequent metamorphosed forms such as Brahmaṇaspati, Bṛhaspati, Tvaṣṭr, Viśvakarman, Prajāpati, 'Ka', Virāj, Hiraṇyagarbha, Skambha, Parameṣṭhin, Svayambhū, Puruṣa, Brahman, etc., belonged to a particular thought-complex associated with creation, having many common characteristics among them, which eventually culminated into the formation of a single divine creative principle.[63] This divine creative principle was not the abstract *brahman* or the individual self of the philosophical tradition, but the more concrete *brahman* who formed a part of the later Hindu trinity as the god of creation.

In the later Saṃhitās and the Brāhmaṇs, a twofold stream is observed in the concept of *brahman*. One stream which tends

to equate it with the inner self of the individual gave rise to the Upanisadic concept of *brahman* which had its final culmination in the Vedānta philosophy. The other stream which purports to identify the creative principle known as Prajāpati with it led to the growth of the solidified creator Brahman of the epico-Puranic tradition. The Supreme Being of Manu, described as Svayambhū or the 'self-existent one', represents an interim stage. The precursor of the creator-god of the Hindu trinity is found in the following verse of Manu.

> The sages declare Brahmā, the creator of the universe, the law, the Great One, and the indiscernible one (to constitute) the highest Order of beings produced by Goodness.[64]

Manu has also brought another concept in which creation is viewed as a procreative process. A sexual dualism in which the affair of creation has been thought of in terms of male-female union is found in a statement of Manu in which he says that "dividing his own body, the Lord became half-male and half-female and with that female he produced Virāj".[65] In the *Bṛhādaraṇyaka Upaniṣad*[66] the same idea is found. Even in the *Ṛgveda* heaven and earth are described respectively as the male and female principles of creation. In post-Ṛgvedic cosmogonic theories, the creative process is sometimes conceived as procreative process and in this connection we come across such terms as *jan, sṛj, garbha, retas, kāma,* etc. In course of time evolved the idea of Prakṛti in place of Pṛthivī or earth who was invoked in the *Ṛgveda* as *matarā* or *janitṛ*.[67] This Prakṛti in the Sāṅkhya has been conveived as the germinal productive principle—the eternal female principle capable of evolving all created things out of herself, but never so creating unless united with the eternal spiritual principle, the Puruṣa. Prakṛti charms Puruṣa, just as a woman charms a man. "Just as a dancing girl, after showing her performance, desists from dancing, so does Prakṛti desist after exhibiting herself to

Puruṣa."[68] Again "as the birth of a child results from the union of male and female so the production of the universe results from the union of Puruṣa and Prakṛti."[69] The viewing of creation as a procreative process reminds us of a very primitive cosmogonical belief, the root of which should be sought not in literature or philosophy but in primitive cults and rituals associated with fertility beliefs.

> So intimate appeared to be the relation between the processes of birth and generation and those of fertility in general that the two aspects of the same 'mystery' found very similar mode of ritual expression under prehistoric conditions.[70]

In *Manusmṛti* man is identified with seed and woman with seed-field: *Kṣetrabhūtā smṛtā nārī vījabhūtaḥ smrtaḥ pumān.*[71]

A theory of secondary creations and dissolutions is found in the *Manusmṛti*[72] in which it is stated that from the union of the male and female aspects of the Supreme Being was created Virāj. From this Virāj sprang Manu Svayambhū who, desiring to produce, performed various austerities and brought into existence ten great sages—Mārīcī, Atri, Aṅgiras, Pulastya, Pulaha, Kratu, Pracetas, Vasiṣṭha, Bhṛgu and Nārada. They created seven other Manus, gods and godlings, great sages of measureless power, the Yakṣas, Rākṣasas and Piśācas, the Gandharvas, Apasarases, Asuras, Nāgas and Sarpas, Suparṇas and several classes of Pitṛs; lightning, thunderbolts and clouds, imperfect and perfect rainbows, falling meteors, supernatural noises, comets and heavenly light of many kinds; horse-faced kinnaras, monkeys, fishes, birds of many kinds, cattle, deer, men and carnivorous beasts with two rows of teeth; small and large worms and beetles, moths, lice, flies, bugs, all movable and biting insects and several kinds of immovable things. Then Manu[73] describes certain aspects of dissolution. The Supreme Being at different *Manvantaras* brings forth co-creators and with them the universe originates and dissolves. Created

beings are subject to the conditions of constantly changing circles of births and deaths. Creation and dissolution are due to two forms of energy of the creator, static and kinetic. When that Divine One wakes, then this world stirs; when he sleeps and universe sinks to sleep, active beings desist from their actions, the faculties leave their corporeal frames. Prior to creation the energy of the creator remains static; when it awakes creation takes place. Again at dissolution the kinetic energy comes back to the source and becomes static. Manu is of opinion that the universe is not eternal. Our visible universe is nothing but a formation in endless span of time. In the past many universes have been created; many have been dissoluted. No indication of such a thought is found in the Vedic literature. Probably it is a fundamental innovation of Manu.

It is noteworthy that in the present day, the idea has been formed of an astronomical year for the measurement of the endless span of time, the anticipation of which is observed in the *Manusmṛti*. Manu says that a worldly year is a day and night of the gods; the half year during which the sun progresses to the north is the day of the gods, that during which it goes southword is night. The *kṛta* (satya) age contains 4000 years of the gods; the twilight preceding it consists of 400 and the twilight following it of 400 years. In the other three ages, with their twilights preceding and following, the thousands and hundreds are diminished by one in each.[74] According to this measurement the *kṛta* or *satya* age comprises 400 + 4000 + 400 = 4800 divine years; the *tretā* age 300 + 3000 + 300 = 3600 divine years; the *dvāpara* age 200 + 2000 + 200 = 2400 divine years; and the *kali* age 100 + 1000 + 100 = 1200 divine years. The four Yugas thus comprise 12000 divine years. One divine year consists of 360 human years. According to the calculation, the total number of years of the four Yugas is 4320000 human years (*kṛta* 1728000, *tretā* 1296000, *dvāpara* 864000 and *kali* 432000). Manu further says:

But know that the sum of one thousand ages of the gods

> (makes) one day of *brahman*, and that his night has the same length.[75]
>
> The before-mentioned age of the gods, (or) twelve thousand (of their years), being multiplied by seventy-one (constitutes what) is here named the period of a *Manu* (*manvantara*). The *manvantaras*, the creations and destructions (of the world), are numberless; sporting, as it were, *brahman* repeats this again and again.[76]

The measurement of the span of time and the system of the division of ages as well as the theory of the successive creations and dissolutions of the universe have been accepted in the Purāṇas.[77] In the *Viṣṇu Purāṇa* it is stated at the end of a *kalpa*, and also at the end of the Day and Night of Brahmā, when the creation was dissoluted, Nārāyaṇa in the shape of a boar raised the earth from beneath the waters and created the four lower spheres—earth, sky, heaven and *maharloka*. This statement is also found in the first chapter of the *Viṣṇusmṛti*, although Manu has given the responsibility of the creation to Brahmā.

Coomaraswamy interprets such formulations in terms of the metaphysical concept of cosmic time, *manvantara*, the transition of one age to another. The dissolution of the world, after completing the term of existence and the beginning of a new span of existence are always intervened, according to him, by a total flood and the ark in the oceanic vastness is symbolic of a patriarchal voyage (*Pitṛyāna*). The end of every *kalpa* or span of time equivalent to a certain extent the Last Judgement of the Christians or the Eddaic *Ragnarok*, the dusk of the gods, and the genesis of a new *kalpa* after the intervening inundation, brought about by a Patriarch of angelic origin (Manu), have been viewed by him as a symbolic representation of what is called the doctrine of reincarnation.[78]

The cosmological theories of Manu undoubtedly influenced the later cosmological theories found in other Smṛtis and Epico-Puranic tradition. The Smṛti of Yājñavalkya[79] accepts them, especially insisting on creation manifested from

the self-existent one, the concept of Puruṣa and the doctrine of elements. Here of course the Sāṅkhya categories are ignored. In the Śāntiparvan of the *Mahābhārata* we come across the doctrine of elements, the Sāṅkhya categories, the golden egg concept, creation emanating from *brahman,* and the division of time from *nimeṣa* to the *yugas* and their characteristics. The *Matsya Purāṇa* begins the topic of creation in the same way as the *Manusmṛti* does—Nārāyaṇa producing from his body cosmic waters and golden egg, the identification of Nārāyaṇa with Prajāpati, creating of the world of beings, the Sāṅkhya scheme of creation, etc. It also states that Brahmā produced a woman (Sātarūpā) from himself and had a son named Manu Svāyambhūva and also Virāj from her. He then called upon Manu and Virāj to create people. The *Brahma Purāṇa*[81] almost quotes Manu in relation to creation emanating from *brahman*.[82] The *Vāyu Purāṇa* devotes five chapters to creation of various kinds.[83] It propounds the Sāṅkhya scheme of evolution which is combined with the cosmic egg theory. It also refers to the Puruṣa Sukta, explains that Nārāyaṇa is so called because he reclines on waters. The *Brahmāṇḍa Purāṇa*[84] deals with the appearance of Hiraṇyagarbha, the Sāṅkhya doctrine of the evolutes of Prakṛti or Pradhāna and a supreme creator equated with Viṣṇu. The *Mārkaṇḍeya Purāṇa*[85] speaks of the creation of Pradhāna, Mahat, Ahaṃkāra, and Tanmātras under the aegis of *brahman,* nine kinds of creation from Viṣṇu and a Theogony-like account of the creation of gods, human beings, animals and the like. The *Viṣṇu Purāṇa*[86] traces the concepts of Puruṣa and Prakṛti, interlinked by *kāla* or time, to *brahman* (equated with Viṣṇu and Vāsudeva) and accounts for the emergence of *mahān* or *buddhi, ahaṃkāra* the organs and the subtle and gross elements to the disbalance in the equilibrium of Prakṛti. The gross elements combine into a compact mass, the world egg, resting on water and surrounded by seven envelops in which the highest deity appears in the form of Brahman and creates all things. The same deity as Viṣṇu sustains and as Rudra destroys the universe after the end of a *kalpa.* The mind-born sons of *brahman* are also described as co-creators.

NOTES

1. *Asiatic Memorial of the Creation, Fall, Deluge, etc., from the Sacred Book of the Hindoos,* Winchester, 1823.
2. *Cosmology of the Ṛgveda,* London, 1887.
3. A Roussel, *Cosmologie Hindoue d'après la Bhāgavata Purāṇa,* Paris 1893.
4. *Uber die Kosmogonischen Grundunschauungen im Mānavadharmaśāstram,* Leipzig 1904.
5. *Cosmogony in Indian Thought,* Banaras, 1942.
6. *History of Dharmaśāstra,* Vol. V, Poona 1962, Sec. IX, Ch. XXXIV.
7. *History of Indian Cosmogonical Ideas,* New Delhi, 1971.
8. *Ancient Cosmologies,* ed. by C. Blacker and M. Loewe, London, 1975.
9. *The Hindu Theory of Cosmology,* Calcutta, 1978.
10. H.W. Wallis, *Cosmology of the Ṛgveda,* London, 1887, p. 50; M. Bloomfield, "Contribution to the Interpretation of Veda" in *JAOS,* XV, 1893, p. 184, Norman Brown, "Theories of Creation in the Ṛgveda" in *JAOS,* LXXXV, 1965, pp. 23-32.
11. See R.N. Dandekar, *Vedic Mythological Tracts,* Delhi, 1979, Appendix.
12. Sukumari Bhattacharji, *The Indian Theogony,* Calcutta, 1978, pp. 330-31.
13. *Genesis* I; E.K. Mitchell in *ERE,* IV, ed. J. Hastings, Edinburgh, 1911, p. 191.
14. Manu I. 5-13.
15. X. 129.
16. X. 2.7; X. 19.6.
17. X. I49.2.
18. X. 63.2.
19. V. 6.4.2; VII. 1.5.1.
20. III. 6.1.
21. VII. 10.11.
22. IV. 6.
23. Cf. *Aitareya* I. 1.3; *Kauṣītaki* I. 7; etc.
24. XI. 1.6.1ff.
25. Muir's trans. *Original Sanskrit Texts,* IV, p. 25.
26. III. 19.
27. *SBE,* I, pp. 54-55.
28. XII. 29-31.
29. Burgess's trans. in *JAOS,* XI, p. 245.
30. I. 10
31. XII. 3.4.1; XIII. 6.1.1.
32. LXXXI. 49-50
33. Cf. *Aitareya,* V. 3; *Maitrī,* III. 2; *Śvetāśvatara* I. 1-3 etc.
34. U. Miśra, *Conception of Matter in Nyaya Vaiśeṣika,* Allahabad, pp. 161ff.
35. I. 6.

36. I. 18.
37. I. 20.
38. *Vaiśeṣika Sūtra,* I. 2-7; VIII. 2-3 etc.
39. Manu I. 75-78.
40. *History of Indian Philosophy,* Vol. II, Poona, 1927, p. 415.
41. *Sāṅkhyakārikā,* XVI, XXXV; *Sāṅkhya Sūtra* I. 63, II. 20, V. 55ff., etc., *Sāṅkhya Pravacana Bhāṣya,* II. 26-42, etc.
42. Manu I, 14-17.
43. *SBE,* XXV, p. 63.
44. Kapilasya tantrasya vedaviruddhatvaṃ vedānusārimanuvacana-viruddhaṃca.
45. Garbe in *ERE,* XI, p. 189; *Aniruddha's Commentary,* Calcutta, 1892, intro XX-XXI; Belvalkar and Renade, *op.cit.,* pp. 412-24; D.P. Chattopadhyaya, *Lokāyata,* Delhi, 1959, pp. 364-72.
46. I. 87.
47. X. 90.
48. XXXI. 18; XXXII. 2.
49. X. 11.
50. Cf. *Aitereya* II. 14; *Copatha* VI. 6.8.
51. I. 11.
52. Cf. *Bṛhadāraṇyaka* III. 10.11.; *Praśna* III. 1.6; *Muṇḍaka* II. 1. 10; etc.
53. I. 1-2
54. III. 12.7.
55. X. 7, 32, 36; X. 8.1.
56. XI. 2.3.1ff
57. II. 8.8.9; II. 8.9.6; III. 12.3.1; III. 12.9.7.
58. *Bṛhadāraṇyaka* II. 6.3; IV. 6.1; VI. 5.4; *Aitareya* V. 3.
59. Cf. *Chāndogya* III. 18.2; *Aitereya* I. etc.
60. I. 1-2.
61. The same list is found in the *Suśrutasaṃhitā,* Śārīrasthāna I. 11 in which Puruṣa and Bhūta are excluded and in the place of Yoni the 'modifications' (*pariṇāma*) of Prakṛti is substituted.
62. S. Radhakrishnan, *Principal Upaniṣads,* London, 1923, p. 706.
63. *The Indian Theogony,* pp. 317-50.
64. XII. 50
65. I. 32.
66. I. 4.
67. *Rv.,* I. 155.3; IX. 85.18; X. 1.7; 35.3; 64.13; X. 110.9.
68. *Sāṅkhyasūtra* III. 68.
69. *Sāṅkhyakārikā,* XXI.
70. E.O. James, *Prehistoric Religion,* New York, 1957, p. 172.
71. IX. 33.
72. I. 31-41.
73. I. 50-55.

74. I. 64, I. 69-70.
75. I. 72.
76. I. 79-80.
77. *Viṣṇu* I, 3; VI. 3; *Mārkandeya* 86; *Brahma* 229-30; *Matsya*, 142-88, etc., cf. *Mahābhārata* I. 149. 11 ff.; *Viṣṇu Dharmasūtra* XX. 1-21.
78. A.K. Coomaraswamy, *Selected Papers*, ed. by Roger Lepsey, Princeton 1977, II. pp. 398 ff.
79. III. 67 ff.; III. 125-28.
80. II. 25-27; III. 5-44.
81. I. 37-39.
82. Manu I. 6-8.
83. Chs. IV-IX.
84. I. 3-5.
85. Chs. XLII - XLVII.
86. Chs. II, IV, V, VII.

Chapter VI

Political Conceptualizations

The seventh chapter of the *Manusmṛti* which deals with Rājadharma or the theoretical and practical aspects of government and statecraft has been studied from different viewpoints by many a writer on ancient Indian polity. Most writers on ancient Indian polity took up the subject as a challenge to the assertion of the western writers that the Indians were a nation of 'philosophers', that Indian intellect was lacking in political or material speculation and that the Indians never knew the feeling of nationality.[1] The discovery of the *Arthaśāstra* of Kauṭilya in 1905 and its publication by Shamasastry in 1909 was an epoch making event, for it provided valuable raw material which could be utilized in ascertaining the Indian viewpoint. With its discovery need was felt to explain the basic aspects of ancient Indian political theories and practices in terms of its comparative study with the contents of other texts, such as the *Manusmṛti*, the *Mahābhārata*, the *Nītisāra* of *Kāmandakī* and so forth. As a result numerous scholarly works came to light, each having its distinctive understanding, field of enquiry, interpretation, argument, speculation and theorisation.

Among the authors, whose views on Rājadharma of Manu evoked much interest and criticism was K.P. Jayaswal, who held that the theory of the divinity of king was advanced by *Manusmṛti* to support the Brāhmaṇa empire of Puṣyamitra and to counteract the Buddhist theory of the origin of the state by contract.[2] According to Jayaswal, Manu's theory of the divine creation of the king has no direct support in earlier literature. In order to substantiate this theory Jayaswal says that Manu has

used, the theory of the politicians' about the peoples' dissatisfaction with the *arājaka* system and the Creator's recommendation of the king at their request, without references to "the theory of election of Manu Vaivasvata". Manu, according to him, took the story of Veṇa but ignored the further tradition of the deposition of this king because of his unlawful rule. Jayaswal also holds that Manu had twisted the import of the Vedic coronation ritual invoking the help of the gods to the elected king "into the doctrine that these gods came into the person of the king". His final suggestion is that Manu developed the references in Kauṭilya to a government spy's speech recalling the resemblance of the king's position to that of Indra and Yama into a theory of the king's divinity and perfect absolutism.

Jayaswal's views were conditioned by his own idealism. His insistence was on a republican and democratic system of administration which Free Indian government should adopt. And his sole effort was to prove that in ancient India the voice of people was the voice of God. So Manu appeared to him as a reactionary with scant respect for public opinion. He described Manu as a champion of orthodoxy and a promulgator of the theory of divine origin of kingship. The views of Jayaswal, as we shall presently see, were criticized by U.N. Ghosal and other writers on Indian polity.

K.V. Rangaswamy Aiyangar (1916)[3] made a comparison between the *Manusmṛti* and the *Arthaśāstra* of Kauṭilya, on the question of Niyoga, courtesans, gambling, widow-remarriage, succession, immunities of Brāhmaṇas in several matters, theories of state and statecraft and so forth, and pointed out the resemblances and differences found in them. According to him, as regards the date of composition, so far as it may be judged from their subject matter, the *Manusmṛti* in its present form belongs to a later date than that of *Arthaśāstra.* He has discarded the view of Sir Henry Maine that the code of Manu does not represent a set of rules actually administered and that it is in great part an ideal picture of that which in the view of

Brāhmaṇas ought to be the laws. According to him, in the *Manusmṛti*, the conception of the state as a natural and necessary institution was bound up with the belief in the entire system of the universe being divinely ordained. Consequently, it did not go beyond suggesting as a justification for government the need for an institution of corrective (*daṇḍa*) to restrain the natural turbulence and depravity of men, leading them to violate the regulations of the different castes and orders of life (*varṇāśramadharma*) and of the divine creation of such a power of chastisement or *daṇḍa*. This theory was enforced by vague references to *śruti* and by the recital of the stories of the divine creation of sovereignty after a non-political stage of lawlessness and confusion and of the compact into which men entered with Manu, the first king pledging themselves to serve him and support him by their contributions in return for his protections. P.N. Banerjea in his '*Public Administration in Ancient India*' (Calcutta, 1966) has referred to the *Manusmṛti* while dealing with the origin and nature of the state. According to him Manu was the exponent of the theory of Divine Origin in contrast with Kauṭilya who was a believer in the human creation of the State.

N.N. Law's work on the aspects of ancient Indian polity (1921) which deals with the forms and types of state, the state council, the royal priest, the regal succession, education of the prince, royal duties, principal state officials, theories of the evolution of kingship and the religious aspects of ancient Hindu polity refers to the views of Manu in many cases. He has shown that in regard to the council meetings, the role of the royal priest, the king's duties and other aspects of administration, the views of Manu tally almost totally with those expressed in the *Mahābhārata* and in the *Arthaśāstra* of Kauṭilya. He has refuted Sir James Frazer's theory regarding the supernatural magical power of the king as is reflected in such passages as Manu IX. 246-47 which says that

In that country where the king avoids taking the property

> of mortal sinners men are born in due time and are long lived. And the crops of the husbandmen spring up, each as it was sown, and the children die not, and no misshaped offspring is born.

According to Law, the *Manusmṛti* seems to suggest that the deification of the Brāhmaṇas was made previous to that of the kings, and that the public relations of the king were influenced by religious conceptions.

U.N. Ghosal's *History of Hindu Political Theories* which first came out in 1923 and went into an expanded edition in 1927, is the first historical presentation of the ancient Indian state and government on the basis of original sources from Vedas down to the works of the late medieval period. This work contains two chapters on the political ideas as found in the Brahmanical works on Sacred Law, especially the *Manusmṛti* and *Yājñavalkyasmṛti.* Ghosal refuted the views of Max Müller and Bloomfield that the Hindus had no conception of state and had no idea to make any provision for the state in their scheme because they had certain non-materialistic and unworldly inherent tendencies in their character. The Western writers of political theories like Janet, Danning and Willoughby held that the Indian Aryans for their inclination towards spiritualism and faith in the supreme divinity, neither thought of developing any political science as an independent branch of knowledge nor did they build up any political theory or political institution like that of the European Aryans. The sole city for the Indians is the city divine. Ghosal criticised those views as half-truth and put his own opinion that the "Indian states contrary to the usual view, were not modelled after a uniform pattern, that of despotic monarchy". Beginning with a brief introductory on the nature of the Brahmanical works on Sacred Law, Ghosal has elaborately dealt with the historical significance of the period, the changing character of the Smṛtis, general character of the political ideas in the works of Manu and Yājñavalkya, ideas of social order, of state law and

justice, of the authority of the king's executive edict, theories of authority and obligation of temporal ruler as well as of sanctions for his obligation, theory of his coercive authority, application of ideas of king's authority, and obligation to the state law, general ideas of kingship, civil rights of classes, theory of property and of ownership of the soil, of state structure, theories of government, principles of government, policy of marching against the foreign enemy, attitude towards fighting and territorial conquest, goal of inter-state relations, doctrine of two powers, theories of Brahmanical immunities and privileges and of the immunity of the Brāhmaṇa desperados. According to Ghosal, Manu's perspective was wide and idealistic. In contrast with Manu, Yājñavalkya appears to have based his view of the sources of state law and their application, exclusively upon the more materialistic Arthaśāstra tradition as represented by Kauṭilya. Criticising the view of Jayaswal that Manu's political theory was laid down to support the rule of the Brāhmaṇa Puṣymitra, he says that it does not bear the test of scrutiny. Assuming that the *Manusmṛti* was written in the reign of Puṣyamitra, the exercise of political authority by a Brāhmaṇa could not be regarded in orthodox Brahmanical codes as an "abnormal state of affairs opposed to the law and tradition". Again Jayaswal's theory that Manu had twisted the Vedic concept of the elected king into the theory of diviṇe origin, Ghosal says that it is a highly speculative formulation having no real basis.

In his lectures on some aspects of ancient Hindu polity, D.Ṛ Bhandarkar,[6] criticised some western writers for unjustified views. He had of course his own view on the origin and development of Hindu political theories. Regarding Manu, he had mostly followed the approach of Jayaswal. Comparing Manu's theory with that of *Mahābhārata*, he observed that the one was practically identical with the other, both holding the king to be a deity but Manu added a new feature by declaring the king to be the creation of the supreme being. This involved according to him, "the first trace of the real divine origin of

kingship similar to that, propounded by the western thinkers". U.N. Ghosal has criticised Bhandarkar's view, on the ground that the *Mahābhārata* passage referred to by Bhandarkar deals with the theory of the king's office and not that of his origin. Manu's theory was anticipated indirectly by one Vedic version of the origin of the king of the gods and directly by an anonymous passage, quoted from a Brāhmaṇa text by Viśvarūpa in his commentary on Yājñavalkya. Ghosal also says that Bhandarkar had confused the Western concept of the theory of divine origin with that of the Indian. There are dissimilarities between the Indians and Western theories on the origin of kingship which are more important than the similarities.

Narayan Chandra Bandopadhyaya's work on Hindu polity[7] (in two parts, 1927, 1938) contains a vast mass of data, excellently arranged in a way to convey to the readers a clear impression of the ancient Indian political theories and institutions, various forms of administrative machinery, social and religious norms and details of economic set-up in a purely historical perspective. Regarding the Dharmaśāstras in general and *Manusmṛti* in particular, he states that, the lawgivers of a reactionary age ushered in an era of social repression and political subjugation. The task of social reconstruction was entrusted to the exponents of the orthodox Dharmaśāstra writers like Manu who repudiated the secular ideals of the *Arthaśāstra* writers and condemned the goal of material prosperity. According to him, Manu had a thorough mastery of the orthodox canon. His knowledge of the diverse views of the socio-ethical schools and his acumen as a lawgiver were bent upon creating a system in opposition to the one which had gained acceptance for centuries. Manu was essentially a reactionary which may be seen from his views on the supremacy of the Brāhmaṇas, the social relation of the castes, the perpetual degradation of the Śūdra, the subjugation of womankind, the blind and immoral advocacy of the absolute authority of father of over family property, its unequal division among the sons and so forth. Bandopadhyaya agrees with

Jayaswal that according to Manu, the Brāhmaṇa is (along with the king) the upholder of the moral order, the highest of the created being, the divine representative of Dharma and the owner of everything of the earth.

Subsequent writers followed mostly the approach towards *Manusmṛti* as outlined above in relation to their study of polity. Beni Prasad wrote three books (1927-28)[8] in which he has dealt with in a general way, the social order in Manu, the laws, kingship, government, judicial procedure, foreign policy, etc. According to him the socio-political ideas of Manu accord closely with those of the *Mahābhārata.* Manu upholds the position of the Brāhmaṇas and in regard to the origin of kingship he advocates the theory of divine origin. In H.N. Sinha's *Sovereignty in Ancient India* (London 1938), the view of Manu that the king was created by the lord in order to protect the mankind is stated. The tradition that Manu was the first king and a gift of Brahmā to the people and that the people pledged one-fifth of their cattle and gold and one-tenth of their grain to him for protection has been explained.

Most works on Indian polity, published in the thirties and forties contain stray reference to the political system as formulated by Manu. But the most important work which deals exclusively with the political system of the *Manusmṛti* was by K.V. Rangaswamy Aiyangar (1946).[9] Aiyangar refuted the views of those scholars who uphold the superiority of Kauṭilya's work over the *Manusmṛti* on the ground that the former was more secular, unorthodox and realist, while the latter was religious, orthodox and idealistic. According to him, the scheme of polity that the *Manusmṛti* outlines is rooted in the general scheme of Hindu life and in the postulates of Hindu social, political and economic organisations. Aiyangar has dealt with the basis of Manu's polity, different scales of political values, theories of the origin of state, glorification of the king, his personal responsibility, check of royal absolutism, ailments of the sate, elaboration of policies and so forth. According to him, the underlying implications of the theories

of the origin of the state and kingship as indicated in the *Manusmṛti* is that the political union under a common ruler is natural and necessary and may be considered as having a divine sanction behind it. It is only the answer to human depravity, unless restrained by a common master. While the divinity in the ruler, so created makes for his lusture and power, he is bound to respect the original convention of righteous rule. But over and above Manu makes the king himself subordinate to a higher power, viz., *Daṇḍa* or the incarnation of the spirit of punishment. It provides not only the Austinian sanction behind the law but also a restriction of the unlimited exercise of the prerogative powers of the king.

In A.S. Altekar's work (1949)[10] there is no separate chapter on the polity of *Manusmṛti* although Manu's view that the king is a part—one of the seven constituents—of the state is mentioned several times. Altekar refers to the Manu mythology according to which in a kingless state the people approached the creator to appoint a king for them and the creator straightway appointed Manu as the first king. The king's very body is formed by the creator by taking particles from the body of the divine guardians of the eight quarters. According to Manu, the king is a veritable divinity and therefore should be obeyed.

V.P. Verma (1954)[11] refers to Manu especially in connection with the theory of kingship. He is of opinion that there are two definite theories on the origin of kingship, the first being the primeval creation of the king and the second, the divine creation. While Kauṭilya is in favour of the former that is the elective origin of kingship, Manu is the champion of the latter. There is a special chapter regarding Manu's theory of divinity of the king in Verma's book. J. Gonda's study of ancient Indian kingship from religious point of view (1955-57)[12] refers to the ruler's functions in terms of those pertaining various gods like Indra, Varuṇa, Agni and others mentioned in Manu IX. 303ff. R.S. Sharma's work (1959)[13] is a treatment of the subject in an historical perspective which refers to various views of Manu, in relation to the Saptāṅga theory of the state, the theories of the

origin of state, influence of religion on the political system, *Varṇa* in relation to law and polities and the functional aspect of the statecraft.

According to Charles Drekmeier (1962)[14] ancient Indian political thought emerged in the context of most conservative large scale society pictured as the one logically consistent expression of the organic conception of the community. The institution of kingship here originated as a response to hostile pressure. The Hindus unlike the ancient Greeks did not view political authority as the natural consequence on the interdependence of man. The state was rationalised in terms of suggesting a compact or was said to have been established through intervention of gods. Drekmeier depended more on the *Mahābhārata* than on Manu in formulating his view of the Indian state, although in other aspects like authority, law and government, diplomacy, etc., he has quoted Manu frequently. John Spellman in his book (1964)[15] quotes Manu while discussing the divine appointment of the king. He refers to the Manu mythology according to which the king was created from the part of various gods. He is not a mere mortal, for he is a great deity in human form. So far as the text of the *Manusmṛti* is concerned Spellman has taken into account the concept of the seven elements, which has also been stressed by Manorama Jauhari (1968).[16] She defines the term Mātsyanyāya in which relation the theory of divine origin was propounded by Manu. Her emphasis has been mainly on the *Mahābhārata*, though as corroborative evidence she has frequently quoted passages from the *Manusmṛti*.

I.W. Mabbett in his *Truth, Myth and Politics in Ancient India* (1971) maintains that in ancient India "there was no state-loyalty transcending the party of the particular king" and that "there were perhaps little idea of government as a more or less technical job". But such was the case of Europe before the advent of the nation states. Prabhabati Sinha's *Smṛti Political and Legal System: A Socio-Economic Study* (1982) deals with the political theories, administrative apparatus and the judicial

system and examines various laws pertaining to property, *varṇa* and family. Discussing the conception of royal divinity and the paraphernalia of kingship she argues that Manu and other law-givers supported the divinity of the king to enable him to obtain passive obedience of his subjects and maintain social order. However, they never sanctioned the divine right theory of kingship in the Western sense of the term. They did not consider the king above law; rather the law was the supreme authority and the king was only to maintain it.

We have thus given an account of the major works dealing with Manu's polity. Manu's chapter on Rājadharma which refers both to administration and legislation and to the study of this department of human activities has been discussed and critically analysed by most writers. That part of life which is political is generally supposed to be concerned with the organisation of social relation with a view to justice and liberty. But according to Manu, political society is not the only form of society and as such his theory of polity is only one section of his social theory. Moreover since his theory of polity is concerned with the general theory of society, its connection with ethics or the study of right action becomes evident. This leads us to make a comparison of Manu's political ideas with those of Greek philosophers especially of Plato and Aristotle. Greek political ideas began with Socrates and are found in Plato's *Dialogues.* Although they are not systematically presented, we can clearly see in the main lines of the Socratic-Platonic analysis and suggestion of social betterment, the spirit of which is also reflected in the *Manusmṛti.* Organised society presented itself to them as a whole—religious, cultural, ethical, political and economic—and the discussion always refers to all the relations or conducts of man with man. Plato's conception of virtues, the conquest of the self matches with Manu's ideas about the conquest of the senses. The ideal of kingship as reflected in the *Manusmṛti* finds parallel in Plato's conception of statesman, who must combine moderation with manliness. Both Manu and Plato appear to prefer their rulers to emerge

from the military class (*kṣatriya*). While we find Plato favouring the enlightened aristocracy as the conscience-keeper of the ruler, Manu is in favour of an elightened Brahmanism.

Manu's seventh chapter begins with the desire to enumerate Rājadharma or the duties of the king and show how a king should conduct himself, how the institution of kingship was created and how the king can obtain highest success.[17] The traditional legends of the origin and development of the Rājadharma are found in ancient works in which it is stated that the first work on Rājadharma was made by Brahmā which was subsequently abridged by authorities including Manu.[18] Though Rājadharma was an integral part of Dharmaśāstra, separate treatises on it were also composed from early times. These were known as Rājaśāstras,[19] Daṇḍanīti (which has been equated in the *Mahābhārata*[20] with Rājadharma), Nīti or Rājanīti,[21] Naya,[22] Arthaśāstra,[23] etc. Medhātithi commenting on Manu VII.1 says that Rājadharma is of two kinds, *dṛṣtārthaka* and *adṛṣtārthaka*. The former consists of the application of *ṣādguṇya*, etc., by which the king protects and enriches his territory. The latter is concerned with such duties as the performance of *agnihotra*, etc., by which the king obtains merit for himself and his subjects. The works of the Arthaśāstra category are principally concerned with the treatment of the *dṛṣṭānta* affairs, the functional aspects of the statecraft, and hence they are called *Dṛṣṭānta* Smṛti.[24] It is most interesting to note that Medhātithi categorically declares that the rules of *rājanīti* are not based on the canonical books of the Dharmaśāstra but mainly on the experience of worldly affairs. According to the *Mahābhārata*[25] Rājadharma is the quintessence of all *dharmas* because the fulfilment of the duties and responsibilities of the rulers to the cause of the stability and orderly development of society and the happiness of the individuals in the state are its chief concern.

According to Manu, a Kṣatriya, who has received according to the rule of the sacrament prescribed by the Veda, must duly protect the world.[26] The *Vīramitrodaya*[27] raises three

important questions in this connection: (1) Is the name *rājā* applied to any and every one doing the work of protecting the people, (2) or only to one belonging to the Kṣatriya caste, (3) or to that Kṣatriya alone who is duly anointed? In popular usage the name *rājā* is applied to any one who owns and performs *rājya*, the functions of the *rājā* or king; and these functions are actually performed by the Brāhmaṇa and other castes also. In the *Nirukta* the etymological meaning of *rājā* is explained as *rājate*, 'one who shines', i.e. with royal glory which results only from protection of the people. When Manu says that a Kṣatriya, duly anointed, should be the ruler he does so in a conventional sense. It was not unknown to the author of the present form of the *Manusmṛti* that the Nandas and the Mauryas were Śūdras. Medhātithi remarks that 'persons of other *varṇas* who subsist by the mode prescribed for the Kṣatriyas have the right to protect people'. According to Kulluka the word *rājan* means 'any person who is crowned king and protects the country and capital' and is not used in the sense of 'a person of the kṣatriya caste'. In the literature on Dharmaśāstras the word *rājan* is understood in the sense of 'one who rules over or protects a country'. Aparārka[28] remarks:

> When he who is not a Kṣatriya becomes a king he should perform all kingly duties because the rule is this that by assuming the position or the work of a particular person one receives what is due to that other. Since the duty of protecting the subjects arises from the fact of receiving taxes from them, any one receiving that must undertake protection to his subjects.

Manu[29] directs a Brāhmaṇa not to stay in a country where the ruler was a Śūdra. Medhātithi explains this by saying that the prohibition applies only to a country where all the seven high functionaries are of Śūdra caste.[30] Kumārila frankly observes that persons of all the four *varṇas* are seen as rulers of kingdoms.[31] The *Harivaṃśa* says *akṣatriyāśca rājano viprāḥ*

śūdropajīvinaḥ.[32] Some of the Purāṇas state that the kings in the Kali age will be mostly Śūdras and that Śūdra kings will celebrate Aśvamedha sacrifices.[33]

According to Manu the king or ruler is one of the seven constituents of the state and there is an organic unity among these constituents. Besides the king (*svāmin*) other limbs are the ministers (*amātya, saciva, mantrin*), capital or fort (*pura, durga*), country (*janapada, rāṣṭra*), treasures (*koṣa*), army (*daṇḍa*) and ally (*mitra, suhṛd*). These seven *aṅgas* or limbs are also called Prakṛti.[34] He says that just as among the three staves of an ascetic, no particular staff is superior to the others, so among the seven elements of the state no particular one can be said to excel the others, since each of them has a particular excellence of its own. He emphasizes the harmonious working or unity of the seven elements though they are diverse in their individual characters. D.R Bhandarkar,[35] K.P. Jayaswal[36] and B.K. Sarkar[37] maintain that this ancient analysis of the state into seven elements shows that the idea of the state as an organism, that is, the organic theory of the state was known to the Hindu thinkers and that this doctrine has correspondence with the definition of the state put forward by Bluntschli and others. This view is, however, contested by H.G. Anjaria[38] who holds that since the Hindu thinkers did not regard the state as a moral organism and since they withheld the liberty of a large segment of population on the ground that they were inferior, the organic concept has nothing to do with the Indian situation. According to Kane all that may be said is that Anjaria tilts the balance to the other side too much.

> The faults he points out in the Hindu theory and practice beset almost all theories of the state almost in all countries. Even in the times of Plato and Aristotle huge population of slaves had no voice in the affairs of the state. Up to the nineteenth century true democracies, never existed even in Europe.[39]

According to Spellman, the organic theory in the first place is a functional concept and not an inherently moral one. Secondly, although the two concepts are often confused, it is useful to distinguish the political organisation from the morality of society. He also says that when the *Matsya Purāṇa*[40] says that the king is the root and the subjects are the tree, it evidently refers to an organic concept.[41] The *Śukranītisāra*[42] presents a perfect organic theory by comparing the seven elements of the state to the organs of the human body. But since the present form of this text seems to be a product of the nineteenth century there is no need of attaching importance to it.[43]

Referring to the origin of the institution of kingship Manu says that if the world is without a king (*arājaka*), it is shaken everywhere owing to fear (*bhayāt*); that is why the Lord (*prabhuḥ*) created the king for the protection of all (*rakṣārthamāsya sarvasya*).[44] This verse is quoted in the *Parāśaramādhava*[45] in which it is stated that the king comes down to the earth for maintaining law and order. The *Vīramitrodaya*[46] explains *arājaka* as meaning 'without a king'. The concept of *arājaka* which seems to have a direct bearing to that of *mātsyanyāya,* the law of the fishes, the bigger ones devouring the smaller ones corresponds to a certain extent with Plato's delineation of the post-Kronotic chaos. The earliest trace of this idea is to be found in the *Śatapatha Brāhmaṇa*[47] in which it is said that "whenever there is a drought, then the stronger seizes the weaker, for the waters are the law". Kauṭilya says:

> But when the law of punishment is kept in abeyance, it gives rise to such disorders as implied in the proverb of fishes (*mātsyanyāyanudhāvayati*), for in the absence of a magistrate (*daṇḍadharābhāve*) the strong will swallow the weak, but under his protection the weak resist the strong.[48]

The concept of *arājaka* in this sense occurs in the *Mahābhārata,*[49]

Rāmāyaṇa[50] and *Matsya Purāṇa.*[51] The term *arājaka* does not, however, necessarily mean anarchy and confusion, but a condition in which there is no king or ruler. According to some scholars it was like a State of Nature as imagined by Rousseau. K.P. Jayaswal, for example, holds that *arājaka* was an idealistic condition, that it was an extreme democracy almost Tolstoian in ideal, that it was based on legal and communal basis and that it was a case of extreme individualism in which the government itself was regarded as an evil.[52] This view has been opposed by Kane who holds that a perusal of the sources—

> Will convince any one not carried away by the over-patriotic desire to find the latest European thought in our ancient books that *arājaka* was viewed as a state of chaos and the negation of any constitution; that when a country was without any ruler no private property in any thing existed or was respected and people preyed upon each other like fishes and that no Tolstoian ideals were present before the eyes of the writers that drew such a harrowing picture of a state without a ruler.[53]

Elsewhere he says that—

> The Śāntiparva[54] narrates that in the Kṛta age there was no king and no punishment, that gradually *kāma* (lust) and *rāga* (passion) began to wield sway and *dharma* dwindled away. This belief in an ideal or perfect past was universal and was probably depicted in order to induce men to rise higher and higher in goodness and virtue and to make them submit easily to the discipline of government and the priestly requirements.[55]

Two theories are recorded in the Indian tradition regarding the origin of the state or government. One ascribes it to a Divine Origin and the other to a Social Contract. According to K.V.R. Aiyangar, both legends are implicit in the *Manusmṛti*,

which, however, does not describe them.[56] As we have seen above, according to Manu, the Supreme Being, finding anarchy and chaos in the absence of a ruler created the king for the protection of the world. The legend given in Kauṭilya is that people finding that for want of a common ruler, they were being ruined by mutual quarrels made Manu Vaivasvata their king and agreed to render a sixth of their harvested grain and so forth. In both legends a pre-political stage is envisaged, which is one of anarchy. Manu follows up his account of creation of the king by stating that he was created from the eternal particles of eight Lokapālas—Indra, Vāyu, Yama, Sūrya, Agni, Varuṇa, Candra and Kubera. So he surpasses all created beings in lusture. Even as a child he should not be taken lightly because he is a powerful divinity in human form. Fire burns one man only but the king's wrath consumes everything. For the attainment of justice he can assume any form. Because of his power the goddess of fortune resides in him, in his valour dwells victory; in his anger abides death. He who hates him is bound to be perished. Therefore no man should transgress that law which the king decrees.[57] The divinity inherent in a king thus springs from a synthesis. The king is not an incarnation of God but of elements of the chief gods. The glorification is not of a king but of kingship. Manu expressly states that because of the lack of virtue kings like Veṇa, Nahuṣa, Sudās, Samukha and Nemi perished.[58] Manu does not follow up the legend of the destruction of Veṇa for his oppressive rule and the installation of his son Pṛthu, after whom the earth is named Pṛthivī. Pṛthu took an oath to subordinate his inclinations to morality and to observe the eternal *dharma*.[59] Almost echoing Manu the *Agni Purāṇa*[60] identifies the king with Vāyu, Yama, Kubera and other deities. The *Matsya Purāṇa*[61] gives essentially the same listing as Manu IX.303-306. The *Nārada Smṛti*[62] says that Agni symbolizes the king's wrath, Indra his regal power, Soma his cheerful countenance, Yama his judgement, Kubera his wealth and so forth. The epics also identify the king with various gods.[63] But as Hopkins[64] points out: "Whatever the

grouping the conclusion is always the same, *mānyāḥ pūjyāśca nityadā*, kings should always be honoured and revered as gods. A god and yet not wholly a god, for besides having a *nararūpa* (human form) the king is 'somewhat human' (*kiṃcid bhavati mānuṣaḥ*). A.K. Sen[65] feels that underlying all the hyperboles, the emphasis was not on the person of the king but on the king's office, otherwise how the fact can be explained that an unrighteous king deserved to be slain by his subjects or were destined to go to the hell. The same is the view of most writers on ancient Indian polity who hold that Manu and others have advocated the divinity, not of the person of the king but of his office because of the resemblance between his functions and those of some deities.[66]

While the divinity in the ruler so created makes for his lusture and power, Manu makes the king himself subordinate to a higher power, namely, Daṇḍa or the incarnation of the Spirit of Punishment.[67] It is Daṇḍa who is the king, the regulator of the entire universe. A guiltless man is hard to find and it is through the fear of Daṇḍa that the world observes *dharma*. Punishment strikes down the king who swerves from *dharma* for Daṇḍa is *dharma* and this implies that the king is under the law, not above it. The power to make new laws or to alter old ones is not vested in the king or any human power. A king, like a judge, merely declares *dharma*; he does not make it. Daṇḍa alone governs all created beings, protects them and watches over them while they sleep. Where Daṇḍa with a black hue and red eyes stalks about, destroying sinners, there people are safe. Daṇḍa possesses a very bright lusture and is hard to be administered by men with unimproved minds. The word Daṇḍa, according to *Nirukta*,[68] may be derived from *dad*, meaning 'to hold' or *dam* meaning 'to restrain'.[69] The epics and Purāṇas hold that Daṇḍa is so called because it restrains and punishes.[70] According to the *Mahābhārata*,[71] for saving the world from anarchy and strife Viṣṇu created Daṇḍa. From that form, having Dharma for its support, the goddess of learning created Daṇḍanīti, the science of chastisement. The

Bhagavadgītā[72] identifies Daṇḍa with the divine Kṛṣṇa: "I am Daṇḍa in the hands of those who control others". Originally Daṇḍa must have stood for the practical aspects of stately functions, as a political expedient by which the king was aided. It was a synonym of punishment, intended for maintaining law and order in order to bring prosperity to the kingdom. In a secondary sense Daṇḍa denoted army, one of the seven elements of the state. But Manu raised the concept of Daṇḍa in an abstract level. Daṇḍa is the moral guardian like the Varuṇa of the past who was in charge of maintaining Ṛta. In Manu's conception Daṇḍa is a blind force like Karma that works independently. The rulers who can understand the principles of its functioning and act accordingly survive with honour, but those who fail to grasp its significance are bound to have an inglorious end.[73]

Thus we find that the grounds on which the obligation to render obedience to the ruler are based on the concept of the king's divinity or semi-divinity, a primeval contract between the ruler and the people, the interdependence of the ruler and the people as parts of one organism and his wielding of Daṇḍa with skill and wisdom for affording protection to the people in regard to their life, liberty and property. That is why Manu has insisted on the qualities and attainments—physical, intellectual and moral—of the ruler as well as his way of life. He should honour the learned Brāhmaṇas, possess a sense of modesty, learn the sacred sciences, shun the ten vices springing from love of pleasure and eight proceeding from wrath and practice self-control.[74] It should be pointed out in this connection that Manu's ideas about the conquest of the senses matches squarely with Plato's conception of virtue as the conquest of the self, 'the internal enemy'. According to Plato, political power and wisdom must meet together, the ruler should be inducted from men of virtue and wisdom, the disinterested lover of truth, the philosopher, alone is qualified to rule, and the ideal state should be founded upon four qualities—wisdom, bravery, temperance and justice.[75] The

hyperboles used for exalting the office and person of the king are meant to emphasize his dedication for his duties. He symbolizes the power of various deities. As Indra showers copious rains he should shower copious benefits; as the sun draws up water with his rays, the king should also draw taxes; as the wind moves everywhere, the king should know and see everything of his kingdom; as Yama is impartial to all, so the king should also be impartial to his subjects; his appearance should be soothing like the Moon and his wrath should be effective like Fire. As the Earth supports all created beings equally, so also the king should support all his subjects.[76]

Following the theory of the seven limbs of the state (*saptāṅga*) Manu says that the king should appoint seven or eight competent ministers coming from noble families for dealing with the affairs pertaining to war and peace, law and order, revenue and welfare activities.

> It is difficult for a person single-handed to accomplish even an easy task. Hence, how can a government, which has great good as its aim, function without helpers?[77]

The most distinguished among the ministers should be a learned Brāhmaṇa who has the king's that much confidence as to advise him on the affairs relating to the six measures of state policy. All administrative understanding must be preceded by consultations with ministers, and the place of consultation should not be heard outside.[78] Apart from the ministers, the king is to appoint other officials who are men of integrity, wisdom, firmness and ability and also an ambassador, well versed in the science of diplomacy.[79] The country should have a good climate which does not cause epidemic, where harvest is abundant, vassals are obedient and people find their livelihood. The king should build a town, erecting for his safety three kinds of fortresses and a palace for himself. He should have a wife, a domestic priest for various Śrauta sacrifices, trusty officers to collect revenue and intelligent supervisors to

inspect various transactions.[80] The king should honour the Brāhmaṇas with gifts, protect the people and ensure their happiness.[81]

> As the weeder plucks up the weeds and preserves the corn, even so let the king protect his kingdom and destroy his opponents. That the king who through folly rashly oppresses his kingdom will together with his relatives, ere long be deprived of his life and of his kingdom.[82]

Manu had laid down elaborate rules for warfare[83] insisting on the principles of war-ethics. The humane rules of warfare, stressed by Manu forbid the use of weapons which are concealed, poisoned or barbed, or the points of which are blazed with fire, and also striking down an enemy who is wounded, engaged in fighting with another, has offered submission, turned to flight, broken his weapon or lost his coat of mail. But he is not unware of the role of power in politics and he says that a king should always display his powers and be ever ready to strike.[84] But the goal of Manu's statecraft seems to be of achieving a balance of power in order to ensure the security of the state, consolidation of state power and welfare of the subjects. In this point he differs from Kauṭilya who was in favour of expansionism, of constantly marching towards *vṛddhi* or success. Manu's strategy is defensive. The king must always be ready to strike, but it is for the protection of his kingdom against onslaught from outside. He should carefully guard himself and observe the movements of his enemies. In his own words:

> His enemy must not know his weakness, but he must know the weakness of his enemy; as the tortoise hides its limbs, even so let him secure the members (of his government against treachery) let him protect his own weak points.
>
> Let him plan his undertakings (patiently meditating) like a heron; like a lion let him put forth his strength; like a wolf let him snatch his prey; like a hare, let him double in retreat.[85]

Like Kauṭilya, Manu also speaks about acquisition, protection, augmentation and bestowal on worthy persons to be the main aims of diplomacy.[86] So far as the inter-state relations are concerned, Manu had in mind the traditional Maṇḍala theory which imparted a symmetrical form to the relationships resulting from the quest of suzerainty and the consequent need of state diplomacy and alliances. The Maṇḍala consists of twelve powers.[87] (1) The Vijīgīsu or the would-be conquerer is placed in the centre. Then, next in geographical order, are five powers in front of him, namely, (2) Ari, the enemy, (3) Mitra, the friend of the Vijīgīsu, (4) Arimitra, the friend of the enemy, (5) Mitra-Mitra, the friend's friend of the Vijīgīsu and (6) Ari-Mitra-Mitra, the friend's friend of the enemy. In the rearward of the Vijīgīsu stand in geographical order, (7) Pārṣṇigrāhi or a rearward enemy, (8) Ākranda, rearward friend, (9) Pārṣṇigrāhasāra, friend of the enemy in the rearward and (10) Ākrandasāra, friend of the friend in the rearward. The circle or Maṇḍala is completed by (11) Madhyama or the intermediary and (12) Udāsīna or neutral. It is assumed in the above enumeration that two adjacent states are normally hostile, and consequently two states with another intervening between them would be friendly, being common enemies of the latter. The Udāsīna is the strongest power in the neighbourhood which normally can rely on its own strength and need not enter into any diplomatic relationship with the neighbouring powers for protection. The Madhyama is intermediate in strength between Udāsīna and the other powers. Manu holds that a king should so arrange matters that neither neutrals nor enemies nor even friends could become superior to him or injure him.

> By all expedients a politic prince must arrange matters so that neither friends nor neutrals, nor foes are superior to himself.[88]
>
> Let him arrange everything in such a manner that no ally, no neutral or foe may injure him; that is the sum of political wisdom.[89]

In order to achieve success in diplomacy Manu like Kauṭilya, speaks about the use of six *guṇas.*[90] This sixfold policy consists of Sandhi (treaty of peace or alliance), Vigraha (war), Āsana (neutrality), Yāna (making preparation for attack without actually declaring war), Saṃśraya (seeking the protection of another) and Dvaidhībhāva (making peace with one and waging war against another). But Manu's interpretation of the six *guṇas* differs to a certain extent from that of Kauṭilya. Manu does not want that the king should always be aggressive. He insists more on the balance of power. According to him each of the *guṇas* has two implications.[91] The expedients are not for the policy-making king alone. They are also meant for his allies so that the greater aim of maintaining peace, conducive to the welfare of the subjects, be achieved through a proper balance of power.[92] Manu holds, in opposition to the view of Kauṭilya, that the strength of the king cannot be demonstrated by taking the path of warfare. Rather a king who is very sure about his superiority to others in strength is capable to conclude peace with absolute success not only in his own favour but for the sake of others as well.[93] The king can go to the path of war only when it is imperative and he is so powerful that success is within his easy grip.[94] At the same time he does not recommend attack on unsuspecting neighbours. Nor does he, unlike Kauṭilya, enjoin that a king should practise guile. According to Manu, the king should resort to *āsana* or neutrality if situation demands it, but he does subscribe to Kauṭilya's view of purposeful neutrality.[95] Manu's approach to diplomacy is thus more ethical. Dvaidhībhāva, according to Manu, is a bifurcation or division of army for the sake of defence,[96] while Kauṭilya considers it as a form of duplicity, making peace with one and waging war against another. Explaining Manu's point of view, Medhātithi says that when a strong enemy attacks the king and the latter is unable to make peace with the aggressor, he should take refuge in a fort with a portion of his army for consolidating his strength and position while the other portion should try to resist the aggressor. According to Manu, a king when weak or harassed may seek Saṃśraya or protection

from another powerful ruler.[97]

According to Manu in regard to diplomacy four expedients are necessary which are *sāma* (making peace or conciliation), *dāna* (granting concession), *bheda* (creating dissension) and *daṇḍa* (use of force) and these should be applied either severally or conjointly.[98] He has insisted on the first three expedients, but he is not in favour of using the fourth expedient, namely, the use of force or the path of war. It may only be taken as an extreme measure. In his own words:

> He should, however, try to conquer his foes by conciliation, by well-applied gifts and by creating dissension, used either separately or conjointly, never by fighting (if it can be avoided).
>
> For when two princes fight, victory and defeat in the battle are, as experience teaches, uncertain, let him therefore avoid an engagement.
>
> (But) if even those three before-mentioned, expedients fail, then let him, duly exerting himself, fight in such a manner that he may completely conquer his enemies.[99]

According to Manu, a treaty should have a threefold objective, namely, acquisition of land, receiving wealth and finding friend, the last objective being most important.

> By gaining gold (*hiraṇya*) and land (*bhūmi*) a king grows not so much in strength as by obtaining a firm friend (*mitra*) who, though weak may become powerful in future. A weak friend even is greatly commended, who is righteous and grateful, whose people are contented, who is attached and preserving in his undertakings.[100]

The success of diplomacy, according to Manu, depends on the king's endeavour to conciliate the conquered territories by various means.

> When he has gained victory, let him duly worship the gods and honour righteous Brāhmaṇas, *let him grant exemptions, and let him cause promises of safety to be proclaimed.*
>
> But having fully ascertained the wishes of all the conquered, *let him place there a relative of the vanquished ruler on the throne* and let him impose his conditions.
>
> Let him *make authoritative the lawful customs of the inhabitants,* just as they are stated to be and let him honour the (new king) and the chief servants with precious gifts.[101]

A study of Manu's Rājadharma leads us to conclude that there was not much difference between the Dharmaśāstra and the Arthaśāstra schools in regard to political conceptualizations and that both Manu and Kauṭilya shaped their ideas from the same source. Both trace the emergence of state-power and kingship to a primeval stage of anarchy and chaos and the institution of rulership to some sort of arrangement, divine or human. Both of them hold that the state is an aggregate of seven elements and that the ruler is one of its constituents. In regard to the practical or functional aspects of the government, the appointment of ministers, officials, ambassadors and other dignitaries and also to that of expedients concerning state policy, diplomacy, inter-state relations and so forth both have identical views, though in regard to their application there is a little difference between Manu and Kauṭilya, the former being more ethical than the latter who has some Machievellian tendencies. Both of them, however, seriously insist on the education, attainments and discipline of the ruler and hold that unless endowed with virtues and distinguished from others by a qualitative greatness in regard to ability and wisdom, the ruler is bound to ruin himself as an ugly despot. But there is also a marked difference between them. This difference is in outlook. As the champion of the Arthaśāstra school Kauṭilya's emphasis is on *artha,* the material aspects of life. But Manu subordinates *artha* to *dharma* and in this respect

he has more affinity with Plato and Aristotle in whose writings we have an echo of Manu's conception of *dharma* which is crystallised in the form of *daṇḍa* and conserved in the form of the human ruler. A comparison between the Greek and the Indian political ideals has been made by eminent scholars like Krishna Rao,[102] B.A. Saletore,[103] N.P. Sil,[104] and others. There are of course some parallels between the Greek thinkers on the one hand and Manu and Kauṭilya on the other especially in their concept of human nature and the role of the ruler in the state, as we have seen above. But at the same time it should not be forgotten that ancient Indian political thought stands by itself and does not fall under any of the accepted categories of Western speculation, having a spirit, a milieu and an atmosphere of its own as different from their Western counterparts as Indian personality, temperament and outlook are different from what one finds in the West.[105]

NOTES

1. Cf. Max-Müller, *A History of Sanskrit Literature*, p. 1. This imperialistic ideology regarding ancient Indian history and particularly the nature of early Indian polity was challenged in the last three decades of the nineteenth century by Bhagawan Lal Indraji, R.G. Bhandarkar, R.L. Mitra, B.G. Tilak and others. Among the important works the following are to be noted: K.A. Nilakantha Sastri, *The Theory of Pre-Muslim Indian Polity*, Madras, 1912; K.V. Rangaswamy Aiyangar, *Some Aspects of Ancient Indian Polity*, Calcutta, 1914, P.N. Banerjee, *Public Administration in Ancient India*, Calcutta, 1916; Ananda Coomaraswamy, 'Hindu Theory of State and Social Compact' in *Hindustan Review*, 1918; R.K. Mookerji, *Local Government in Ancient India*, Calcutta, 1919; R.C. Majumdar, *Corporate Life in Ancient India*, Oxford, 1919; R. Shamasastri, *Evolution of Indian Polity*, Calcutta, 1920; N.N. Law, *Aspects of Ancient Indian Polity*, Oxoford, 1921; B.K. Sarkar, *Political Institutions and Theories of the Hindus*, Allahabad, 1921; U.N. Ghosal, *A History of Hindu Political Theories*, Oxford 1923; K.P. Jayaswal, *Hindu Polity*, Calcutta, 1924; Ajit Kumar Sen, *Studies in Hindu Political Thoughts*, Calcutta, 1926; D.R. Balakrishna, 'Evolution of the State', *IHQ*, Vol. III, No. 2, 1927; N.C. Bandopadhyay, *Kauṭilya or An Exposition of His Social and Political Theory, I. Art of Good Government*, Calcutta, 1927; *Development of Hindu Polity and Political Theories;*

2 Vols., Calcutta, 1927, 1938; Beni Prasad, *Political Theories in Ancient India*, Allahabad, 1927; *Theory of Government in Ancient India*, Allahabad, 1928; *The State in Ancient India*, Allahabad, 1928; V.R.R. Dikshitar, *Hindu Administrative Institutions*, Madras, 1928; *Mauryan Policy*, Madras, 1932; K.P. Jayaswal, *Manu and Yājñavalkya*, Calcutta, 1928, Pramatha Nath Bose, *Public Administration in Ancient India*, London, 1930; E.W. Hopkins, The Divinity of Kings in *JAOS*, LI, New Haven, 1931; B.B. Naik, *Ideals of Ancient Hindu Politics*, Dharwar, 1932; S.V. Venkateswar, *Public Life and Political Institutions*, London, 1932; J.J. Anjaria, *The Nature and Ground of Political Obligation in the Hindu State*, 1935; R. Pratapgiri, *Problems of Indian Polity*, 1935; C.P. Ramaswamy Aiyar, *Indian Political Theories*, Madras, 1937; K.M. Panikkar, *The Origin and Evolution of Kingship in India*, Baroda, 1938; H.N. Sinha, *Sovereignty in Ancient India*, London, 1938; B.N. Datta, *Studies in Indian Social Polity*, Calcutta, 1944; Jagadish Lal Shastri, *Political Thoughts in the Puranas*, Lahore, 1944, C.J. Gadd, *The Divine Rule in the East*, London, 1944; Frankfort Henri, *Kingship and Gods*, Chicago, 1948; K.V. Rangaswamy Aiyangar, *Aspects of Social and Political System in the Manusmṛti*, Lucknow, 1949; V.P. Varma, *Studies in Hindu Political Thought and Its Metaphysical Foundation*, Delhi, 1954; M.M. Ghosal, On Some Recent Interpretations of the *Mahābhārata* Theory of Kingship, *Indian Historical Quarterly*, Vol. XXXI; 1955; T.V. Mahalingaon, *South Indian Polity*, Madras, 1955; J.C. Heesterman, *Ancient Indian Royal Coronation*, The Haque, 1957; J. Gonda, *Ancient Indian Kingship from Religious Point of View*, Rep. from NUMEN, Vols. III and IV, 1955-57, Leiden, 1966; A.S. Altekar, *State and Government in Ancient India*, 3rd Ed. Banares, 1958 (1st Ed. Banares, 1942); R.S. Sharma, *Aspects of Political Ideas and Institutions in Ancient India*, Delhi, 1959; B.P. Sinha, 'The Kauṭilyan State' in *Journal of Bihar Research Society*, XL, No. 3, Charles Drekmeier, *Kingship and Community in Early India*; Standford, 1962; Jhon W. Spellman, *Political Theory of Ancient India—A Study of Kingship from the Earliest Times to A.D. 300*, Oxford, 1964; Manorama Jauhari, *Politics and Ethics in Ancient India*, Varanasi, 1968; I.W. Mabbett, *Truth, Myth and Politics in Ancient India*, Delhi, 1971; Prabhabati Sinha, *Smṛti Political and Legal System: A Socio-Economic Study*, New Delhi, 1982; etc.

2. *Hindu Polity*, Calcutta, 1924, pp. 224-28. This work was serialized in the *Modern Review* between 1912-15.
3. *Ancient Indian Polity* (Sir Subrahmanya Aiyar Lecture, 1914) Madras, 1916, pp. 25-34, 50-57, 78-80, 91-92.
4. *Aspects of Ancient Indian Polity*, Oxford, 1921, Rep. Delhi, 1986, pp. 31 ff.
5. Expanded Edition under the title *A History of Indian Political Ideas*, Oxford University Press, 1959, Rep. with corrections 1966, pp. 307-36.

6. *Some Aspects of Ancient Hindu Polity*, Banaras, 1929, pp. 145-47, 157.
7. *Development of Hindu Polity and Political Theories*, (two parts), Calcutta, 1927, 1938, edited in a single volume, N.N. Bhattacharyya, New Delhi, 1980.
8. *The Political Theories in Ancient India*, Allahabad, 1927. *The Theory of Government in Ancient India*; Allahabad, 1927, *The State in Ancient India*, Allahabad, 1928.
9. *Aspects of Social and Political System in the Manusmṛti* (R.K. Mookerji Lectures, Lucknow University, 1946), Lucknow, 1949.
10. *State and Government in Ancient India*, Banaras, 1949.
11. *Studies in Hindu Political Thought and its Metaphysical Tradition*, Delhi, 1954.
12. *Ancient Indian Kingship from Religious Point of View*, NUMEN, III-IV, 1955-57, Leiden, 1966.
13. *Aspects of Political Ideas and Institutions in Ancient India*, Delhi, 1959.
14. *Kingship and Community in Early India*, Stanford, 1962.
15. *Political Theories of Ancient India: A Study of Kingship from c.A.D. 300*, Oxford, 1964.
16. *Politics and Ethics in Ancient India*, Varanasi, 1968..
17. VII. 1.
18. *Mbh.* XII. 58. 1-3; XII. 59,30,79; XIII. 39.8; Kauṭilya I.8; V.5, etc. *Nītiprakāśikā*, ed. Oppert, I. 21-22.
19. Cf. *Buddhacarita*, I. 46.
20. XII. 63. 28.
21. Cf. *Kāmandaka* I. 6; *Raghuvaṃśa* XVII, 68; *Bhagavadgītā* X. 38.
22. *Kauṭilya* I. 2.
23. *Mitākṣarā* on *Yājñavalkya* II. 21.
24. Cf. *Vīramitrodaya*, Chowkhamba ed., *Paribhāṣā*, p. 16.
25. XII. 63.25. For details XII. 56-130.
26. Manu VII. 2.
27. Chowkamba ed. *Rājanīti*, p. 10.
28. On Yājñavalkya I. 366.
29. IV. 61.
30. Cf. *Āpastamba Dh. S.* I. 11.32.18.
31. *Tantravārtika* (Anandasrama ed.), p. 580.
32. III. 3-6.
33. Cf. *Matsya* CXLIV. 40,43; *Liṅga* XL. 7, 42; etc.
34. IX. 294-97. The word Prakṛti is also used for the constituents of the circle of states (*maṇḍala*), Manu VII. 156; Kauṭilya VI. 2. In the inscription of Khāravela (*Ep. Ind.* XX, p. 79) and in *Raghuvaṃśa* VIII. 18 it means subjects.
35. *Some Aspects of Ancient Indian Polity*, pp. 66-89.
36. *Hindu Polity*, II, p. 9.
37. *Positive Background of Hindu Sociology*, II, pp. 34-39.

38. *Nature and Grounds of Political Obligations in the Hindu State,* Ch. IV.
39. *Op. cit.,* III. p. 20.
40. CCX. 34.
41. *Political Theory of Ancient India,* p. 9.
42. I. 61-62.
43. See L. Gopal. *The Śukranītisāra: A Nineteenth Century Text,* Varanasi, 1978.
44. Manu VII. 3.
45. *Ācāra,* Bib. Ind. ed., p. 301.
46. *Rājanīti,* Chowkhamba ed., p. 15.
47. XI. 1.6.29.
48. I. 4; Shamasastry's trans., p. 8.
49. XII. 63. 3ff.
50. II. 67. 8-31.
51. CCXXV. 8-9.
52. *Hindu Polity,* I. pp. 97-98, 134, 173.
53. Kane, *op.cit.,* III. p. 30.
54. *Mbh.* XII. 59. 13ff.
55. Kane, *op. cit.,* p. 244.
56. Aiyangar, *op. cit.,* pp. 171-72.
57. Manu VII. 4-13.
58. Manu VII. 41.
59. *Mbh.* XII. 9. 106-08.
60. CCXXVI. 17-20.
61. CCXXVI. 9-12.
62. XVIII. 26-31.
63. Cf. *Rām.* III. 40; *Mbh.* XII. 89.
64. 'The Divinity of Kings' in *JAOS,* LI. p. 312.
65. *Hindu Political Thought,* p. 34.
66. Cf. Altekar, *State and Government in Ancient India,* p. 61.
67. Manu VII. 14-32.
68. II. 2.
69. Cf. *Gautama Dh. S.* XI. 28.
70. Cf. *Mbh.* XII. 15.8; *Matsya* CCXXV. 17; *Agni* CCXXVI. 16.
71. XII. 122. 19-25.
72. X. 38.
73. VII. 33-34.
74. VII. 35-53.
75. *The Republic of Plato,* trans. by Francis M. Cornford, London, 1941, rep. 1972, pp. 29ff.
76. Manu IX. 303-11.
77. VII. 55; cf. *Kauṭilya* I. 7; *Mbh.,* XII. 106-11; *Matsya* CCXV. 2-3.
78. VII. 147-50; cf. *Kauṭilya* I. 15; *Agni* CCXXV. 9, etc.
79. VII. 54-68, cf. *Kauṭilya* I. 16; *Kam.* XII. 1-24. *Matsya* CCXV. 12-13.

80. VII. 69-81.
81. VII. 82-88.
82. VII. 110-11.
83. VII. 89-108.
84. VII. 102.
85. VII. 105-106.
86. VII. 99.
87. VII. 156.
88. VII. 177.
89. VII. 180.
90. VII. 160.
91. VII. 162.
92. VII. 163-66.
93. VII. 169.
94. VII. 170-71.
95. VII. 173.
96. VII. 168.
97. VII. 168.
98. VII. 107, 159, 214.
99. VII. 198-200.
100. VII. 208-09.
101. VII. 201-03.
102. *Studies in Kauṭilya*, 1958, rep. Delhi 1978, pp. 21ff.
103. *Ancient Indian Political Thought and Institutions,* London 1963, pp. 191-290.
104. *Kauṭilya's Arthaśāstra: A Comparative Study*, Calcutta, 1985.
105. Cf. Beni Prasad, *Theory of Government in Ancient India*, Allahabad, 1927, p. 337.

Chapter VII

Legal Conceptualizations

We have already had the occasion to say that the Western interest in the *Manusmṛti* was due to the impelling necessity of the British rulers for managing a country which differed significantly from the norms of Western civilization. The *Manusmṛti* was treated by most scholars as the sourcebook of Hindu law and studied especially for legal purposes, though the legal portion of the text does not amount to more than one-fourth of the whole. Colebrooke's *Digest* (1797-98)[1] contained copious quotations from Manu which subsequently became the basis of modern legal literature intended for the European practitioners and their Indian counterparts who were required to know the basic contents of the Dharmaśāstras in general and the *Manusmṛti* in particular along with those of their commentaries. Among subsequent publications of Indian law, mention may be made of Sir Thomas Strange's *Hindu Law* (1830), Gibelin's study on the civil law of the Hindus (1846)[2] and Wilson's *Glossary* (1855)[3] which still remains indispensable for the students of Indian law. West and Bühler's *Digest* (1867-69)[4] which was based mainly on later Smṛtis discussed in detail the laws prevalent in then Bombay Presidency and it was extensively used by A. Mayr (1873)[5] who had tried to prove that Sir John Lubbock's (Lord Avebury) theory about the primitive family and particularly the theory that women were originally the common property of the clan might also be traced in Indian law. J.D. Mayne (1878)[6] made a comprehensive study of the Hindu laws and their various forms of application in different parts of the country. Rao

Bahadur V.N. Mandlik's researches (1880)[7] brought to light various new sources and manuscript materials, not very easily available at that time, which contributed a lot for the reconstruction of the history of the Smṛtis. Leist (1884, 1889, 1892)[8] wanted to reconstruct the earliest form of the Aryan or Indo-European legal system on the basis of a comparative study in which he had taken into account the history of Indian law as well, while Kohler (1891)[9] dealt with the same from the standpoint of comparative jurisprudence with particular reference to customary law which he had constructed systematically on the basis of the Gazetteers.

The Tagore Law Lectures instituted by the University of Calcutta were instrumental in bringing out a good number of legal publication of the highest merit. Among the experts whose lectures were published in book-form mention may be made of E.B. Cowell (1870-72),[10] Sir Gurudas Banerjee (1828),[11] T. Mitra (1881),[12] R. Sarvadhikari (1882),[13] Julius Jolly (1885),[14] G.C. Sarkar (1891),[15] Priyanath Sen (1918),[16] and others. In all these works the Code of Manu and its various commentaries have been copiously utilised and variously interpreted. Subsequently there has been a multifarious growth of legal literature. Julius Jolly's *Recht and Sitte* (1886)[17] is one of the best handbooks on the ancient legal system which deals with the sources of Indian law; the family law and and the law of inheritance; law of property and control; crime, penance and punishment; judicial procedure; and customs and usages. According to him, the classification of law made by Manu in eighteen titles is worthy of notice not only as a first attempt, but seems to have been taken directly from actual life. Comparing Manu with Kauṭilya in his subsequent works he says that the general tendency of the *Arthaṣāstra* is directed towards *artha* or gain as the name of the book implies, whereas Manu lays down rules or *dharma,* i.e. of dutiful and pious conduct, and ordains superiority of *dharma* whenever it comes into conflict with *artha.*

Among the works of the subsequent writers on the ancient

Indian legal system reference may be made to those of J.C. Ghosh (1906)[18] who insisted more on its theoretical aspects, D.H.H. Ingalls,[19] D.F. Mulla (1912),[20] J.N.C. Ganguly,[21] M.M. Ganganath Jha (1930),[22] and K.P. Jayaswal (1930).[23] The last two authorities deserve special mention. According to Jha, whose contribution to the study of *Manusmṛti* we have already had the occasion to refer the law of the Hindus—like everything else conducive to the welfare of man—has its source in the revealed words of the Veda. Though this source is eternal and immutable, it has an inherent tendency to bear signs of being distinctly progressive, taking into account the varying conditions of time and space, which gave rise to the Smṛtis marking the second stage in the development of Hindu law. As regards the works included under the generic name Smṛti there is some difference of opinion among the ancient authorities. As regards the exact number and names of the works belonging to Smṛti category, there is no unanimity of opinion. This diversity in the list of authorities on law also bears testimony to the progressive spirit at work in this branch of literature. The next stage is presented in the Nibandhas in which we find the writers laying far greater stress on the Smṛtis than on the Śruti. This may have been due to the simple psychological reason that they found the Smṛti texts more ready to hand and more easy to comprehend and manipulate than the archaic Śruti texts. All this points to the fact that in the domain of law there has all along been a progressive spirit at work. Jha also has criticised the view of some modern scholars that *vyavahāra* occupies but a small fragment of their energy which is all spent on *ācāra* and *prāyaścitta* and refuted the view of Sir Henry Maine that—

> The code of Manu does not represent a set of rules ever actually administered in Hindustan. It is in great part an ideal picture of that which, in the view of the Brāhmaṇas, ought to be law.[24]

Jayaswal's Tagore Law Lectures on *Manu and Yājñavalkya* are chiefly concerned with the analysis of the jural ideas of the two works. Yājñavalkya, as we have seen above, treats of almost all subjects that we find in Manu, but his treatment is more concise. According to Jayaswal it represents a liberal recension of Manu and is influenced more by Kauṭilya than by contemporary Dharmaśāstra theories. Yājñavalkya represents the view of Hindu Law as it prevailed in the Sātavāhana regime. He devotes larger space to the consideration of the problems of civil law. He deals with contract generally and with patnership of sea-traders and artisans and the law of corporations is also considered by him. Jayaswal was criticised by some scholars, especially by S. Varadachariar, U.N. Ghosal and P.V. Kane, for his insistence on the hypothesis of a rivalry between the *Arthaśāstra* and the Dharmaśāstra of Manu, which was likened to that between the work of a statesman and a priest. Much was made of the former's secular outlook and features, as contrasted with the religious or 'superstitious' attitude of its rival. He was also criticised for his theory that the present version of the *Manusmṛti* was a composition to justify the Śuṅga usurpation, which has been dealt with in the preceding chapter.[25] But to his credit it may be said that he has given forceful expression to some novel views which a historian cannot reject outright. Next come in succession the works of Radhabinod Pal (1938),[26] P.V. Kane (1946),[27] C.P. Ramaswamy Aiyer (1949),[28] R.S. Davar and K.D.P. Madan (1950),[29] N.C. Sengupta (1953),[30] L. Sternbach (1965-67),[31] D.M. Derrett (1968, 1976)[32] etc. There are some works dealing with the ancient Indian sources of international law as well.[33]

Manu is very often charged for mixing law with religion, but this is an oversimplified and unhistorical assertion. It is a fact that Manu has claimed a divine origin for his laws. But it is to be remembered that ancient peoples almost without exception regarded their laws as of divine origin. Though in its progress, the legal order appears to have tried to meet the new demands arising out of a multitude of unsatisfied social de-

sires, human agency did not claim the authorship of law. In ancient Egypt law was attributed to the gods.[34] The Mosaic Law or Hammurabi's Code or the *Manusmṛti*, each one in its own way, claimed to be based upon divine inspiration. The *Old Testament* represents Jahweh as dictating the Ten Commandments to Moses. There it is also stated that all the laws found in the *Exodus, Leviticus* and *Numbers* were a direct revelation from God through Moses. At the top of the front side of the stele containing the famous Code of Hammurabi, the Sun God Shamash is pictured in a bas-relief seated on a throne and presenting the king the laws which follow. In the epilogue to his code Hammurabi declares:

> If a man heeds my words which I have written upon my monument, does not efface my words, does not alter my monument, so may Shamash prolong his reign.[35]

According to Demosthenes, men ought to obey the law because—

> Laws are prescribed by God, because they were a tradition taught by the wise men who knew the good old customs, because they were deductions from an eternal and immutable moral code, and because they were agreements of men with each other binding them because of a moral duty to keep their promises.[36]

Cicero declared: *Lex nihil aliud nisi recta et a numine deorum tracta.* He believed that justice and the whole system of social life depended upon gods and men's belief in them. The law, according to Roman ideas, had a double foundation, being based partly upon divine revelation (*fas*) and partly upon human ordinance (*ius*).

It is said that the code of Manu contains a great deal more about *ācāra* or established practices, that is, observance of caste, domestic ceremonies, funeral rites, oblations to the

manes and to the gods, rules of diet, and other religious questions including purely religious and philosophical discussions than on the subject of secular laws. On which Manu really insisted, as we have seen in the fourth chapter, was a way of life in accordance with the spirit of the Vedas which was also interpreted by him in his own way. His insistence on the sacraments, rituals, penances, daily duties, offering oblations to deities, self disciplining and so forth reflects the beliefs and customs of the people living in this subcontinent. Every people of the ancient world felt strongly that their customs and rituals were peculiar to themselves and presented a marked contrast to those of other peoples. These have nothing to do with any particular religious system or outlook, but represent a totality of cultural tradition of various shades as is reflected in the *Twelve Tables* of Rome. Manu's special discourses on religious and philosophical matters are also part of this cultural tradition. A comprehensive study of ancient laws in the world would reveal that they do not make any distinction between beliefs, rituals, customs, ethics or morality on the one hand and the provisions of what may be called the positive law on the other. According to Manu, the whole Veda is the source of *dharma* or law, and next is the tradition of those who know the Vedas, further, the usages of various men and self-satisfaction.[37] Kane takes the view that the *ācāra* mentioned by Manu has to be taken by itself and not as qualified by the words *śrutyukta* or *smārta.* Manu and other Smṛtikāras show that the customs and usages of which notice has to be taken pertain to districts, towns, villages, castes, families, guilds and corporations or groups.[38] Vijñāneśvara while commenting on Yājñavalkya II. 118-19 categorically says that the texts in the section are mostly recitals of what actually prevails among the people. In this way the laudable objet of bringing the provision of the divine law into the line with popular usages and customs was achieved.

It would thus appear that during the early stages of the development of law, with due recognition of all its sources, what were regarded as rules of law were invariably assumed to

have divine origin, and they purported to receive their sanction from the fact that they embodied the dictates of providence. Each age has expressed the conviction that law is not a mere human convention, but is conditioned by the eternal nature of things and behind nature is the working of the divine intelligence and will. Even Blackstone in the eighteenth century says that the law of nature being coeval with mankind and dictated by God himself, is superior in obligation to any other. It is binding over all the globe, in all the countries and at all times. No human laws are not gone to this extent. According to him law is a divine revelation, but it has come down to the earth through human agency, and this agency is not of average mortal human being but of sages or seers whose worldview is not restricted to a narrow strip of land. In this respect the views of Manu correspond to those of Plato who holds that it is the state and not the individual that can set the standard of moral and law. But this 'state' of Plato is not the existing city-state of his time, but an ideal common-wealth which is capable of setting and maintaining the standard of law and justice.[40] The legal philosophy of Manu centres on the concept of *dharma* which is the rational and moral reflection of the law-governed universe. The word is clearly derived from the root *dhṛ*, 'to uphold, to support, to nourish'. The word *dharma* passed through several transitions of meaning and ultimately, its most important significance came to be the privileges, duties, and obligations of a man, his standard of conduct as a member of the community and of the caste, and as a person at a particular stage of life. Jaimini defines *dharma* as a desirable goal or result that is indicated by injunctive passages.[41] According to Kane, the idea of *dharma* replaced the earlier concept of *ṛta* which in the *Ṛgveda*[42] denotes the supreme transcendental law or the cosmic order by which the universe and even the gods are governed.[43] On the relation between *ṛta* and law Kane quotes Berolzheimer[44] who says:

Closely connected with the religious and philosophical

> views of the Aryans are certain fundamental positions in regard to the philosophy of law which in turn became the antecedents of later legal and ethical developments among the Greeks and the Romans. Foremost among these philosophical conceptions is *ṛta* which is at once the organised principle of the universe and the divine ordering of earthly life; as the former it regulates the appearance of the sun and the moon, of day and night, and embodies the unchangeable principles that pervade the succession of phenomena; as the latter it is affiliated with purpose and human benefit and is exemplified in the flow of the rivers which fertilise the fields; in the cattle useful to men; in the institutions of marriage, of the monarchical state, of the patriarchal home, and in man's sense of responsibility for his sins. The derivative conceptions of *vrata*, *dharma*, *dhāma*, *svadhā* represent special aspects of *ṛta*; thus *vrata* refers to any specialised embodied *ṛta*; while *dharma* refers specifically to the moral function of rewarding good and punishing evil.[45]

The law-governed physical universe, is thus, according to Manu, the source of an eternal and universal law, a justice equally valid for all peoples and for all times. The king is not above the law, but is under it. In one place[46] Manu says that no one should defy the law which the king makes. But it does not mean that the king is entitled to make special laws according to his personal whims. The next verse[47] refers to *daṇḍa* and its creation, through which alone the king is able to maintain his authority, which is superior to the king, and will strike down the king swerving from *dharma* with which *daṇḍa* is identical. Among the four sources of judicial proceedings one is *rājaśāsana* (royal decree). But these *rājaśāsanas* are not new laws made by the king over and above those given in the Dharmaśāstras. The king cannot transgress *dharma* or issue an edict that does so. According to Grote, Zeus or the human king on earth is no law-maker but a judge, and his judgements divinely inspired,

constitute law.[48] Referring to Manu VII. 13 Kulluka says that the king has the right to issue occasional ordinances or edicts provided they are in conformity with *dharma* or are not in conflict with it. Medhātithi takes it to refer to orders that a king may issue, as the situation demands, in the course of administration and in consonance with *dharma* and customs. A functional liberty has been given to the king, because there are so many affairs and problems which are to be faced by the king in his day-to-day administration and these are not specifically mentioned in the Dharmaśāstras. Such edicts should be made in conformity with the spirit of Dharmaśāstra and Medhātithi says that "when such orders are issued by beat of drum, they should be obeyed". But he categorically warns that "the king has no power to make ordinances relating to *dharma* and religious duties, nor rules about *varṇa* and *āśrama*". According to K.V.R. Aiyangar, the *rajaśāsanas* are isolated or consolidated rules of procedure made by the king as a judge.

> The courts will be bound by them. Or they may contain authoritative interpretations of obscure points of *dharma* (law) decided by Pariṣads. The alleged 'royal edict' will thus correspond to the praetor's edict in ancient Rome, which *declared* but did not *make* new law."[49]

Manu has been severely criticised by most modern scholars for the one-sidedness of his approach, the discriminating nature of the legal procedure which is conducive to the interest of the privileged or Brahmanical classes and detrimental to the interest of common men, those belonging to the lower ranks of the caste-hierarchy. Previously we have had the occasion to refer to the views of N.C. Bandyopadhyaya according to which Manu took upon himself the task of presenting a social ideal which was more for conservation than for progress. He upheld the supremacy of the Brāhmaṇas, the doctrine of social inequality, the perpetual degradation of the Śūdras, the denunciation of womankind, the absolute authority of the

father over family property, unequal division among sons, the institution of slavery, the sacerdotal ideal and the blind and immoral advocacy of royal absolutism.[50] But it is to be remembered that even today all over the world equality is a fiction and most laws are in favour of the powerful and the privileged. The Code of Hammurabi recognises the *amelu*, freeborn person of high birth and standing, the *mushkenu*, free-born but the lower rank, and the *wardu* or the slave. These three classes are separately treated in the Code. According to Plato, the essence of law is the distribution of rights and duties on the principle of not meddling with the concerns of others. The privilege of each class—thinkers, fighters and workers—must be strictly proportionate to its responsibilities.[51] As Plato puts it,

> The shoemaker is to be only a shoemaker and not a pilot also; the farmer is to be only a farmer and not a judge as well; a soldier is to be a soldier and not a man of business besides; and if a universal genius, who through wisdom can be everything and do everything comes to the ideal city-state, he is to be required to move on.[52]

His teachings portrayed an ideal aristocratic state, based on slave labour and watched over by soldiers or 'guardians'. Below these free citizens were the 'handicraftsmen'.[53] Aristotle's 'justice in general' deals with the moral precepts brought under the cognizance of the state by its laws, while his 'justice in particular' deals more specially with proportionate distribution of rights and duties pertaining to various classes of society.[54] According to him, justice is a condition in which each keeps within his appointed sphere. Inequality being the basic feature of life the individuals are to be treated according to their worth. No social class has the right to transgress the limit assigned to it.[55]

Manu has used the term *vyavahāra* to denote 'law-suit' or 'dispute in a court' and 'legal procedure'.[56] That branch of

dharma which deals with secular law is known by the word *vyavahāra*. According to Kātyāyana, since *vi* means 'various', *ava* means 'doubt' and *hāra* means 'removal', the etymological meaning of the word *vyavahāra* indicates that it is that branch of law which removes various doubts.[57] The view that *vyavahāra* refers to secular law is supported by the *Mahābhārata* which says that the authority of the *vyavahāra* law is as sacred and great as that of the *dharma* law. While the latter has its origin in the Vedic law, the former in political governance which is also of divine inspiration.[58] The word *vyavahārasamatā* occurs in an Aśokan inscription[59] and *vyavahāravidhi* in the Hathigumpha inscription of Khāravela.[60] A *vyavahārikā-mahāmātra*, minister of justice, occurs in the Ceylonese chronicles.[61] Among other meanings of *vyavahāra* we have 'transaction in dealing'[62] 'legal capacity to enter into transactions',[63] 'the means of deciding a matter',[64] etc. In a wider sense *vyavahāra* includes every aspect of legal system. But in a narrower sense it denotes a contract and a litigation which is fought in a court. And it is in this second sense that it forms one of the four feet of *vyavahāra*- in-general, the other feet bring *dharma, cāritra* and *rājaśāsana*.[65] By *dharma* is meant the sacred law and truth. *Cāritra* means the usages of a country, village or family which are means of decision in certain cases apart from the question whether they are supported by the Smṛtis or not. Written documents also fall within this category. *Rājaśāsana* is royal decree, when a king issues an order, which is not opposed to the Smṛtis or local usages, which comes out of the king's wisdom, or which is issued to decide a matter when the authorities on which of the two sides are equally strong. According to Yājñavalkya[66] the four feet of *vyavahāra* are the plaint, the reply, the proof and the decision.

Manu, for the first time, gives a regular classification of law (*vyavahārapada*) under eighteen heads or titles.[67] These are (i) non-payment of debts (*ṛṇādāna*), (ii) deposit and pledge (*nikṣepa*), (iii) sale without ownership (*asvāmīvikraya*), (iv) concerns among partners (*sambhūya-samutthāna*),

(v) resumption of gifts (*dattasyānapākarma*), (vi) non-payment of wages (*vetanadāna*), (vii) non-performance of agreements (*saṃvidvyāti-krama*), (viii) rescission of sale and purchase (*krayavikrayānuśaya*), (ix) dispute between the owner and his servants (*svāmipālavivāda*), (x) dispute regarding boundaries (*sīmāvivāda*), (xi) assault (*vākpāruṣya*), (xii) defamation (*daṇḍapāruṣya*), (xiii) theft (*steya*), (xiv) robbery and violence (*sāhasa*), (xv) adultery (*strīsaṅgrahaṇa*), (xvi) duties of man and wife (*strīpuṃdharma*), (xvii) partition and inheritance (*vibhāga*), and (xviii) gambling and betting (*dyūtasamāhvaya*). Almost all these items occur in the third book of Kauṭilya's *Arthaśāstra*, but are not specified in a systematic manner, though some scholars have divided them into eighteen titles of law.[68] According to Manu, the enumeration of eighteen titles is only a matter of convenience; they do not embrace all disputes, but only those which are most important.[69] There is some difference about the number and nomenclature of the titles between Manu and other Smṛti writers. All do not mention them in the same order as in Manu VIII. 4-7. Yājñavalkya (Ch. II) does not enumerate all of them in one place as Manu and Narada do. He omits 'the duties of husband and wife' from the eighteen topics of *vyavahāra*, splits 'rescission of sale and purchase' into two, adds two other titles concerning 'miscellaneous wrongs' and thus gives twenty topics. Nārada[70] maintains fifteen topics of Manu (in some cases under slightly different names), omits three topics, splits two and adds two.

Greatest insistence on justice and equity has been laid by Manu. According to him, he who violates justice is always despicable. Justice is the only friend who follows men even after death. One quarter of the guilt of an unjust decision falls on the offender; one quarter on the false witness; one quarter on the judge; and one quarter on the king. Unprejudiced and impartial justice can alone make the king virtuous.[71]

> Where justice, wounded by injustice, approaches and the judges do not extract the dart, there they also are wounded by the dart of injustice.

> Where justice is destroyed by injustice, or truth by falsehood, while the judges look on, there they shall also be destroyed.
>
> Justice, being violated, destroys; being preserved, preserves: therefore justice must not be violated, lest violated justice destroy us.[72]

Manu says that "either the court must not be entered or the truth must be spoken; a man who either says nothing or speaks falsely, becomes sinful".[73] A similar verse occurs in other law books as well. Nārada[74] explains this in the following way:

> Either the judicial assembly must not be entered at all, or a fair opinion should be delivered. That man who stands mute or delivers an opinion contrary to justice is a sinner.

The *Mitākṣarā* or *Yāj* II.2 supports a similar view that the assessors, duly appointed, incur sin if they do not check the king in the event of his taking an illegal course; but as regards other people present, these incur sin only if they either speak falsely or suppress the truth—and not for not checking the king.[75]

According to Manu, justice should be primarily dispensed by the king who combines in him both the original court and the appellate tribunal. He should normally preside over the law-courts and be assisted by the Brāhmaṇas and experienced councillors to examine the business of the suitors.[76] The same is held by Yājñavalkya[77] who says that "the king shall try cases, accompanied by learned Brāhmaṇs, in strict accordance with legal scriptures, being free from anger and avarice," which is also echoed in the Dharma Sūtras of Gautama[78] and Vasiṣṭha[79] in various Smṛtis and digests. Manu says that the king shall decide the cases which fall under the eighteen titles of law according to the principles drawn from local usages and from the institutes of the sacred law.[80] In this context Vasiṣṭha[81] says

that Manu has declared that the peculiar law of countries, castes and families may be followed in the absence of revealed texts. Gautama[82] says that the king's administration of justice shall be regulated by the Veda, the institutes of sacred law, the subsidiary sciences and the Purāṇas. The local laws, the customs of castes and families, which are not opposed to the sacred laws, have also authority. Cultivators, traders, herdsmen, moneylenders and artisans have the authority to lay down rules for their respective classes. Having learnt the state of affairs from those who have authority to speak, the king shall give his decision. Manu says that when due to pressure of other works the king is unable to attend to the work of administering justice, he should appoint a learned Brāhmaṇa together with three Sabhyas (assessors) to decide the disputes.[83] The same is held by Yājñavalkya[84] who says: "The Brāhmaṇa knowing the entire *dharma* shall be appointed by the king to try law-suits if, under pressure of business, he is unable to look into them himself."[85] As regards the number of Sabhyas or assessors the later law-givers have divergence in opinion.[86] Kauṭilya, however, is in favour of three assessors presiding over such courts as should be established on the borders, for a group of ten villages (*samgrahaṇa*), for a district as well as for a province.[87]

Regarding evidence Manu says that if the defendant denies the charge, the complainant must call witnesses or adduce other evidence. Trustworthy men who are free from covetousness are admissible as witnesses. Those who have an interest in the suit, who are known friends or branded enemies of the parties, who were formerly convicted of prejury or tainted by moral sin and who are suffering from illness must not be made witnesses.[88] According to Medhātithi and Kulluka 'those who have an interest in the suit' pertain to 'those who are connected by money, i.e. creditors or debtors of the parties' while according to Nandana it means 'men who have received benefits from one of the parties'. All clean persons are admissible as witnesses irrespective of caste and creed, but Manu urges that women, twice-born men, Śūdras and men of

the lower castes should give evidence only on behalf of people of the same rank or class—women for women, Brāhmaṇa for Brāhmaṇa and so forth. But every person who has personal knowledge of a murder, or of acts done in the interior of a house or in a forest should be called as witness, particularly in cases of violence, adultery, defamation and assault. The witnesses should be strongly exhorted to speak the truth and severe penalties have been laid down for giving false evidence.[89] The personal qualities and trustworthiness of the witness as an individual should also be taken into account:

> On a conflict of the witnesses the king shall accept as true the evidence of the majority; if the conflicting parties are equal in number that of those distinguished by good qualities; on a difference between equally distinguished witnesses that of the best among the twice-born.[90]

In case there were no witnesses the judge should resort to the policy of investigation. For example, in order to find truth about deposits in the absence of witnesses the judge should employ an investigator who can even go to the extent of cleverly seducing the party through a double-dealing for the sake of proving his guilt, of course if he is really guilty.[91] In case there were no witnesses the judge could ascertain the truth by means of oath or ordeal.

> If the two parties dispute about the matters for which no witnesses are available, and the judge is unable to really ascertain the truth, he may cause it to be discovered even by an oath.
>
> Let no wise man swear or oath falsely, even in a trifling matter; for he who swears an oath falsely is lost in this world and after death.
>
> Let the judge cause a Brāhmaṇa to swear by his veracity, a Kṣatriya by his chariot or the animal he rides on and by his weapons, a Vaiśya by his kine, grain and gold and a

> Śūdra by imprecating on his own head the guilt of all grievous offences.
>
> Or the judge may cause the party to carry fire or to dive under water, or severally to touch the heads of his wives and children.[92]

Manu's rules regarding evidence has been systematised by Yājñavalkya who mentions three kinds of proofs, namely documents, witnesses and possession,[93] and he adds that ordeal is another kind or evidence in the absence of any of these. Where both witnesses and documents are wanting. Nārada[94] allows as a last alternative recourse to the ordeal. Nārada's long and detailed account of the different kinds of ordeals is matched only by Bṛhaspati, but it is necessary to quote it here. Kauṭilya does not refer to ordeals but gives gruesome details of eighteen kinds of torture to elicit confession of guilt. According to Kauṭilya,

> If witnesses differ, judgement may be given in accordance with the statements of a majority of pure and respectable witnesses; or the mean of their statements may be followed, or the amount under dispute may be taken by the king.[95]

Manu has also laid insistence on the social purpose of justice. According to him, the king must protect the inherited and other forms of property of a minor until the latter returns from his teacher's house or becomes adult. In the like manner care must be taken of barren women, of those who have no sons, of those 'whose family is extinct'. Of wives and widows and of women affilicted with diseases.[96] According to Nārada[97] and Kulluka 'the minority ends with the sixteenth year' of a boy. The second term is intended, according to Medhātithi and Kulluka, to provide for the case of those who finish their Veda study before the sixteenth year. Medhātithi gives also a second view according to which this second term pertains to the Śūdras. As for the phrase 'of those whose family is extinct'

Govindarāja says that it means 'maidens in that condition'. According to Medhātithi it means 'those who have quitted their families and become prostitutes'. Those who appropriate the property of such females are to be punished like thieves.[98] The king should keep for three years as deposit the property, the owner of which is missing. If the owner comes back within this stipulated period, the king will return the property to him. A false claimant is to be severely punished. If someone finds a treasure-trove, the king may take one-sixth or one-twelfth part of it from him, but not from a Brāhmaṇa. If the king himself obtains a treasure-trove he should bestow one half of it to the Brāhmaṇas. Property stolen by thieves must be restored by the king to its owner. A king who knows the sacred law must enquire into the laws of castes, of districts of guilds and of families and thus settle the peculiar law of each.[99]

Caste privileges and disabilities are reflected in the criminal laws of Manu, especially on matters of morality and social hygiene. Different punishments are laid down for identical offences in accordance with the caste of the criminal and the victim. Manu prescribes capital punishment for the murder of the Brāhmaṇas, women and children, tampering with the loyalty of ministers, treason and false proclamations. But as a general rule, Brāhmaṇas are to be exempted from capital punishment.

> Let him never slay a Brāhmaṇa, though he has committed all possible crimes; let him banish such an offender, leaving all his property to him and his body unhurt.
>
> No greater crime is known on earth than salying a Brāhmaṇa; a king, therefore, must not even conceive in his mind the thought of killing a Brāhmaṇa.[100]

Manu allows that the law may be taken into one's own hand on certain occasions, as in self-defence, and permits recovery of debt by artful management or even by force.

> Twice-born men may take up arms when they are hindered in the fulfilment of their duties, when destruction threatens the twice-born castes in evil times.
>
> In their own defence, in a strife for the fees of officiating priests, and in order to protect women and Brāhmaṇas; he who under such circumstances kills in the cause of right commits no sin.
>
> One may slay without hesitation an assassin who approaches with murderous intent, whether he be one's teacher, a child or an aged man, or a Brāhmaṇa deeply versed in the Vedas.
>
> By killing an assassin the slayer incurs no guilt, whether he does it publicly or secretly; in that case fury recoils upon fury.[101]

Various severe forms of punishments have been recommended by Manu. Apart from capital punishment, mutilations are prescribed for robbers, cut-purses and for those who obstruct popular well-being. Banishment is prescribed for acts which are calculated to endanger public safety and also for gamblers, cruel men, heretics, forbidden professionals, and so forth. Damages and fines are recommended for various offences. But one thing which one should bear in mind is that all the forms of punishment are to be inflicted after very careful consideration. For example capital punishment is prescribed for murder, but all murders do not deserve capital punishment. There are cases of accidental or unintentional homicide. There is the question of motive and so forth. That is why Manu says:

> Let the king, having fully ascertained the motive, the time and place of the offence, and having considered the ability of the criminal to suffer and the nature of the crime, cause punishment to fall on those who deserve it.
>
> Unjust punishment destroys reputation among men, and fame (after death), and causes even in the next world

> the loss of heaven; let him, therefore, beware of inflicting it.
>
> A king who punishes those who do not deserve it, and punishes not those who deserve it, brings great infamy on himself and (after death) sinks into hell.
>
> Let him punish first by gentle admonition, afterwards by harsh reproof, thirdly by a fine, after that by corporal chastisement.
>
> But when he cannot restrain such offenders even by corporal punishment, then let him apply to them even all thc four (modes conjointly).[102]

Manu requires the king to make the debtor repay his debt to the creditor in whatever way he can do it.[103] If the liability is denied by the debtor, then the only method is to file a suit for the recovery of the debt. But if the liability is admitted by the debtor, then there are five means of recovery viz., *dharma* (persuasion), *vyavahāra* (legal proceeding), *cala* or *upadhi* (trick), *carita* (sitting down at his door) and *bala* (compulsion to do the work or confinement).[104] But on the denial of the debt by a debtor the complainant has to prove his case in the court by calling witnesses or adducing other evidence.[105] Manu also lays down that if a debtor is unable to pay a debt then he should be made to do work suitable to his caste in the house of his creditor in order to gradually liquidate the debt, and a Brāhmaṇa debtor should be made to pay by easy instalments.[106] The son, though he has taken the ancestral estate, is not liable to pay the following debts of his father, viz., those incurred as a surety, for drinking or gambling, those arising from idle promises, debts for promises made under the influence of wrath or illicit love to women, the balance of a fine or toll and so forth.[107] The monthly interest on debt is allowed at the rate of two, three, four or five per cent according to the order of the castes. But in a pledge in which profit accrues no extra interest is taken.[108] The enjoyment of property for ten years gives a prescriptive right to it, but—

> A pledge, a boundary, the property of infants, an open deposit, a sealed deposit, women, the property of the king and the wealth of a Śrotriya are exempted from the operation of this rule.[109] A contract made by a person intoxicated or mentally disordered or wholly dependent or below the age of maturity or very aged or by an unauthorised party is invalid; and so also is the agreement which is 'contrary to law or to the settled usage'.[110]

Manu says that a gift or sale or pledge made by one who is not the owner should be considered as null and void.[111] Any unlawful purchase should be rescinded by the king or the judge. If the buyer purchases through ignorance in market overt from one who is not the owner, he incurs no blame or punishment, but he may have to hand over the article to the real owner. But if the purchase is made in the presence of a number of witnesses, there is no difficulty. Adulterated commodities must not be sold as pure, and so also commodities less than proper quantity or weight.[112] Manu extends the rule about the distribution of fees at a sacrifice among the priests to the secular joint undertakings, to the partnership of traders, craftsmen, etc.[113] Regarding resumption of gift, Manu says that where a man desires to resume what has been given by him to another as gift, because it has been improperly given by him in a manner opposed to the law, or the specific purpose of the gift is not served, the gift is to be regarded as invalid.[114] Wages of hired workmen or servants should be paid according to the agreement between the master and his men, but if the latter, apart from illness or valid reason, do not dutifully perform their work they will be fined and no wages will be paid to them.[115] If a man, belonging to a corporation inhabiting in a village or a district, after swearing to an agreement breaks it through avarice, the king should banish him from his kingdom or inflict on him various punishments.[116] The disputes arising from the transgressions of the owners of the cattle and the

herdsmen should be settled in terms of the previous agreement between the two parties as well as in terms of the duties and responsibilities vested on each of the both parties.[117] In the case of the dispute between two villages concerning a boundary the task of its settlement rests on the ruler. Manu states that in disputes boundaries should be settled in accordance with the visible and concealed signs, by reliance of long former enjoyment and by the constant flow of water and that if there be doubt even after observing the signs then the dispute has to be decided on the evidence of witnesses.[118]

It is in the *Manusmṛti* that we first come across a regular exposition of the legal system which was further followed in later Dharmaśāstras. The *Arthaśāstra* of Kauṭilya also deals with legal topics. Kauṭilya was probably not far removed from the time when *Manusmṛti* was composed. We have already had the occasion to refer to the basic or generic similarity of the two works and tried to explain this similarity in terms of the fact that both the works derived their main impulses from a common traditional source. But there are many functional differences which ought to be narrated here. While Kauṭilya allows levirate (*niyoga*) in its ancient fullness, Manu condemns it. Kauṭilya legitimises the courtesans while Manu considers them as a public scourge though Medhātithi is of opinion that Manu's reference to those 'whose families have become extinct' refer to prostitutes who have the right to have legal protection from the king. Kauṭilya attempts to regulate gambling and drinking while Manu condemns them as sin. Kauṭilya knows of remarried widows and unmarried mothers, but Manu has nothing for them. Manu strongly disapproves for heresy but Kauṭilya does not. They differ in regard to the shares to be allotted to sisters on inheritance. Kauṭilya forbids suicide and disapproves of Sati whereas Manu does not seem to renounce Sati expressly though he prescribes an alternative to it. While Manu would only discourage the pursuit of astrology as a profession, Kauṭilya condemns addiction to it. Regarding the status, privileges and concessions to be enjoyed by the

Brāhmaṇas, there is a marked difference between Manu and Kauṭilya. Manu says that capital punishment must not be inflicted on the Brāhmaṇas even for the most serious crimes. But Kauṭilya provides death penalty for a Brāhmaṇa guilty of high treason. Regarding the Śudras and women Kauṭilya is more lenient than Manu. Kauṭilya holds that *dharma, vyavahāra,* customs and royal ordinance are the four legs of law-suits and the latter in each case supersedes the former. This is an important innovation by which the king becomes the highest authority for promulgating law. Still more revolutionary is Kauṭilya's dictum that 'wherever sacred law (*śāstra*) is in conflict with rational law (*dharmanyaya*) then reason shall be held authoritative'. This is denied by most Dharmaśāstras which place the sacred law above all, even above the royal decree.

The legal formulations of the *Manusmṛti* were further followed in the later Dharmaśāstras, especially in those of Yājñavalkya, Nārada and Bṛhaspati. One of the chief merits of the Smṛti of Yājñavalkya lies in arranging the materials of the *Manusmṛti* in a more systematic and concise fashion. Yājñavalkya's description of the royal court of justice, agrees with that of Manu. But unlike Manu who only hints at the process of judicial procedure, Yājñavalkya describes them systematically, as we also find in the third book of the *Arthaśāstra.* The laws of Yājñavalkya relating to documents and witnesses closely resemble those of Manu. The *Nārada Smṛti* is admittedly based upon the extant *Manusmṛti,* but it has a number of original features. As compared with Manu and Yājñavalkya, Nārada introduces us to a highly complex legal procedure. According to Jolly, the impression that the *Manusmṛti* is the basic work upon which Nārada has made improvements is strengthened by the fact that he fully agrees with Manu in the arrangement of the subject matter. Nārada frequently refers to Manu and in a manuscript Nārada is even directly called *mānava dharmasastra Nāradaproktā saṃhitā.*[119] Close as the connection of Nārada with Manu, Bṛhaspati's work is very

often described to be a *vārtika* on the *Manusmṛti*, as he has not only given Manu the first place among all law-givers, but explains, amplifies and occasionally modifies the rules of the *Manusmṛti* on various topics of law. Even where he does not expressly mention Manu, he always adheres to his teachings.[120] Manu's influence on subsequent legal treatises has already been discussed in the third chapter.

NOTES

1. *A Digest of Hindu Law on Contracts and Succession with a Commentary of Jagannath Tarkapanchanan translated from the Original Sanskrit.* 4 Vols. Calcutta, 1787-98.
2. E. Gibelin, *Etudes sur le droit civil des Hindous,* 2 Vols., Pondichery, 1846-47.
3. *Glossary of Judicial and Revenue Terms,* London, 1855.
4. *Digest of Hindu Law,* Bombay, 1867-69.
5. *Das indische Recht,* Vienne, 1873.
6. *A Treatise on Hindu Law and Usage,* London, 1878.
7. *Hindu Law,* Bombay, 1880.
8. *Graco-italische Rechtsqeschichte,* Jena, 1884, *Alt-arisches Jus qentium,* Jena, 1889; *Alt-arische Jus Civile,* Jena, 1892.
9. *Altind, Processrecht,* Stuttgart, 1891.
10. *Hindu Law,* Calcutta, 1870-72.
11. *Hindu Law of Marriage and Strīdhana,* Calcutta, 1878.
12. *The Hindu Widow,* Calcutta, 1881.
13. *Law of Inheritance,* Calcutta, 1882.
14. *Outlines of an History of the Hindu Law of Partition, Inheritance and Adoption,* Calcutta, 1885.
15. *Hindu Law of Adoption,* Calcutta, 1891.
16. *General Principles of Hindu Jurisprudence,* Calcutta, 1918.
17. Eng. trans. by B.K. Ghosh under the title *Hindu Law and Custom,* Calcutta, 1928.
18. *Principles of Hindu Law,* Calcutta, 1906.
19. "Authority and Law in Ancient India", Supplement of *JAOS,* XXXI, 1911.
20. *Principles of Hindu Law,* Bombay, 1912.
21. "Hindu Theory of Property" and "Philosophy of Law", *IHO,* Vols. I-II, 1925-26.
22. *Hindu Law and its Sources,* Allahabad, 1930.
23. *Manu and Yājñavalkya: A Comparison and a Contrast,* Calcutta, 1930.
24. *Ancient Law,* London, 1861, p. 15.

25. S. Varadachariar, *Hindu Judicial System,* R.K. Mookerji Endowment Lecture, Lucknow, 1946, pp. 38ff. Kane is very critical about Jayaswal. He says: "A separate treatise would have to be written for exposing the hollowness of some of his assertions", *HD,* I, Part I, p. 447.
26. *History of Hindu Law,* Calcutta, 1938.
27. *History of Dharmaśāstra,* Vol. III. second Ed., Poona, 1973.
28. *The Philosophical Basis of Indian Legal and Social Systems,* Madras, 1949.
29. *General Principles of Indian Law,* Bombay, 1950.
30. *Evolution of Ancient Indian Law,* Calcutta, 1953.
31. *Judicial Studies in Ancient Indian Law,* London, 1965-67.
32. *Religion, Law and State in Indian,* London, 1968, *Essays on Classical and Modern Hindu Law,* Leiden, 1976.
33. P.N. Banerjee, *International Law and Custom in Ancient India,* Calcutta, 1920, S.V. Visvanath, *International Law in Ancient India,* London, 1925; H. Chatterjee, *International Law and Inter-State Relations in Ancient India,* Calcutta, 1958.
34. J.H. Breasted, *History of Egypt,* London, 1906, p. 242.
35. 'Code of Hammurabi' in J. Hastings' *Dictionary of the Bible,* Vol. V, p. 584. For details see R.P. Harper, *The Code of Hammurabi,* Chicago, 1904; also H.W.F. Saggs, *The Greatness that was Babylon,* London, 1962, pp. 196-232.
36. Roscoe Pound, *An Introduction to the Philosophy of Law,* London, 1946, p. 22.
37. II. 6; cf. Yājñavalkya I. 7.
38. *HD,* III. pp. 875-76.
39. W.A. Dunning, *History of Political Theories: From Rousseau to Spencer,* Indian ed., Allahabad, 1970, pp. 73 ff.
40. *Republic,* II. 368 ff., IV. 433, VII. 519.
41. I. 68.2; I. 105. 12; 136. 2; I. 142.7 ; I. 164. 11; II. 28.4 ; IV. 3. 8-16; X. 190.1.
43. *History of Dharmaśāstra,* III. pp. 244-45.
44. *The World's Legal Philosophies,* Eng. trans. by Jastrow, New York, 1929, pp. 37-38.
45. Cf. V.M. Apte in *ABORI,* XXV, pp. 55-60.
46. VII. 13.
47. VII. 14.
48. H. Maine, *Ancient Law,* London 1861, p. XVI.
49. *Aspects,* p. 185.
50. *Development of Hindu Polity,* Rev. ed. by N.N. Bhattacharyya, New Delhi, 1986, p. 256.
51. *Republic,* IV. 433.
52. Pound, *op.cit.,* p. 76.
53. B. Farrington, *Greek Science,* I, pp. 105-06.
54. *Ethics,* BK. V.

55. Pound, *op.cit.*, p. 77.
56. VIII. 1.
57. Kane, *HD*, III. p. 246.
58. *Mbh.* XII. 121. 49-57.
59. *CII.* I, p. 123.
60. *EI.* XX, p. 79.
61. *Mahāvagga* I. 40.3 : *Cullavagga* VI. 4-9.
62. *Āp. Dh. S.* II. 7. 16-17; *Mbh.* V. 37. 30.
63. *Gaut. Dh. S.* X. 48.
64. *Ibid.* XI. 19.
65. Cf. Kauṭilya IV. 1; *Nārada* L. 10.
66. II. 8.
67. VIII. 3-7.
68. Cf. N.C. Bandyopadhyaya, *Kauṭilya,* Calcutta, 1927, p. 219.
69. Cf. Medhātithi and Kulluka on Manu VIII. 8.
70. I. 16-19.
71. Manu VIII. 16-19.
72. VIII. 12, 14-15.
73. VIII. 13.
74. III. 10, III. 14.
75. Jha. *Explanatory Notes,* p. 401.
76. Manu VII. 1-2.
77. II. 1.
78. XIII. 26.
79. XVI. 2.
80. Manu VIII. 3.
81. I. 17; XVI. 4-5.
82. II. 19-24.
83. Manu VIII. 9-11.
84. II. 3.
85. Cf. Gautama. XIII. 26; Vasiṣṭha XVI. 2; Bṛhaspati I. 24.
86. Cf. Bṛhaspati I. 5.
87. III. 1.
88. XIII. 64.
89. Manu VIII. 60-100.
90. VIII. 73.
91. VIII. 182-84.
92. VIII. 109, 111, 113-114.
93. II. 22.
94. I. 239, 260-61.
95. Shamasastry, p. 225.
96. VIII. 27-28.
97. III. 37.
98. Manu VIII. 29.

99. VII. 27-41.
100. VIII. 380-81.
101. VIII. 348-51.
102. VIII. 126-30.
103. VIII. 47-48.
104. VIII. 49, cf. Nārada IV. 122; Bṛhaspati (*SBE*, XXXIII, p. 329).
105. VIII. 51-61.
106. VIII. 177; cf. Yāj., II. 43, Nārada IV. 131.
107. VIII. 159.
108. VIII. 142-43.
109. VIII. 145-49.
110. VIII. 163-64.
111. VIII. 199.
112. VIII. 200-03; *cf. Visnu Dh. S.* V. 164-65.
113. VIII. 206-11; Cf. *Yājñavalkya* II. 265.
114. VIII. 213-14; cf. *Nārada* VII. 2-5.
115. VIII. 215-17; cf. *Nārada* IX. 2-3; *Yājñavalkya* II. 194-98.
116. VIII. 219-28.
117. VIII. 229-44.
118. VIII. 245-66.
119. For Nārada's relation to Manu see Jolly, *SBE*, XXIII, Oxford, 1889, intro., pp. XII-XV.
120. For the relation of Bṛhaspati to Manu see Jolly, *Outlines of the History of Hindu Law* (TLL, 1885), pp. 60-62, Bühler in *SBE*, XXV, intro., p. CVIII; Kane, *HD*, I, p. 207.

Chapter VIII

Ritualistic Conceptualizations

The ritualistic conceptualizations of Manu derived their main impulses from primitive beliefs and practices by which the social and religious life of various ethnic groups were conditioned and characterised at the dawn of Indian history. It is said that the ideals contributing to the growth of a civilization are to a great extent observed in the rituals of a people more explicitly than in any other cultural traits. But to define the terms 'ritual' is a matter of proverbial difficulty.[1] The word has its root in Latin *ritus* meaning 'a custom'. In the lexicons the meaning attributed to 'ritual' is 'prescribed order of performing religious service'. It is said that ritual and prayer are the two expressions in act and word of man's sense of dependence on divine or supernatural powers and represent the practical aspect of religion, as distinguished from the theoretical one consisting of the body of beliefs held by men regarding these powers. But this definition is not correct since there are many rituals which possess a hot self-sufficiency and absolute disregard for the supernatural. There are many rituals which pertain to secular activities as well. In a broader sense 'ritual' may denote certain simple or complex performances in conformity with the world-view of a given people acting severally or conjointly on their individual or collective well-being and comprise rites, customs, ceremonies, observances, sacraments and other related practices. Here the Mīmāṃsā concept of *apūrva* may be used in order to explain the term 'ritual'. In connection with the question of causation of Mīmāṃsakas formulated the theory of potential energy (*śakti*) according to which there is an imperceptible power in

every cause, producing the effect. This theory of potency (i.e. power for generating the fruit of an action) seeks to explain how an action like sacrifice can bear fruit long after its performance. Literally, *apūrva* means yielding of that which did not exist before.

At the simplest level of life the rituals employed are instinctive in character. These are concerned with birth, puberty, marriage, parentage, eldership, death, etc. In the Indian tradition rituals associated with such aspects of life are known as *saṃskāras* and pertain to the *āśrama* theory dividing the stages of life into distinct categories. Just as there are seasons in the arc of man's days, so there are seasons of natural year which man must observe, such as the rites of seed-time and harvest. Above this level comes the cultural grade wherein ritualism is modified to reflect and sustain social organisation and its religious superstructure. In India this religious superstructure is found in the Yajña rituals, the Śrauta sacrifices pertaining to mankind in general and the Gṛhya rites in particular. It is at this level that ritual generates myths; in fact divinities are born of rituals.[2] The later Saṃhitās and the Brāhmaṇa literature categorically hold that the gods are products of sacrifices. Yajña is the First Principle to which gods are subordinate. As Jane Harrison observes: "The Maypole or harvest-sheaf is half-way to a harvest-maiden; it is thus a goddess is made. A song is sung, a story told, and the very telling fixes the outline of the personality".[3] The rites of annual decay and revival of plant-life, current in olden days, undoubtedly gave rise to the myths and legends pertaining to death and resurrection. Especially in Indian context it gave rise to the doctrines of transmigration, metempsychosis and *karma.* The legends outlining the personality of a divinity were thus at the root of the development of literature, the miming of such legends and their visual representations being conducive to the growth of drama and visual art respectively. The dialogue-hymns of the *Ṛgveda* and the *pāriplava ākhyānas* recited during the Vedic sacrifices may be referred to in this connection.[4]

According to Manu the rites, norms and rules, observances, conduct, behaviour, customs and kindred characteristics pertaining to different stages of individual, family, communal, social and religious life fall within the purview of *ācāra*. These are described in detail under different categories and specific terms. For individuals there are *ācāras* belonging to the Śrauta category connected with the cleanliness of the body. The *saṃskāras* or sacraments connected with different stages of individual life form *ācāra* of a different category. *Vratas* or religious rites belong to another class which being effected make a particular thing or person fit for a specific purpose. *Āhnika* belongs to the daily duties of an individual. *Saṃdhyā* is its branch which is the act of prayer at the daybreak, noon and sunset. The principal matters of *śauca* are related to the rules of bodily purity. *Tarpaṇa* is a remembrance of the deities, sages and fathers. The central point of the five *mahāyajñas* or daily observances is the discharge of duty to the creator, the ancient sages, the fathers and to the whole universe with its myriads of creatures of various grades and intelligence. *Dāna* or making gifts and *pratiṣṭhā* or installation of temples, dedication of wells, tanks, parks, etc., also fall in the category of non-obligatory *ācāras*. Apart from the codified *ācāras*, there are customary ones connected with harvest, seasonal changes, etc. For example, *āgrayana* or *navaśasyeṣṭi* is the rite of the offering of the first corn; and so is *navānna* which is performed after the harvest has been gathered. *Navarātra* is the ritual of nine nights in autumn with the consecrated pitcher and holy water and nine kinds of herbs and roots. In many places it is a part of Durgā worship which indicates the connection of the goddess with vegetation and fertility. A few rituals of such categories like Holi, Dīpāvalī, Car-festival etc., have transcended the limits of their original significance and have assumed a national character.

"From the cradle to the grave", said E.O. James,[5]

Human existence has seemed to be in a flux 'never

> continuing in one stay', a dying to be born again, exemplified in the decay and regeneration in nature. This has called forth a series of *rites de passage* at the critical junctions to obtain a fresh outpouring of life and power.[6]

This primitive belief was probably the driving force behind the Indian concept of the *saṃskāras*. Etymologically the term signifies 'putting together', 'forming well', 'making perfect', 'accomplishment', 'embellishment', 'purification', 'cleansing', 'preparation', 'dressing', 'refining', 'polishing', etc. From a religious point of view it denotes sacraments, rituals, purificatory acts, etc. Sabara[7] explains *saṃskāra* as that which being effected makes a certain thing or person fit for a certain purpose. More precisely in the Hindu tradition it denotes a sacred or sanctifying ceremony, one which purifies from the taint of sin contracted in the womb and which leads to regeneration. Twelve such ceremonies are enjoined by Manu.[8] The Dharmasūtra of Gautama, however, speaks of forty *saṃskāras*.[9] The twelve *saṃskāras* of Manu are *garbhādhāna* (rite of pregnancy), *puṃsavana* (rite to ensure birth of a male child), *sīmantonnayana* (rite of parting the hair), *jātakarman* (the ceremony after birth), *nāmakaraṇa* (rite of naming of child), *niṣkramaṇa* (the first leaving of the house), *annaprāsana* (first feeding with rice), *cuḍākaraṇa* (rite of tonsure), *upanayana* (initiation), *keśānta* (rite of clipping the hair), *samāvartana* (rite of returning home after completing education), and *vivāha* (marriage).[10]

The rite of impregnation is known as *garbhādhāna*. Since the procreative process was regarded as a sacred act in primitive belief, sexual intercourse on the appointed day with *mantras* and purificatory observances has been insisted by Manu.[11] In the Vedic texts procreation is conceived in terms of *yajña* or sacrifice.[12] *Garbhādhāna* is also identified with *niṣeka* and *caturthīkarma* or *caturthīhoma*.[13] In some texts *niṣeka* is identified with *ṛtu-saṅgamana* or union of married pair after the menstruation of the wife. This right may be a relic of the

primitive custom of ceremonial defloration. In the Dharmasūtra of Gautama[14] it is said that a girl should be given to marriage at puberty and that she is allowed to remain virgin until her third menstruation. Manu holds three opinions. The first is that a maiden may rather live unmarried, but the father should never give her in marriage to one who is devoid of good qualities. Again he says that a maiden after attaining puberty may wait for three years but after this period she may find out a man for her. In another place he says that a man of thirty should marry a girl of twelve while a man of twenty-four should marry a girl of eight years.[15] Manu also shares the deeply ingrained dread which the ancients entertained of the menstrual blood:

> A Caṇḍāla, a village pig, a cock, a dog, a menstruating woman and a eunuch must not look at the Brāhmaṇas while they eat.
>
> Let him, though mad with desire, not appraoch his wife when her courses appear; nor let him sleep with her in the same bed.
>
> For the wisdom, the strength, the sight and the vitality of a man who approaches a woman covered with menstrual excretions, utterly perish.[16]

Menstrual blood is also dreaded in the Mosaic law book of the *Holy Bible*[17] as well as in the *Quran*[18] both of which prescribe seclusion of women during their courses. Pliny's account of the effects produced by a menstruating woman expresses substantially the beliefs expressed by Manu which are still current among the rural population of the world and prevalent in rural India even today. According to Pliny, if a woman during her menstruation happens to approach or go to a vessel of wine, it will become sour; if she touches any standing corn in the field it will wither away; if she walks on a bed of grass it will go dry; if she passes by a garden the young buds will catch a blast; if she sits under a tree its fruits will fall; if she looks at

herself on a mirror, its brightness will become faded; if she looks upon a sword or knife or tool, it will catch rust; if a dog tastes her blood it will go mad.[19]

There is no need of dealing with the rites to be made after the birth of the child and those of its naming, its first leaving of the house, its first feeding with rice and so forth which have only a passing reference in the *Manusmṛti.* But it is the rite of *upanayana* which is of greatest importance, because this custom is on the one hand an adaptation or development of tribal puberty rites of the past and on the other it is suggestive of the concepts like second birth or *dvijatva* which has not only characterised the primitive tribal rites of life-cycle but also has made way into the principles underlying various rituals and customs, ideas and institutions, including the education system of antiquity, the procedure of religious initiation, the theoretical standpoint of the doctrine of *karma,* the transmigration of soul and so forth. In the tribal world an entrance into the adult group requires the observation of certain customs or the performance of certain rites. The qualification for admission into the adult group is not birth, but rebirth restricted only to those who have undergone the appropriate rites and customs. The rebirth of the initiate is often represented dramatically by a magical representation of the act of dying and being reborn from the womb.[20] A vivid description of the ritual of rebirth of the initiate is found in the *Aitareya Brāhmaṇa*[21] many features of which are found in the *upanayana* ceremony.

In a verse of the *Ṛgveda*[22] Bṛhaspati is addressed as an 'all-pervading one' and also as a 'Brahmacārī' who had received against his services a wife who was formerly taken away by Soma. This passage is very much obscure, but it reflects a primitive belief, mentioned elsewhere in the same text[23] that a girl is enjoyed by Soma, Gandharva and Agni before her marriage, a belief which has something to do with the primitive concept of ceremonial defloration. In the *Ṛgveda*[24] the sacrificial post has been compared with a young person dressed in the robe of initiation. In the *Atharvaveda*[25] we come across

a complete hymn in praise of Brahmacārī. In the *Taittirīya Saṃhitā*[26] we also come across the functional conception of Brahmacārī and Brahmacarya. The *Śatapatha*[27] and *Gopatha*[28] Brāhmaṇas contain details about the life of a Brahmacārī which bear a close similarity with the principles of *upanayana*.[29] In the Upanisad systematic rites of *upanayana* find expression and in the Sūtra literature we come across elaborate rules about this special type of initiation.[30] The word *upanayana* literally means 'leading or taking near' (to the *ācārya* or teacher for instruction). Manu says that the highest age limit of *upanayana* is 16 years for the Brāhmaṇas, 22 years for the Kṣatriyas and 24 years for the Vaiśyas,[31] and that it is a second birth, because it is an initiation into manhood by which the initiated one has the right over the Śrauta and Smārta works.[32] This shows that the candidate should at the time of his initiation attain some sort of mental and intellectual maturity so that he may grasp the essentials of his subject of study. When Manu says that marriage is the Vedic *Upanayana* of women[33] we cannot help speculating that the ceremony has something to do with the maturity of the candidate concerned. In the case of the girls we have seen that there is a close relation between puberty and marriage, between the first menstrual flow and the age of marriage. Kauṭilya[34] says that a girl attains maturity at twelve and a boy at sixteen. The Gṛhya Sūtras though prescribe the 8th, 12th and 16th years as the proper age of the *upanayana* admit the 16th, 22nd and 24th year as the highest age limit.[35] It is also important to observe that supreme importance is attached to the question of *brahmacarya*, and the initiated one has to observe a number of sexual taboos. In fact a boy of eight years does not require any sexual taboo, since his impulses are not matured, but in the case of a boy attaining the age of maturity such restrictions are inevitable. The ritual of *upanayana*, described by Manu, is as follows:

> Let students, according to the order of their castes wear as upper dresses the skin of black antelopes, spotted deer,

and he-goats, and lower garments, made of hemp, flax or wool.[36]

The girdle of a Brāhmaṇa shall consist of a triple cord of *muñja* grass, smooth and soft, that of a Kṣatriya, of a bow-string, made of *mūrvā* fibres; that of a Vaiśya, of hempen threads.[37]

If *muñja* grass and so forth be not procurable, the girdles may be made of *kuśa, asmantaka,* and *balbaja* fibres, with a single threefold knot, or with three or five knots according to the custom of the family.[38]

The sacrificial string of a Brāhmaṇa shall be made of cotton, shall be twisted to the right and consist of three threads, that of a Kṣatriya of hempen threads and that of a Vaiśya of woollen threads.[39]

A Brāhmaṇa shall carry according to the sacred law, a staff of *bilva* or *palāśa*; a Kṣatriya of *vaṭa* or *khadira* and a Vaiśya of *pilu* or *udumbara.*[40]

The staff of a Brāhmaṇa shall be made of such length as to reach the end of his hair; that of a Kṣatriya to reach his forehead; and that of a Vaiśya to reach the tip of his nose.[41]

Having taken a staff according to his choice, having worshipped the sun and walked round the fire, turning the right hand towards it, the student should beg alms according to the prescribed rule.[42]

Manu says that the student should first beg to his mother, sister or mother's sister, or another female who will not refuse.[43] Food obtained by begging is supposed to be pure.[44] The initiated one has to perform *saṃdhyā* or daily prayer at least twice.[45] The principal feature of the prayer called *saṃdhyā* are *ācamana* or sipping water,[46] *prāṇāyāma* or restraint of breath,[47] *mārjana* or sprinkling water by means of *kuśa* grass[48] *arghya* or offering water out of respect to the sun[49] *upasthāna* or worship of Mitra and Varuṇa,[50] and the recitation of *gāyatrī* hymn (*Rv.* III. 62.10 addressed to Savitṛ or the sun).[51] An

interesting question may be raised. Whether women ever had *upanayana* performed or whether they had to wear *yajñopavīta* or sacred thread. In the *Gobhila Gṛhyasūtra*[52] there is categorical mention of a bride wearing sacred thread slung from her left shoulder. In the *Āśvalāyana Gṛhyasūtra*[53] we come across some post-*samavartana* rites for women. The *Saṃskāraprakāśa* quotes the law book of Yama which says that in former times maidens desirous of learning Vedas and reciting of Savitr used to wear sacred thread, the girdle of *muñja*.[54] This was also known to Manu who says:

> This whole series of ceremonies must be performed for females also, in order to sanctify the body, at the proper time and in the proper order, but without the recitation of sacred texts.[55]

Entry into the second stage of life was thus to be after one has undergone the *saṃskāra* of *upanayana*. The probationary period lasted for twelve years and it was known as *brahmacarya* which was regarded as the first stage or *āśrama* of life. The students were known as *brahmacārī*. Certain rules and observances were prescribed for them. Avoidance of certain types of food, offering fuel-sticks (*samidh*) to the fire, begging for food, sleeping on a hard place, working for the teacher and several other observations were to be continued throughout the period of studenthood. The rules relating to the conduct of the student are too numerous to be set out in detail. The student should not look at the sun and should avoid honey, flesh, perfumes, garlands, sleeping by day, rubbing oil on the body, putting collyrium in eyes, going in a cart, wearing shoes, and holding an umbrella, love affairs, anger, covetousness, infatuation, worthless and proud discussions, playing on musical instruments, luxurious bath with hot water, making his teeth attractively clean, ecstatic state of mind, dancing, singing, dazing at women, touching young women, shampooing the wife of the teacher, gambling, serving a low person, injury

to animals, obscene talk, drinking of wine, and so on.[56] The *brahmacārī* should sip water, face the north, fold both hands together and wear light clothes. He should clasp the feet of the teacher at the beginning and end of the study.[57] Manu says that ten persons deserve to be taught, viz., one who is the son of a teacher, one who gives service to the teacher, one who gives some knowledge in exchange, one who knows *dharma* or one who is pure in body and mind, one who is truthful, one who is able to understand, one who gives money, one who is well-disposed, and one who is a relative of the teacher.[58]

Some points should be noted in this connection. The Śūdras, though pronounced as not needing sacraments for which they are supposed to lack in worth, are allowed by Manu[59] to go through the ritual of the *dvijas*, 'without incurring sin but winning praise' without repeating the prescribed *mantras.* Secondly, Manu has laid emphasis on Vedic and not on knowledge of secular sciences. According to him, the *saṃskāras* which punctuates life are designed for the purpose of making the human body sanctified for the residence of the purified self. If this human frame is to be made a suitable mansion for the Soul (*brāhmiyam kriyate tanuḥ*)[60] the preparation must be made with the holy rites laid down by the Veda, in the due performance of the rites of sacraments like *garbhādhāna*, the *homas* during pregnancy, the *jātakarma*, *caula* and *mauñjībandhana* (initiatory ceremony). The transfiguration of man is to be accomplished by a process spread throughout the life.[61] The life of the *bramacārī* had two sides of activity that devoted to the acquisition of knowledge in the highest sense (*vidyā*) and that in which the mind, soul and body were disciplined by a course or rigorous adherence to vows (*vrata*) of continence, truthfulness and poverty.

The return of a student to his paternal home from his teacher's house, after the successful completion of his period of studentship, was signalised or formalised by the rite of *samāvartana* (lit. return) which took place just before his actual re-entry to his paternal abode.[62] A ceremonial bath

(*snāna*) was the main feature of the rite and that is why a student who was supposed to have completed his course of study and taken the ceremonial bath was known as *snātaka*. Elaborate procedure of the *samāvartana* is found in the Gṛhyasūtras.[63] Manu says that "having bathed, with the permission of his teacher, and performed according to the rule the *samāvartana*, a twice-born man shall marry a wife of equal caste who is endowed with auspicious bodily marks."[64] *Samāvartana* is a pre-condition of marriage, but is not necessarily an essential precondition. However, with its completion an individual enters the second stage of life, the *āśrama* known as *gārhastha*. A *snātaka* becoming householder after marriage should perform daily the rites prescribed for him in the Veda; he should not seek wealth by forbidden occupations; and his way of life should be in conformity with the highest ethical standard.[65] Among the rituals to be performed by a householder Manu says the following:

> Teaching and studying is the sacrifice offered to *brahman* (*brahmayajña*); the offering of water and food called *tarpaṇa* is the sacrifice to the manes (*pitṛyajña*) the burnt oblation is the sacrifice offered to the gods (*devayajña*); the *bali* offering is that offered to the *bhūtas* (*bhūtayajña*); and the hospitable reception of guests is the offering to men (*manuṣyayajña*).[66]

Collectively these are called *mahāyajñas*. These differ from the Śrauta sacrifices in two respects. Firstly, the chief agent is the householder himself who does not need the help of a professional priest. Secondly, the central point of the five yajñas is the discharge of duty to the creator, to the fathers, to the gods, to men and to the whole universe with its myriads of creatures of various grades and intelligence. But in the Śrauta sacrifices the main spring of action is the desire to secure some specific ends.[67] Among other rituals to be performed by the householders Manu says:

> A Brāhmaṇa shall always offer Agnihotra at the beginning or at the end of the day and of the night and the Darśa and Paurṇamāsa (*iṣṭis*) at the end of each half-month.
>
> When the old grain has been consumed the *Āgrayana iṣṭi* with new grain, at the end of the three seasons the *cāturmāsya* sacrifices, at the solstices an animal sacrifice, at the end of the year Soma offerings.[68]

Agnihotra is the simple rite of kindling, maintenance and worship of fire employed to attain manifold ends. Oblations thrown into fire are supposed to reach the sun that sends rain which produces crops. Jaimini[69] holds that since Agnihotra is obligatory it may be undertaken even by those who are not able to perform every detail of it in its entirety. Darśa-Paurṇamāsa which is performed at the time of the new and full moon was a simple agricultural rite desiring prosperity, happiness and fulfilment of human desires. One of its functions is known as the *haviṣkṛt* call or the invocation of Mother Earth as the Corn Mother followed by beating the grains of rice and baking *purodāsa* cakes on potsherds.[70] Āgrayana is the rite of the offering of first corn.[71] Cāturmāsya is the seasonal celebration lasting for a period of four months. Soma offering was originally connected with the rites of pressing the Soma plant to extract wine. It thus appears that for the householders Manu has prescribed such rituals as are consistent with their material aspirations and entail no special strain. In such rituals the priests have no place. Moreover, emphasis has been laid on the symbolic aspects of the rituals and not on the details of their performance. The Manuṣya-yajna, for example, is nothing but honouring the guests, feeding poor persons and the like.

Manu allows entry into Vānaprastha or the third stage or *āśrama* of life only after one has fulfilled his duties in domestic life. His renunciation is only of his associates and his dwelling and the choice of an *araṇya* or forest for dwelling is to enable him to practise undisturbed different forms of austerities.[72] He

may go alone to the forest leaving his wife under the care of his sons or take his wife with him. He is to live on the forest produce, but is allowed to beg his food from adjoining villages. He has to carry the household fires with him, maintain the five fires and bathe thrice a day.[73] Though living in the forest, he has to observe some of the rituals of his previous *āśrama*, such as performing the *bali* offering with such food as he eats, giving alms according to his ability, the new moon and full moon sacrifices at proper time, the *nakṣatreṣṭi*, the *āgrayana*; the *cāturmāsya*, etc.[74] But all these are to be done in a very simplified form. For example, with grains which naturally grow in spring and autumn in the forest region he is to prepare sacrificial cakes (*puroḍāsa*) and the boiled messes (*caru*).[75] In food habit he should observe restraint. While bathing at the three *savanas*—sunrise, midday and sunset—he should offer libation of water to the manes and the gods and practise austerities.[76] He who has taken refuge to the third *āśrama* is allowed to commit suicide by starvation while the ascetic, belonging to the fourth *āśrama* must await his natural death; the former has no penance to do or punishment to undergo if he reverts to his house, while the latter who gives up *sannyāsa* becomes for life the slave of the king. It is also interesting to note that Manu has recommended the study of the Upaniṣads for the Vānaprasthin.[77]

In the fourth *āśrama*, the Sannyāsa, there is no ritual to be performed. Of course there are a few rites to be performed for entering the order of the ascetics.

> Having performed the *iṣṭi* sacred to the Lord of Creatures (Prajāpati), where he gives all his property as the sacrificial fee, having reposited the sacred fires in himself, a Brāhmaṇa may depart from his house as an ascetic.[78]

After the formal entry, the ascetic is to provide himself with a drinking vessel, a staff made of three bamboos tied together, a water jar and tattered garment. He is debarred from using

metal vessels, owning money, having any contact with the world or worldly affairs, recalling his old name and associates, speaking to women and from remaining in the same place for over three days except during the rainy season. He must pursue the steps in meditation, which are indicated in outline in the twelfth book of Manu, so at first to withdraw his mind from the world and then, concentrate it on the Self. He should live on food collected after the householder's hearth has been extinguished, i.e. in the afternoon. He should wander alone, remain celibate and spend his time in reciting or calling to his recollection the Vedic texts. He should not desire to die; he should not desire to live; he should patiently bear hard words and should not return the same.[79] Premature entry into ascetic life of one whose passions have not been conquered and who is physically still subject to sensual impulses can only spell disaster. According to Manu, one shuld take up the career of asceticism only after successfully completing the duties of the three previous *āśramas.* Only he is entitled to take up the career of asceticism who after passing from order to order, after having studied the Vedas in accordance with the rule, after having begotten sons according to the sacred law and after having offered sacrifice according to his ability can direct his mind to the attainment of final liberation.[80]

The ritual-cycle of an individual's life is thus completed through the performance of the sacraments outlined above. The purpose of the *saṃskāras* has to be inferred from the stress laid on each of them. Generally they may be regarded as developing the personality of the person for whom they are done, as external symbols, or reflections of inward and invisible changes that take place as the consequence of doing them. But there is a point of culmination where the ritual-cycle completes its course yielding rise to another cycle, and this culminating point is death to be followed by a resurrection or rebirth. Funeral rites are therefore regarded as one of the *saṃskāras* to be performed by the twice-born with Vedic *mantra*[81] and by women and Śūdras without Vedic *mantras.*[82] The word *antyesti*

is used in a wide sense which includes apart from the disposal of the dead (*mṛtyusaṃskāra*), all sorts of post-mortem rites. Funeral rites and rites after death vary in accordance with caste and religious position, nature of death, time and space factors, etc., connected with the deceased.

The Śrauta and Gṛhya Sūtras differ among themselves in many details of the same topic. Moreover, the procedure became more elaborate in medieval and later times. Manu[83] makes it clear that the three ancestors of a man, viz., the father, the grand father and the great-grand father are respectively to be identified with the three orders of superintending *pitṛ* deities, viz., Vasus, Rudras and Ādityas, when performing a Śrāddha which is the ritual for the spiritual welfare of departed ones, accompanied by the desire to keep in constant touch with the dead by means of ceremonials. More particularly Śrāddha is the offering with faith of an article of food or some substitute thereof intending it for the benefit of the departed.[84] The distant ancestors are known as *pitṛs* and those who have lately departed as *pretas*. The second finds expression in the funeral rites following immediately after and in the *ekoddiṣṭa* and *sapiṇḍīkaraṇa* Śrāddhas. In the *ekoddiṣṭa* only one *arghya* (respectful offering of water) and one *piṇḍa* (food-lump) are offered. *Sapiṇḍīkaraṇa* can secure the admission of a *preta* to the order of the manes. This ceremony takes place after death and is performed each year by the descendants of the dead. Water and food-lumps are offered to the dead and his three ancestors with *mantra* from *Rv.* X.191. 3-4. The first finds expression in the daily *pitṛyajñas*, the monthly Śrāddha and the *aṣṭakā* and *anvaṣṭakā* rites in which the *pitṛs* are honoured. The *pitṛyajña* which Manu defines simply as *tarpaṇa*[85] is a Śrauta rite in which *piṇḍas* are offered to the more distant ancestors.[86] It was on account of the supposed power of the *pitṛs* to benefit or harm the living that the cult of the dead became a prominent feature in primitive societies. Offerings and ceremonies which may have in most ancient times been prompted in part at least by the desire to placate the ancestors

are continued as tokens of pure affection and remembrance.

Apart from the *saṃskāras* or sacraments, daily and periodical duties and ceremonies as well as the hygienic rules have also acquired a ritualistic significance in the *Manusmṛti*. Although the scheme of the four *āśramas* have been outlined in detail, special importance has been attached to the second or *gārhasthya* stage. Manu states that as all creatures live by receiving support from the air, so other *āśramas* subsist by relying for support on the householder.[87] He divides the Brāhmaṇa householders into four varieties, viz., one who possesses enough to fill a granary, one who possess that much filling a corn-jar, one who collects as much as will satisfy his need for three days, and one who makes no provision for the morrow.[88] Yājñavalkya divides on occupational basis.[89] Other two categories of the twice born and the Śūdras have not been classified in this way. But the rules pertain to all sections and though most of them are simply hygienic they are to be followed as if serving an important religious purpose. Thus there are rules regarding urination, answering call of nature, brushing the teeth, cleansing the body, and so forth.[90] This cleansing of the body is only a part of the general *śauca.* According to Manu[91] there are twelve impurities of the human body, viz., fat, semen, blood, marrow, faeces, mucus of the nose, ear-wax, phlegm, tears, rheum of eyes and sweat. The first six are removed by water and earth and others by water. Special importance is attached to *snāna* or bathing. All the *varṇas* have to bathe and the Brāhmaṇas have to do it with Vedic *mantras.*[92] No bathing is allowed for any one at night except when there is an eclipse, a marriage, a birth or death or when a *vrata* is undertaken with some object. Bathing should be in natural water.[93] Tarpaṇa or offering water to gods, sages and manes is a subsidiary constituent part of bathing which is to be done while standing in the water.[94]

There are other aspects of ritual cleansing which fall in the category of *śuddhi* or purification. *Śuddhi* includes within its purview facts relating to the sacred and the profane. The law-

books employ the word *śuddhi* in relation to purification after *āśauca.* The word *āśauca* is formed from *śuci* or 'pure'.[95] Another word which is often used as a synonym for *āśauca* is *agha.* Manu refers to two kinds of *śuddhi,* viz., *pretaśuddhi* (purification after a man is dead) and *dravyaśuddhi* (purification for things).[96] The observance of ritual impurity implies seclusion for a period and it is removed after a ceremonial bath. For example, a woman in her monthly courses is impure. She will remain secluded for three days. Such rules hold good for all castes. In the case of an abortion the mother remains untouchable for a few days; after childbirth the same rule pertains. During this period no religious rite can be performed. Practices observed among ancient peoples as also in tribal societies, show that the most important taboos were on the dead, on women in their menstruation and on women in childbirth. In the *Old Testament,*[97] childbirth made a woman unclean and the number of days that she was to be unclean depended on whether the child was a male or a female. So far as the *āśuca* of death is concerned, it depends on the nature of death, time and place and the relation of the observer to the deceased. Manu says that if one who had gone abroad dies, his relatives should on hearing of his death remain untouchable for the days that remain out of the proper period of impurity.[98] If one's *ācārya* dies, the pupil has to observe *āśauca* for three days, but only one day if he dies in another village.[99] A *yati* or a *brahmacārin* has to observe no *āśauca.*[100] Medhātithi commenting on Manu V.58 says that there is a distinction as regards the period of *āśauca* and the persons affected by it in several ways. As to the *āsuca* on death numerous distinctions arise. The duration of *āśauca* depended on the age of the departed one, on nearness of blood, i.e., whether the person affected in a *sapiṇḍa* or a *samānodaka,* on the nearness or distance from the place of death; on the time that is elapsed before the event of death came to the knowledge of the relative, and on other subsidiary factors.

According to Manu the *śuddhi* on purification of an object

means the removal of a taint attaching to a thing, and it is of two kinds, purification of the body and the purification of an external object.[101] But at the same time he says that of all kinds of purity, mental purity is the highest. A man who makes wealth by unfair means cannot be pure even if he bathes many times a day or smears his body with earth.[102] Manu states that the following are always pure: what is not seen to be polluted; what is washed with water; what has been commended as pure by a Brāhmaṇa; what has the smell, colour and taste of a pure substance; the hand of an artisan or a craftman; articles exposed for sale in a market; alms collected by *brahmacāriṇ;* the mouth of a woman (at the time of dalliance); meat of animals seized or killed even by dogs, caṇḍālas and carnivorous birds; rays of the sun, fire, dust, the shadow of a tree, part of the body above the navel, and so forth.[103] He provides that sprinkling with water is the mode of purification when large quantities of corn or cloths are polluted, but when the quantity is small they must be washed with water.[104] The general rule about the purification of things or bodies that are smeared with foul matter is that water and earth are to be employed for purification till the foul odour and the contact with the foul thing is entirely removed.[105] The body is cleansed by water; internal organ by truthfulness; metal, gems and anything made of stone by ashes; earth and water; gold and silver by water and fire; copper, iron, brass, pewter, tin and lead by alkaline, acid or water; liquids by passing two blades of *kuśa* grass through them; sacrificial goods by water; skins, vegetables, roots, fruits, conch shell, horn, bone, ivory etc., by water; silk and woollen stuffs by alkaline earth; blanket by *ariṣṭa* fruit; *aṃśupaṭṭa* by *bel* fruit; linen with a paste of yellow mustard; and land by sweeping and other means.[106] Bath is prescribed for the purification of the body when a person touches one who is *patita* (an outcast owing to murder or other serious crimes), a woman freshly delivered, a woman in her monthly illness, and a corpse.[107] Having voluntarily followed a corpse, whether that of a paternal kinsman or of a stranger, a person becomes pure by bathing,

dressing in his clothes, by touching fire and eating clarified butter.[108]

Food habit also acquired a ritual significance. According to Manu death overtakes an individual owing to the absence of Vedic study, giving up the performance of proper duties, laziness and blemishes attaching to the food taken.[109] He says that if one facing the east eats food, it tends to long life, if one facing the south eats food its leads to fame; if he eats turning to the west he will have prosperity; if he faces the north it will lead him to truthfulness. One should eat with a concentrated mind after performing an ablution, should worship the food and eat it without contempt. Food is to be worshipped because it gives strength. The remnants of food one has eaten should not be given to any one. One should not eat between the two meal times. Excessive eating is detrimental to health, fame and spiritual merit.[110] Manu says that one should not eat from a broken vessel and that eating in same dish with wife is prohibited.[111] Those who sanctify the company of diners when they sit down for eating are known as *paṅkti-pāvanas* and those who defile the company of diners by their presence are known as *paṅkti-duṣakas.*[112] Manu says that one who understand the Veda, one who expounds the Veda, a *brahmacārin,* one who is a liberal donor, one who has reached the age of one hundred, are all fit to grace a dinner party. Elaborate rules are laid down about what food should or should not be eaten and from whom food may or may not be taken.[113] It is interesting to note that Manu is not in favour of animal killing and flesh eating because of his insistence on *ahiṃsā* or non-violence. He permits to kill animal only for some special sacrifices and in rites for gods and manes but on no other occasions.[114] He says that no sin is incurred in flesh-eating when one's life is in danger owing to famine or diseases. Or when flesh is given to him by another out of what is prepared for offering to gods and manes.[115] But elsewhere Manu takes up the position of total abstention from killing animals even in sacrifices.[116] He says that no flesh can be had without killing living beings and

killing such being cannot lead to heaven; therefore one should give up flesh.[117] His final conclusion is that it is better not to eat flesh, but if someone eats in a limited scale and under certain specific condition there is no sin.[118] He gives a long list of birds, the flesh of which is forbidden. All birds like vultures that subsist on raw flesh, the Cātaka, parrot, Haṃsa, birds that dwell in a village, Baka, birds that subsist on filth, etc., are forbidden while wild cocks and peacocks are permitted.[119] He regards fish-eating as the worst form of flesh-eating and forbids all fish, but then makes an exception in favour of fish called Pāṭhina and Rohita if used in rites and fish called Rājīva, lion-faced fish and fish having scales.[120] Regarding milk Manu says that the milk of a cow that is *sandhinī* ('a cow in heat' or 'that gives milk once a day' or 'that yields milk on account of another calf being brought to it, its own being dead'),[121] the calf of which has died, that gives birth to twins and that has not passed ten days after delivery is forbidden.[122] Among the vegetables he forbids garlic, onion, *gṛñjana*, mushrooms and all herbs that spring from impure soil, red resins and red sap and cough-producing fruits.[123] Cooked food which has become sour or rotten should not be eaten.[124] He forbids all kinds of intoxicants to Brāhmaṇas at all stages of life.[125] A wife who drinks liquor is to be abandoned.[126] Drinking is the most pernicious of all the vices of the kings.[127]

Rules about sleeping, viz., as to the position of the head, what kinds of bed to use, where the sleep and what texts to recite and so on, have also been set forth in a ritualistic framework.[128] The same holds good in the case of sex life. Manu says that after intercourse the husband and wife should take a bath or at best wash, sip water and sprinkle water over the body and then should sleep on separate beds.[129] The rite which signalises the opening of the session for Vedic study in the year is itself called *upākarma* or *upākaraṇa* which should begin, according to Manu, during the full moon of Śrāvaṇa or Bhādrapada (August-September).[130] Likewise the cessation of Vedic studies for a certain period in a year is known as *utsarjana*

or *utsarga.* Manu says that after studying the Veda for four months and a half after *upākarma, utsarga* should take place when the moon is in the Puṣya star in the bright half of Māgha (mid-January).[131] There are certain days of *anadhyāya* on which the Veda should not be studied.[132] Manu has also laid down rules regarding making and accepting gifts (*dāna*). Its acceptance is lawful for Brāhmaṇa,[133] but in some cases it is dangerous, especially when the donee develops the bad habit of receiving, when it is given or received without a full knowledge of the rules prescribed in the sacred law and when gifts of attractive and costly objects are concerned.[134] Receiving gifts from wicked and low persons is forbidden[135] except when offered unasked or in time of distress.[136]

Regarding the means of reducing consequences of sins Manu holds that the more a man's mind loathes his own evil deed the more he is free from unrighteousness.[137] The ritual of confession consists in the person's proclaiming his lapses while begging at seven houses.[138] Self-disciplining and restraint of the breath (*prāṇāyāma*), if performed every day, purify the mind and help a person to become free from guilts.[139] By performing *tapas* or austerity a man can become free from all sins.[140] Manu says that a Brāhmaṇa becomes free from all distresses when he performs *homa,* the rite of kindling the fire and making offerings into it with the prescribed *mantras*[141] but at the same time he says that the performance of *japa* (muttering of Vedic passages as prayer) is ten times more efficacious than the sacrifices.[142] Vedic study is also efficacious which consumes guilt caused by evil deeds just as a fire burning strongly consumes even green grass.[143] *Upavāsa* or fasting is prescribed by Manu as a means of getting free from sins[144] as also *dāna* or gift. Medhātithi commenting on Manu XI.139 remarks that the verse implies that as to sins arising from injury to living beings, gifts are the principal expiations. Manu says that sins committed unintentionally are destroyed by penances or *prāyaścittas.*[145] Among the penances, Manu mentions *aghamarṣaṇa* which is chanting of *Ṛgveda* X.1-3 along with

fasting and donation of a milch cow;[146] *Cāndrāyana* which is increasing and decreasing of the consumption of food in imitation of the increase and decrease in the course of the phases of moon;[147] *pañcagavya* which is drinking a mixture prepared from cow's urine, dung, milk, curds and clarified butter;[148] *prājāpatya* which comprises four periods of three days, each following one another, in which there is respectively eating once only by day, once only by night, once only without asking for it and complete fast;[149] *yaticāndrāyana* in which the sinner eats only eight mouthfuls of sacrificial food only once in the noon for a month;[150] *śisucāndrāyana* in which the sinner eats for a month four mouthfuls in the morning and four after sunset;[151] and also various *kṛchras* or rigorous self-disciplining.

To sum up, the ritualistic features of the *Manusmṛti* widely vary in content and quality. They reflect the relics of the primitive infrastructure of Indian social life. The *Manusmṛti*, though deals with an advanced stage of social development, not only retains in its body some beliefs and usages derived from remote antiquity, but attempts as well as restructure them in a changed social phenomenon. The original forms of the rituals which must have been consistent with the imagination and aspiration of our remotest ancestors sum up all that passed for wisdom when the world was young. They are spontaneous transformations of an elemental rationalism, and the forms they take are normal for primitive mind, though in modern society the same phenomena are apt to be pathological. In the language of Frazer:

> Crude and false as that philosophy may seem to us, it would be unjust to deny it the merit of logical consistency. The flaw of the system lies not in its reasoning but in its premises; in its conception of the nature of life, not in any irrelevancy of the conclusions which it draws from that conception.[152]

But Manu's ritualism reflects a higher stage in which it is

modified to sustain social organisation—a point to which we have referred in the beginning of this chapter. The primitive *rites de passage* at the turning points of the life-cycle have been re-organised as *saṃskāras*, given a religious flavour and brought in relation to the *āśrama* theory clearly differentiating the four stages of life, each endowed with special privileges and duties. The purpose of each *saṃskāra* has been specified with reference to the results to be obtained. *Garbhādhāna* is meant for good progeny; *upanayana* is initiation into studenthood. Even marriage is a sacrament. As a bride is required by an accomplished student (*snātaka*) to enable him to set up as a householder and establish the fire and perform the five daily duties to *brahman*, the gods, the fathers, the spirits and the human beings, the gift of a bride according to Manu, is the greatest of all gifts which has unseen benefits. To what a wife is entitled springs from *dharma*. As marriage is a duty, anything that might diminish the chances of a man or a woman discharging it, must go against *dharma*. The rituals like *agnihotra*, *darśa-paurṇamāsa*, *cāturmāsya*, *āgrayana* etc., were intimately associated with the facts of the day-to-day life. Supreme emphasis has been laid on the huseholders. Religious and ritualistic significance has been attributed even to the hygienic rules, physical cleanliness, attitude to things belonging to the sacred and profane categories, various processes of purging off the impurities caused by contamination, monthly sickness of the females, childbirth and death, purification of metals and various things, food habit, daily life of a person, giving and receiving gifts, even penances and expiations for moral lapses so that people should follow the rules as part of their obligatory rituals divinely ordained.

NOTES

1. W.H.R. Rivers remarked that there is no more depressing and hopeless task than that of trying to discover why people perform rituals. According to Sir John Woodroffe and application of the term 'ritualistic' to any phenomenon is a means to hide one's ignorance.

E.B. Tylor approached ritual with his theory of animism or belief in an elementary soul; Herbert Spencer with his theory of ancestor worship; Robertson Smith, F.B. Jevons and Emile Durkheim with totemism; Bishop Codrington, R.R. Marett and E.S. Hartland with pre-animistic belief in the unexpected wonder-working power of any object; Sir James Frazer with magic or primitive association of ideas on the analogical principles of similarity and contiguity; Marcel Mause with total social facts in reference to symbolic performances; B. Malinowsky with social relationship; Levi Strauss with structural coherency and cultural diffusion; G.G. Jung with 'collective unconscious'; M. Eliade with typological analysis based on the concept of archetypes; and so forth. See E.B. Tylor, *Primitive Culture*, London, 1871, II, pp. 277-328; E.S. Hartland, *Ritual and Belief*, London, 1914; pp. 26-66; J.G. Frazer, The *Golden Bough*, London, 1913, V. pp. 233-35, 263-76; VI. pp. 37-48, 236-52; VII. pp. 14-34, 168-70; VIII. pp. 325-29, IX. pp. 394-96; R.R. Marett, '*The Threshold of Religion*, London, 1914, pp. 1-28, 80-81, 98-121; E. Durkheim, *Elementary Forms of Religious Life*, tr. London, 1912, pp. 178ff. Levi Strauss, *Structural Anthropology*, New York, 1964; etc.

2. The theory that ritual generates myth was advanced by Andrew Lang, Jane Harrison, Gilbert Murray and others. See Lang, *Myth, Ritual and Religion*, London 1899; Harrison, *Ancient Art and Ritual*, Cambridge 1913, pp. 37ff; S.K. Hooke (ed), *Myth, Ritual and Kingship*, London, 1958; J.E. Fonten-Rose, *Ritual Theory of Myth*, London, 1966; etc.
3. *Prolegomena to the Study of Greek Religion*, Cambridge, 1908, pp. 64, 187, 304.
4. For the ritualistic basis of Greek drama see George Thomson, *Aeschylus and Athens*, London, 1950. In the Indian context it is also possible to demonstrate. See N.N. Bhattacharyya, *Ancient Indian History and Civilization: Trends and Perspectives*, New Delhi, 1988, pp. 292-98.
5. *Prehistoric Religion*, New York, 1957, p. 143.
6. For details see A. Van Gennep, *Les Rites de Passage*, Paris, 1909, Eng. trans. London, 1960; also M. Eliade, *Birth and Rebirth*, 1958, N.N. Bhattacharyya, *Indian Puberty Rites*, Calcutta, 1968, second ed. New Delhi, 1980; *Ancient Indian Rituals*, New Delhi, 1975.
7. On Jaimini III. I.3.
8. II. 26 ff.
9. VIII. 14-24.
10. The *saṃskāras* have been dealt with Kane's *History of Dharmasastra*, Vol. II. B.N. Datta, *Dialectics of Hindu Rituals*, 2 Vols., Calcutta, 1951-56; C.G. Diehl, *Instrument and Purpose: Studies in Rites and Rituals of South India*, Gleerup, 1956; Raj Bali Pandey's *Hindu Saṃskāras*, 2 Vols., Banaras, 1949; Sec. ed., Banaras, 1966, H. Yogi, *Saṃskāras: The*

Genius behind Sacramental Rites, Madras, 1951; H.N. Chatterjee, *Studies in some Aspects of Hindu Saṃskāras in Ancient India*, Calcutta, 1965.

11. II. 16, 26, 142.
12. *Av.* V. 25; *Br. Up.* 4.13. 19-22.
13. Manu, II. 16.26; *Yājñavalkya*, I. 10-11; *Śāṇ. Gr.*I. 18-19: *Pār. Gr.* I. 11; *Āp. Gr.* VIII. 10-11.
14. XVIII. 20-23.
15. IX. 89-90. 94.
16. Manu III. 239; IV. 40-41; cf. *Yama* 56-62; *Atri* 271-80; *Āpastamba* VII. 4; *Aṅgiras* 35-39; *Parāśara* VII.19; *Varāha Purāṇa*, CXLII; etc.
17. *Leviticus* XV.
18. II. 122; II. 228.
19. *Natural History* VII. 64 ff. For details see Bhattacharyya, *Indian Puberty Rites*, New Delhi, 1980, pp. 11-30.
20. H. Webster, *Primitive Sacred Societies*, New York, 1932, p. 40.
21. I. 3; cf. A.B. Keith, *Ṛgveda Brāhmaṇas*, HOS XXV, 1920 Rep. New Delhi, 1971, pp. 108-09.
22. X. 109. 5.
23. X. 85. 45.
24. III. 8.4.
25. XI. 7.
26. VI. 3.10.5.
27. V. 1.5.17; XI. 3.3 2-3; XI. 5.4. etc.
28. II. 5-7.
29. Cf. Chāndogya, IV. 3.5. etc.
30. *Āśv. Gr.* I. 19-22; *Āpas Gr.* X; *Pār. Gr.* II. *Hir. Gr.*I; *Baudh Dh.S.* I., *Gaut. Dh. S.* I; *Āpas Dh. S.* I, *Vas. Dh. S.* X-XII etc.
31. II. 38.
32. II. 169-71.
33. Manu II. 67.
34. Kauṭilya III. 59.
35. *Āpastamba* X. 2; *Śāṅkhāyayana* II. 1; *Baudhyāyana* II. 52 *Bhāradvāja* I. 1; *Gobhila* II. 10.1.
36. II. 41; cf. *Āpas Dh. S.*, I. 2. 39 ff; *Vasiṣṭha Dh.S.* XI. 61-67, *Baudh. Dh. S.* I. 3.14; *Par.Gr.* II. 5.
37. II. 42; cf. *Gaut. Dh.S.* I. 15; *Vas. Dh.S.* XI. 58-60. *Gaut. Dh. S.* I. 3.13.
38. II. 43.
39. II. 44; Cf. *Gaut. Dh. S.* I. 36; *Vas. Dh.S.* XIII. 14; *Baudh. Dh.S.* I. 5.5.
40. II. 45; Cf. *Āpas. Dh.S.* I.2.38; *Gaut. Dh.S.* I. 22; *Vas. Dh. S.* XI. 51-52. *Baudh. Dh. S.* I. 3.15.
41. II. 46.
42. II. 48.
43. II. 49-50.
44. II. 51-55.

45. II. 101.
46. II. 58-62; cf. *Yājñavalkya* I. 18.21; *Gobhila Gr.* I. 1.2.
47. II. 75; cf. VI. 69-71; XI. 200. 202. 249.
48. II. 75; *Yāj.* I. 22.
49. *Mānava Gr.* I. 2.1-5.
50. *Baudh. Dh. S.* II. 4. 11-15.
51. Manu II. 77, 83.
52. II. 1.19.
53. III. 8. 11.
54. Chowkhamba ed., pp. 402-03.
55. II. 66.
56. Manu II. 108, 170 ff; cf. *Āśv. Gr.*I. 22.17 ff; *Pār Gr.* II. 5; *Khadira Gr.*II. 4.33; *Hiraṇya Gr.* I. 8.2; *Yāj.* I.33 ff.
57. Manu II. 70-74.
58. II. 109.
59. X. 126-27.
60. II. 28.
61. II. 26-28.
62. II. 245.
63. *Āśv.* III. 8-9; *Pār* II. 6; *Gobhila* III. 4. 31-34.
64. III. 4.
65. IV. 13 ff.
66. III. 70.
67. Cf. *Śāt. Br.* XI. 5.61; *Taitt. Ār.* I. 10; *Āśv. Gr.* III. 1.1.4; *Āp. Dh.S.* I. 4, 12-13; *Baudh Dh.S.* II. 6.1.8. etc.
68. IV. 25-26.
69. VI. 3.1.10.
70. For details see. *Āp. Sr.* III. 14.12.13.
71. Cf. *Āśv. Gr.* II. 2; *San. Gr.* III. 8; *Pār Gr.* III. 1; *Gobhila Gr.* IV. 8.9.24; *Khadira Gr.* III. 3.6-15.
72. Manu VI. 1 ff.
73. VI. 3-5.
74. VI. 6-10.
75. VI. 11.
76. VI. 24.
77. VI. 29.
78. Manu VI. 38; for details see *Baudh. Dh. S.* II. 17.
79. Manu VI. 33-85. Manu also speaks of a type of renunciation which allows an informal ascetic to remain in his own house under the protection of his son (IV. 257-58; VI. 95-95). But he has to give up performance of enjoined rites, assume the ascetic's robe and live a detached life.
80. VI. 34-36.
81. II. 16; Yāj. I. 10.

82. II. 66. X. 127; Cf. *Āśv. Gr.* I.15.12; I. 16.6; I. 17.12.
83. III. 284; cf. Yaj. I.268; *Agni Purāṇa* CLXIII. 40-41.
84. Mit. on *Yāj.* I. 217.
85. Manu III. 70; cf. *Rv.* X. 16.10.
86. For details about the Śrāddha ritual see Manu III. 122-126.
87. III. 77-78; VI. 89-90; cf. *Gaut. Dh. S.* III.3; *Vas Dh.S.* VIII. 14-16; *Visṇu Dh. S.* LIX. 27-29.
88. IV. 7.
89. Mit. of *Yājñavalkya* I. 28.
90. Manu IV. 47; V. 126, 134, 136 etc.
91. V. 135, cf. *Viṣṇu Dh. S.* XXII. 81.
92. II. 76; IV. 82, cf. *Baudh. Dh. S.* II. 44.
93. IV. 203. cf. *Yāj.* I. 159.
94. II. 176.
95. Cf. *Pāṇini.* V.I. 131; VII. 3.30.
96. V. 57.
97. *Leviticus* XII. 2-5.
98. V. 75-76.
99. V. 86.
100. V. 82.
101. V. 110.
102. V. 106 etc. *Viṣṇu Dh. S.* XIII.89; *Mbh.* XIII. 108. 12.
103. V. 127-33; cf. *Yāj.* I. 186, 191-93; *Viṣṇu Dh. S.* XXIII. 47-52; *Baudh. Dh. S.* I. 5.56 ff. *Mārk Pu.* XXXV. 19-21; etc.
104. V. 118; cf. *Yāj.* I. 184; *Viṣṇu Dh. S.* XXIII. 13.
105. V. 126.
106. V. 109-26.
107. V. 85.
108. V. 103.
109. V. 4.
110. II. 52-57.
111. IV. 43, IV. 65.
112. Cf. III. 184-86.
113. VI. 207-23; cf. *Āpas.Dh. S.* I. 5-6; *Vas. Dh. S.* XIV. *Yāj.* I. 167-181.
114. V. 27-44.
115. V. 27. 32.
116. V. 45-55.
117. V.48. cf. *Viṣṇu Dh. S.* LI. 69-78.
118. V. 56.
119. V. 11-14; cf. *Āpas Dh. S.* I. 5.17; *Vas. Dh. S.* XIV. 48; Yaj. I. 172-75.
120. V. 14-16; cf. *Vas. Dh. S.* XIV. 41-42; *Gaut. Dh. S.* XVII. 36; Yaj. I. 177-178.
121. *Mit.* or *Yāj.* I. 170.
122. Manu V. 8-9; cf. *Gaut.* XVII. 22-26; *Vas.* XIV. 34-35 etc.
123. V. 5-6; cf. *Yāj.* I. 176; *Vas. Dh. S.* XIV. 33.

124. V. 10. 24-25.
125. XI. 93-94.
126. IX. 80.
127. VII. 42-52.
128. IV. 34, 175-76, cf. *Gaut.* II. 13; IX. 90; *Yāj.* I. 36.
129. IV. 4; V. 144.
130. IV. 95.
131. IV. 96.
132. IV. 119.
133. I. 88; X. 75-76. 115.
134. IV. 186-91.
135. III. 179; IV. 84-91; XI. 24-25; 42. 70.
136. IV. 247-52, X. 102-14.
137. XI. 229-30; cf. *Viṣṇu Dh. S.* II. 73, 131-32.
138. XI. 122; cf. *Gaut. Dh. S.* XXIII. 18.
139. XI. 248. cf. *Baudh. Dh.S.* IV. 1.31.
140. XI. 239-41.
141. II. 34.
142. II. 85-87.
143. XI. 261-62.
144. IV. 34. ff; XI. 203.
145. XI. 45-47, cf. *Yāj.* III. 226.
146. XI. 259-60; cf. *Baudh. Dh.S.* IV. 2. 19-20; *Vas.Dh.S.* XXVI. 8.
147. V. 21; XI. 27, 215, 221, etc.
148. XI. 165.
149. XI. 211.
150. XI. 218.
151. XI. 219.
152. *The Golden Bough* (abridged ed.), p. 263.

Chapter IX

Socio-Economic Conceptualizations

The social and economic contents of the *Manusmṛti* have been utilised in almost all the works pertaining to the social and economic life of ancient India. In such works the socio-economic materials have been collected from the *Manusmṛti* and compared with facts obtained from other literary and epigraphical sources with a view to understanding the real state of affairs in an historical perspective. A good number of works belonging to this category have been referred to in the preceding chapters in connection with the studies in polity, law and ritual. In 1966, R.S. Sharma made a survey of such works (limited to the publications till the middle of 1950s) especially dealing with the approaches of their authors belonging to the imperialist, nationalist and Marxist tradition under the title "Historiography of the Ancient Indian Social Order".[1] It was followed by Suvira Jaiswal's 'Studies in Indian Social History' (1979-80) which dealt with subsequent important publications on social history.[2] Other works will be mentioned in the present chapter while dealing with the specific aspects of the social and economic formulations as found in the *Manusmṛti*. There is another category of works as well which purports to deal with the sociology of Manu based on subjective observations of eminent thinkers. These works mostly stand for absolute idealisation and in some cases for a rationalistic appreciation.[3] Again, there are some works which seek to prove that Manu was basically an obscurantist, a champion of Brahmanical tyranny and orthodoxy whose defence of a class-caste ridden society had jeopardized the progress of the Hindus.

The sociological formulations of Manu were evidently worked out on an existing structure which was determined by various economic factors. It has to be remembered in this connection that the present form of *Manusmṛti* was composed at a time (c. 200 B.C. to A.D. 200) when the socio-political system of India assumed a distinct shape. The shadow of the Maurya empire was still there, but at different places of the country new kingdoms were coming into existence. Most of the new royal dynasties had a tribal past and Kṣatriyahood was visibly nowhere. The ruling dynasties in Magadha—the Nandas, the Mauryas, the Śuṅgas and the Kāṇvas—were not Kṣatriyas, and this held good in the case of many other ruling dynasties, though some of them claimed Kṣatriyahood by virtue of their being in power. Manu himself knew about the Śūdra kings and ministers[4] and the real situation of his time corresponded to what the *Harivaṃśa*[5] and some other *Purāṇas*[6] had depicted as the awful degeneracy of the Kali age in a prophetic strain that the kings would be mostly Śūdras and that the Śūdra kings would perform Aśvamedha sacrifice. The ideal of *varṇaśrama* which since its inception had remained simply as an ideal could not be enforced. None of the four *varṇas* had any homogeneous existence, each of which was a conglomeration of numerous castes and subcastes. Owing to their adoption of various callings even the Brāhmaṇas ceased to remain a single and solidified social class. And that is why Manu had to recommend that if a Brāhmaṇa was unable to subsist by the occupations prescribed for him in the Śāstras he was at liberty to take up the professions of the Kṣatriyas and the Vaiśyas.[7]

From an historical point of view such a condition was not at all discouraging; rather it was conducive to sort of social, economic and political mobility. When the present form of the *Manusmṛti* was composed the Mauryas were probably not in the scene, but the ideals of the Maurya empire had a great impact on the subsequent monarchies. The Mauryas stood for militarism, bureaucracy and centralisation, and all these

required immense economic resources in the hand of the state. And this fund-raising was not possible only be taxation. To a certain extent, state-control on the production and distribution system and in certain specific cases state ownership and even monopoly were required.[8] This point of view is reflected in the *Arthaśāstra* of Kauṭilya, and an echo of this is also found in the *Manusmṛti.* That is why in both their works *koṣa* (treasury or finance) is regarded as one of the seven limbs of the state. Kauṭilya says that a king with depleted treasury ruins the vitality of his people and that since all undertakings depend upon finance, the king should pay foremost attention to the treasury.[9] Likewise the *Mahābhārata*[10] calls upon the king to guard his finances with great effort. The *Viṣṇudharmottara*[11] says that *koṣa* is the root of the tree of state. Manu says that while the army depends on the official placed in charge of it and war and peace depend on the ambassador, the treasury and administration depend solely on the king, both being his personal concern.[12] Following Manu, Yājñavalkya also states that *kosa* or treasury depends on the personal competence of the king.[13] Of the seven limbs of the state, the *koṣa* and army are frequently joined together both by Kauṭilya and by Manu. In the *Arthaśāstra* as well as in the *Manusmṛti* a mass of rules and principles relating to various branches of royal revenue and expenditure as well as the forms and methods of revenue administration are given in details. According the U.N. Ghoshal, the principles of revenue and expenditure occur explicitly in the former and implicitly in the latter as part and parcel of the art of statecraft or government.[14]

One fundamental conception of the Indian tradition as recorded in the ancient texts is that taxes are the king's dues for the service of protection. The Dharmasūtras[15] justify the king's levy of taxes on the ground that he is charged with the duty of protecting his subjects. "Even the theory of the king's ownership of the soil in Manu has to be buttressed with that of the king's claim to one-half of the treasure-trove and of the output of mines".[16] This deep-rooted concept of protection

may be connected with the maxim that the king shares in the spiritual merits as well as demerits of his subjects. Manu categorically says:

> A king who duly protects his subjects receives from each and all the sixth part of their spiritual merit; if he does not protect them, the sixth part of their demerit also will fall on him.
>
> Whatever merit a man gains by reading the Veda by sacrificing, by charitable gifts or by worshipping *gurus* and gods, the king obtains a sixth part of that in consequence of his duly protecting his kingdom.
>
> A king who protects the created beings in accordance with the sacred law and smites those worthy of corporal punishment, daily offers, as it were, sacrifices at which hundred thousands are given as fees.
>
> A king who does not afford protection, yet takes his share in kind, taxes, tolls and duties, daily presents and fines will soon sink into hell.
>
> They declare that a king who affords no protection, yet receives the sixth part of the produce, takes upon himself all the foulness of his whole people.[17]

So strictly is the notion of the king's responsibility for protection carried out to its logical conclusion that Manu requires him to make good the equivalent of the stolen property that he has failed to recover.[18] But the doctrine of protection was rather theoretical. The term protection has a wide denotation and its significance is variously explained. Manu, Kauṭilya and other law-givers did not look upon taxation as returning to the people in 'fertilising showers'. Kālidāsa describes king Dilīpa as receiving the taxes from his subjects for their own welfare like the sun who extracts water in order to render it back a thousand-fold.[19] This is no more than a poetic hyperbole. The inner significance of the doctrine of protection, as we find in Manu or Kauṭilya, is that the king

needed money for consolidating his power and position, for meeting the expenditure of warfare and for satisfying his manifold ambitions. Taxation was one of the principal sources of royal income and since kingship was regarded as a divine or semi-divine or socially approved institution meant for the protection of the people any type of royal expenditure was regared as meant for the welfare of the people. That is why, according to Manu, protection may even denote preparedness for or participating in war. He categorically says that -

> The king's peculiar duty is conquest, and he must not turn back in danger (*sadharmo vijayastasya nāhave syāt parāṅmukhaḥ)*; and having thus protected the trading community by his weapons, he may cause the legal tax to be collected.[20]

The Dharmasūtra of Gautama[21] also says that "to stand firm in battle and not to turn back is the duty of the king".

The most complete account of the methods and principles of taxation occurs in the *Manusmṛti* which is corroborative to other sources as well. Manu says that the king should fix the taxes upon merchants after examining the matters relating to purchase and sale, the distance travelled, the provisions consumed and the charges for securing the merchandise.

> Having well considered the rates of purchase and of sale, the length of the road, the expense for food and condiments, the charges of securing the goods, let the king make the traders pay duty.
>
> After due consideration the king shall always fix in his realm the duties and taxes in such a manner that both he himself and the man who does work receive their due reward.[22]

The same is said in the *Mahābhārata*.[23] This rule undoubtedly shows an appreciation of the difficulties attending the

assessment of merchants' profits and indicates an attempt to throw the burden of taxation upon the net profits instead of charging the same upon the capital. As to the general principles of taxation Manu declares that the taxes should be fixed by the king in such a way that he himself and the producer may participate in the result. He states that the king should not destroy his own substance, nor that of his subjects, by showing excessive greed.

> As the leech, the calf and the bee take their food little by little, even so must the king draw from his realm moderate annual taxes.[24]
>
> Let the king having carefully considered each affair, be both sharp and gentle; for a king who is both sharp and gentle is highly respected.[25]

As the sun during eight months (imperceptibly) draws up the water with his rays, even so let him gradually draw taxes from the kingdom; for that is the office in which he resembles the sun.[26]

According to the *Mahābhārata*[27] just as a bee draws honey but at the same time leaves the flowers uninjured, so the king should take wealth from men without harming them. Elsewhere it is stated in the *Mahābhārata*[28] that the intelligent king should milk his kingdom on the analogy of a calf; when the calf is given nourishment, it grows strong and is capable of enduring fatigue, but when the cow is milked too much the calf cannot perform any work; so does a kingdom, which is drained too much, fail to perform any great service. Kauṭilya says that the king should pluck the ripe fruits from his kingdom just as one gathers from a garden, but should not take unripe fruits which cause provocation, lest this should bring about his own ruin.[29] That is why he says that the king shall bestow on cultivators only such favour and remission *(anugrahaparihārau)* as will tend to swell the treasury and shall avoid such as deplete it.[30] The practical consequence of this dictum is aptly expressed in the

Manusmṛti which states that the king, even though reduced to straitened circumstances, should not take what ought not to be taken, nor even though he is affluent he should forego his just dues.

> No king, however indigent, shall take anything that ought not to be taken nor shall he, however wealthy, decline taking that which he ought to take, be it even so small. In consequence of taking what ought to be taken, or of refusing what ought to be received a king will be accused of weakness and perish in this world and after death.[31]

According to Manu and other writers the principle of taxation was that the king could not levy taxes at his pleasure or sweetwill and that the rates of taxes which the king was entitled to levy were fixed. The rates varied only according to the commodity and also according as the times were normal or there was danger of invasion or some other calamity impending. With taxation were connected the maxims that taxation should not destroy the substance of the people, but should have ample margin for their subsistence, that the taxes should be levied by slow almost imperceptible degrees and not in lump and that it should be levied at the time and place most suited for the subjects.[32] Ghoshal has referred to the view of Plehn who on the authority of Burnell and Hopkins quotes a maxim of Manu which, according to him anticipates the doctrine of progressive taxation and teaches that taxes should not be levied on the capital but on the income of the tax-payers. We have already observed that the latter principle is implicitly embodied in one of Manu's rules of taxation. But no text of Manu can be held to imply the doctrine first mentioned. The nearest approach to this doctrine is made by Medhātithi who understands Manu VII. 128 to mean that there is no rule for fixing the taxes in the case of merchants' profits, and that where the profits are large, even an excessive rate may be levied.[33]

In the *Manusmṛti* we meet with descriptions of the branches of revenue which are neither so full nor so well arranged as those of the *Arthaśāstra* of Kauṭilya. In so far as the sources of land revenue and similar charges in these works are concerned Manu refers to *bali.* The word *bali* is perhaps the oldest which occurs even in the *Ṛgveda*[34] in the sense of tribute payable to the chief and in the Brāhmaṇa literature[35] in almost the same sense as that of tax. The Jātakas also refer to *bali.*[36] Though the *Amarakoṣa* treats *bali, bhāga* and *kara* as synonymous, Aśoka in his Rummendei pillar inscription makes a difference between *bali* and *bhāga* in which it is said that the village of Lumbini was made free from the payment of *bali,* but had to pay one-eight as *bhāga* (*atabhāgiya= aṣṭabhāga*).[37] According to the *Arthaśāstra* while *bhāga* may be rightly taken to be the king's customary share of the produce levied on the ordinary revenue-paying lands, *bali* was additional impositon, an undefined cess over and above the king's normal share. Manu employes the word *bali* in the sense of the produce that the king levied as tax.[38] The significance of the term *bhāga* has been explained above. According to Manu, *bhāga* may be one-sixth, one-eighth and even one-fiftieth of the produce.[39] The term *kara* appears to mean tax in general. According to Manu *kara* is that form of tax which is imposed on merchants and manufacturers at various rates,[40] and on common inhabitants (*pṛthag-janam)* who subsist on ordinary occupations levied at a minimal rates.[41] The word *śulka* generally means tolls or custom duties. Manu says that expert custom officials were acquainted with the settlement of tolls and duties and skilful in estimating the value of all kinds of merchandise (*śulkasthāneṣu kuśalāḥ sarvapaṇya-vicakṣaṇaḥ*) should fix the value of each saleable commodity and king will take one-twentieth of that.[42]

Elsewhere[43] Manu while mentioning a list of the king's receipt distinguishes between the terms *bali, kara, śulka, pratibhāga* and *daṇḍa.* We have already explained *bali* and *śulka.* Among other terms *kara* is that form of tax which is received in kinds on commodities. According to Kulluka it is

the tax payable by the inhabitants of villages and towns every month or according to the rule of payment in Bhādra, Pauṣa and other months. Rāghavānanda holds that it is the tax payable by the inhabitants of the villages every month. The interpretations of Kulluka and Rāghavānanda are very much is accordance with Bhaṭṭasvāmin's explanation of the same term occurring in Kauṭilya. According to Sarvajñanārāyaṇa it is the tax in cash payable on land while Rāmacandra describes it to be the king's dues paid at military stations and so forth. Ganganath Jha in his translation renders it as 'what is paid in cash'.[44] According to U.N. Ghoshal *kara* would thus be a periodical tax levied originally upon agricultural land over and above the king's normal grain-share. He also refers to Jain lexicon which mentions that while the villages were liable to the *kara*, the towns were immune from the the same.[45] As to the term *pratibhāga*, it is explained by Medhātithi in the sense of offering of fruits, flowers, roots, grains and the like, for elsewhere Manu says that "those articles which the villagers ought to furnish daily to the king, such as food, drink and fuel, the lord of one village, shall obtain."[46] For *pratibhāga*, Sarvajñanārāyaṇa and Rāghavānanda have the reading *pratibhoga*, Govindarāja has *bhūtibhoga*. It has been explained in Keśava's *Kalpadrukośa*[47] in the practically identical sense of presents of vegetables, etc. It may be added that the *Agni Purāṇa*[48] applies the term *bhoga* to the perquisites of the officers in charge of one, ten and one hundred villages as well as the governor of the district.

Manu exhorts the king to appoint officers for the collection of revenue in mines, manufactories and storehouses.[49] The word *ākarakarmanta* used in this connection may mean, according to Bühler, for superintending mines and manufactories because *ākāra* has very frequently that double meaning. Medhātithi says that *karmānta* means 'management', 'sugar mills', 'distilleries' and so forth. Kulluka and Govindarāja add 'storehouses of grain'. Nārāyaṇa explains it as manufactories of ornaments and weapons and so forth. Elsewhere Manu says

that for various branches of business the king should appoint intelligent supervisors who are to inspect the transactions of businessmen.[50] We have already had the occasion to refer to Manu VIII. 198 according to which the king should take one-twentieth of that which the experienced commercial tax officers may fix as the value for each commodity. Medhātithi and Sarvajñanārāyaṇa take it to refer to one- twentieth of the amount of merchandise while Govindarāja, Kulluka and Rāghavānanda refer to one-twentieth of the profit derived for the same. We have already referred to the fact that a state-controlled economy and state monopoly of certain articles of trade are indicated in the *Manusmṛti* which exhorts the king to confiscate the whole property of a trader who out of greed exports goods of which the king has a monopoly or the export of which is forbidden.[51] Medhātithi says that among the articles of state monopoly there were elephants, saffron from Kashmir, fine cloth and wool from certain regions, horses from the western region, precious stones and pearls from the southern region and so forth.

> He who avoids a custom-house or a toll, he who buys or sells at an improper time, or he who makes a false statement in enumerating his goods shall be fined eight times the amount of duty which he tried to evade.
>
> Let the king fix the rates for the purchase and sale of all marketable goods, having duly considered whence they come, whither they go, how long they have been kept, the probable profit and the probable outlay.
>
> Once in five nights, or at the close of each fortnight, let the king publicly settle the prices for the merchants.[52]

The aforesaid injunctions prove a kind of state control, The rules regarding the administration of *śulka* and the policy of its collection correspond to the system of the *Arthaśāstra*. Thus Manu prescribes a fine of eight times the amount of the duty upon persons evading the taxes. In thorough accord with

the *Arthaśāstra* again Manu forbids the exportation of what is proclaimed as suited for the king's use and of the country while the collection of tolls on merchants by official agency and the state regulation of prices were the general rule. Medhātithi commenting on Manu VIII.41 says that a verbal agreement between the king and the guilds of merchants was possible according to which the latter would pay a fixed amount to the king irrespective of their profit or loss. Regarding the rate of taxation, the sources of revenue, tolls transit duties, customs and the like Manu says:

> A fiftieth part of (the increments on) cattle and gold may be taken by the king, and the eighth, sixth or twelfth part of the crops.
>
> He may also take the sixth part of trees, meat, honey, clarified butter, perfumes, herbs, substances used for flavouring food, flowers, roots and fruits.
>
> Of leaves, pot-herbs, grass, objects form of cane, skins, of earthen vessels and all articles made of stone.
>
> Let the king make the common inhabitants of his realm who live on traffic, pay annually some trifle which is called *kara*.
>
> Mechanics and artisans, as well as Śūdras who subsist by manual labour, he may cause to work for himself one day in each month.[53]

Turning to the next branch of revenue we may mention that Manu, like Kauṭilya, apparently contemplates a tax to be derived from weights and measures. Manu says that all weights and measures must be duly marked and the king should examine them once in six months.[54] Apart from weights and measures Manu mentions ferry charges (*tārya* or *tārika*) which has its precise parallel in the *Arthaśāstra*.

> At a ferry an empty cart shall be made to pay one *paṇa*, a man' load half a *paṇa*, an animal and a woman one-quarter

> of a *paṇa,* an unloaded man one-half of a quarter. Carts laden with vessels full of merchandise shall be made to pay toll at a ferry according to the value of the goods; empty vessels and men without luggage some trifle. For a long passage the boat-hire must be proportioned to the places and time; know that this rule refers to passages along the banks of rivers; at sea there is no settled freight.[55]

State receipts from gambling and betting, fines and contributions from artisans were also sources of revenue. Regarding gambling and betting Manu seems to hold a view which is different from Kauṭilya and Yājñavalkya. According to Manu, in a former *kalpa,* the vice of gambling became the cause of enmity and disaster. A wise man therefore should not practice it even for amusement. Gambling and betting amount to open theft. The gamblers are thorns of society. So the king should corporally punish the gamblers or instantly banish them from his kingdom.[56] On the other hand, Yājñavalkya[57] provides that gambling should be brought under control of single officer and that the keeper of the gambling-house should give the king his proper share. Nārada[58] also states that gamblers may play in public provided they pay the king his stipulated dues. *Daṇḍa* or fine has been regarded by Manu as one of the five special forms of royal income which is levied from wrong-doers, defeated litigants and so forth. While the later Dharmaśāstras contemplate that the artisans and craftsmen should pay their taxes in cash Manu says that the craftsmen, artisans and those living by manual labour should work for the king one day in each month.[59] Income from mines, gardens, forests and herds has been mentioned above. Manu while mentioning the mines as a source of revenue, for which trusted officials are to be employed by the king,[60] enjoins that the king should take only one-half of the metals found underground.[61] As regards the treasure-troves Manu says that when a person claims the treasure and proves his title thereto, the king should take from him one-sixth or one-twelfth. On

the other hand, if a person lays a false claim to the treasure he is to pay a fine of eight times the value of his property. When a Brāhmaṇa finds a treasure, he is to give one-half to the Brāhmaṇas and send the other half into his own treasury.[62] Medhātithi commenting on the views of Manu in regard to treasure-troves says that the rule permitting the Brāhmaṇas to take the treasure applies only when it belongs to them. When, however, the owner of the treasure is not known, the king's share of one-sixth has to be paid by the finder, even though he is a Brāhmaṇa. The same argument has also been put forward by Govindarāja and Sarvajñanārāyaṇa as well as by Devanabhaṭṭa, the author of the *Smṛticandrikā.* The author of the *Vīramitrodaya,* however, holds that the verses of Manu mean that the king should keep the remaining half of the treasure with the object of restoring it to the rightful owner.

A notable feature of the revenue system embodied in the literature of law and polity is that is seeks to provide for the exceptional needs of the king or the state during grave emergencies. The most complete account of the branches of emergency revenue occurs in the *Arthaśāstra.*[63] Manu says that if a king after protecting his subjects to the best of his ability takes in time of his distress even the fourth part of the crops, he incurs no sin. The king has to engage himself in warfare which is for his self- protection and also for the protection of his subjects from external attacks. He cannot turn back. The prosperity of the trading community depends on the power and stability of the state. So the king has legal right to levy extra-taxes on the manufacturers, traders, agriculture and wealth-producing occupational groups.

> One-eighth as the tax on grain, one-twentieth (on the profits of gold and cattle) which amount at best to one *kārṣāpaṇa*; Śūdras, artisans and mechanics shall benefit the king by doing work for him (*dhānye'aṣṭamaṃ viśāṃ śulkam vimśam kārṣāpanavaraṃ karmopakaraṇāḥ śūdrāḥ kāravah śilpinastathā*)[64]

According to Medhātithi the first line refers to the profits of subjects dealing in corn or in gold. From the former the king may take in time of distress one-eighth and from the latter one-twentieth. The second line indicates that though the normal rule is that mechanics and artisans as well as the Śūdras who subsists by manual labour should give their service to the king for one day in a month (VII. 138), in time of distress they may be made to work more for the king. According to Kulluka, the producer should give one-eighth of his surplus in king's distress instead of the usual one-twelfth (VII. 130), but in the direct distress caused by the king's war-efforts to protect the prosperity of his peoples, especially the trading communities, it may be raised to one-fourth (cf. x. 118). Likewise in the time of crisis there will be an extra surcharge on gold and so forth (amounting to more than one *kārsāpaṇa*) which is one-twentieth instead of one- fiftieth. According to Nārāyaṇa one-eighth of the tax is to be paid by the Vaiśyas on grain and on everything else at least one *kārṣāpaṇa* out of twenty. The principle was that the king could not levy taxes at his pleasure or sweetwill, that the rates of taxes were ordinarily fixed at various percentages and that under exceptional circumstances where was the danger of invasion or some other calamities, the king could levy surcharges. Kauṭilya says that during emergency the king should beg of the people (*yācata*) an extra amount for which he uses the word *praṇaya* at the time of distress.[65] The word *pranaya* occurs in this sense in the Junugadh inscription of Rudradāman.[66]

The frequent mention of money in connection with taxation, sale and purchase, pledge, surety, fine, debt, interest and so forth testifies that Manu thought in terms of money-economy. He categorically says that certain quantities of copper, silver and gold (*tāmrarūpyasuvarṇānām*) which are generally used for business transactions have technical names (*lokasaṃvyavahārārthaṃ yāḥ, saṃjñāḥ prathitā bhuvi*).[67] According to Manu, the smallest particle which is not bigger than a dust is called *trasarenu*, eight of which form a *likṣā;* three *likṣās* constitute a

rājasarṣapa (one grain of black mustard seed) and three of the latter a *gaurasarṣapa* (one grain of white mustard seed); six grains of white mustard seed constitute one middle-sized barley-corn (*yava*) and three *yavas* one *kṛṣṇala*, which is *raktika* or *guñja-berry*.[68] This *kṛṣṇala* or *raktika* or *rati* or *guñja*-berry which weighs approximately *118—*122 grammes is the primary unit. It is still used by jewellers and goldsmiths. The word *kṛṣṇala* occurs in the *Taittirīya Saṃhitā*.[69] Five units of *kṛṣṇala* or *guñja-berry* constitute a *māsa*, and sixteen *māsas* a *suvarṇa*. Four *suvarṇas* make a *pala* and ten *palas* a *dharaṇa*. Two silver *kṛṣṇalas* make a *māsaka* and sixteen of these make a silver *dharaṇa* or *purāṇa* (= 32 *ratis*). A *kārsā* of copper is a *paṇa* (= 80 *ratis*) and hence the name is *kārṣāpana*. Ten *dharaṇas* of silver make one *satamāna*; and four *suvarṇa* are equal in weight to *niṣka*.[70] Of the *suvarṇa* of standard gold coin of 80 *ratis*, we have no specimen, but numerous specimens of silver *purāṇas* and *dharaṇas* of 32 *ratis* as well their various multiples and subdivisions have been discovered. The tables of Manu are substantially in agreement with those of Kauṭilya, Yājñavalkya, Nārada and Bṛhaspati.

The canon of taxation, as enumerated in the *Manusmṛti*, shows that it was meant for such a society which was pluralistic in nature with a considerable degree of mobility at all levels which was not at all consistent with the traditional concept of classical *varṇa* division. It has also to be remembered in this connection that whatever ages may be assigned to the *Arthaśāstra* and the present *Manusmṛti* the two works cannot be separated from each other by more than a century and therefore the economic conditions of the one may be held to have not differed much from those to which the other refers.[71] Manu had to accept the reality of this times and though he refers to the 'pure occupations' prescribed for each *varṇa*, he has to recognise in principle the validity of downward occupational mobility of the higher *varṇas*. The reverse, that is, the upward occupational mobility of the lower *varṇas* was a matter of rare occurrence in those days, as it is even today all over the world.

The 'pure occupations' were, in the case of the Brāhmaṇas, teaching, study, worship, officiating in worship, making gifts and accepting gifts: in the case of the Kṣatriyas, study, worship, making gifts, profession of arms and offering protection to others; in the case of the Vaiśyas, study, worship, making gifts, agriculture, cattle-rearing and trade; and in the case of the Śūdras, service, production of wealth, arts and crafts. But these pure occupations were theoretical and that is why it was suggested that if the Brāhmaṇas and the Kṣatriyas were not sufficiently competent to follow the 'pure occupation' prescribed for them, or the situation did not permit them to follow, or in distress caused by various conditions, they could, for the sake of their livelihood, adopt the occupations of the Vaiśyas and even some of the Śūdras. But although the Brāhmaṇs and Kṣatriyas, for the sake of their livelihood, were forced to take up lower occupations, their social status would be lowered in accordance with the status of the occupations they took up. For example, Manu says that a Brāhmaṇa should always and assiduously study the Veda alone.[72] Compared to him the status of a temple priest is low. A Brāhmaṇa who performs service before the image in a temple is unfit to be invited in a Śrāddha or to officiate in a sacrifice for gods.[73]

Manu lays down that the persons of three higher *varṇas* should, if they cannot maintain themselves by the peculiar occupations of their *varṇa*, resort to the means of livelihood prescribed for the *varṇa* which is immediately below their own.

> A Brāhmaṇa, unable to subsist by his peculiar occupations, just mentioned, may live according to the law applicable to the Kṣatriyas; for the latter is next to him in rank. If it be asked, 'how shall it be, if he cannot maintain himself in either of these occupations', the answer is, he may adopt a Vaiśya's mode of life, employing himself in agriculture and rearing cattle.[74]

So the profession of arms was not prohibited to the Brāhmaṇas. In fact from very ancient times the Brāhmaṇas appear to have followed the profession of arms. Among the heroes of the *Mahābhārata* many were Brāhmaṇas. In the historical period the Brāhmaṇa Puṣyamitra Śuṅga, who was a *senāpati* or general, wrested a kingdom from the last king of the Mauryas. The Kāṇva and Kadamba princes were Brāhmaṇas and also warriors at the same time. Kauṭilya refers to army composed of all the four *varṇas* including the Brāhmanas and the Śūdras.[75] Manu categorically says:

> Twice-born men may take up arms when they hindered in the fulfilment of their duties, while destruction threatens the twice-born castes in evil times.[76]

The very fact that the twice-born persons can take up the profession of arms proves that there was professional mobility among the three higher *varṇas*. Regarding the Vaiśyas Manu says that they should be always attentive to the business, tend cattle, know the respective value of gems, pearls, metals, cloth, purfumes and so forth and be acquainted with the art of agriculture, weights and measures, excellence and defects of commodities, advantages and disadvantages of different countries, profit and loss of the merchandise, wages of the servants, various languages of men and should exert themselves to the utmost to increase their property in a righteous manner.[77] Also from the list of restrictions imposed upon the Brāhmaṇas who follow the profession of the Vaiśyas, we can have a fair idea about the specially privileged calling of the Vaiśyas. Manu says:

> But a Brāhmaṇa, or a Kṣatriya, living by a Vaiśya mode of subsistence, shall carefully avoid the pursuit of agriculture, which causes injury to many beings and depends on others. Some declare that agriculture is something excellent, but that means of subsistence is blamed by the

> virtuous; for the wooden implement with iron point injures the earth and the beings living on earth.[78]

This apathy towards agriculture is also found in the *Baudhāyana Dharmasūtra*[79] which says that "the study of the Veda tends to the loss of the study of the Veda. One who has the capacity to look after both may resort to both, but he who is unable to look after both should give up agriculture." It is interesting to note that Plato also showed a similar apathy to agriculture.[80] So the best way, according to Manu, for the Brāhmaṇas and Kṣatriyas to follow the Vaiśya mode of life, is to take up trade as occupation.

> But he who, through a want of means of subsistence, gives up the strictness with respect to his duties, may sell, in order to increase his wealth, the commodities sold by Vaiśyas, making however, the following exceptions.[81]

The exceptions comprise trade in such commodities as all sorts of cooked food, sesamum, stones, salt, cattle, human beings, dyed cloth, cloth made of hemp, flax or wool, fruits, roots, medical herbs, water, weapons, poison, meat, wine, purfumes of all kinds, fresh milk, honey, sour-milk, clarified butter, oil, wax, sugar, *kuśa* grass, beasts of the forest, animals, with fangs or tusks, birds, spirituous liquor, indigo, lac, one-hoofed beasts, flesh, etc.[82]

This list of commodities, the sale of which is forbidden to the Brāhmaṇas and the Kṣatriyas, were really meant for the trade of the Vaiśyas. In the *Dharmasūtra* of Gautama[83] it is also said that a Brāhmaṇa should not engage in the sale of fragrant things such as sandalwood, purfumes, etc., fluids such as oil, clarified butter and so forth, cooked food, sesame, hemp, linen, deer-skin, dyed and cleanly washed clothes, milk and its products, roots, flowers, fruits, herbs, honey, meat, grass, water deleterious drugs, animals, men and slaves, barren cows, land, rice, barley, goats and sheep, horses, bulls, freshly

delivered cow, etc., but these restrictions do not apply to a Kṣatriya engaging in trade.[84] Manu also states that exchange or barter of those articles that are forbidden to be sold cannot be resorted to, but adds that barter is allowed in cases where things are similar.

> Condiments may be bartered for condiments, but by no means salt for other condiments; cooked food may be exchanged for other kinds of cooked food and sesamum seeds for grain in equal quantities.[85]

Apart from agriculture and trade money-lending was also a business of the Vaiśyas which a Brāhmaṇa or a Kṣatriya could adopt under compelling circumstances. According to Manu, there are seven lawful modes of acquiring wealth, namely inheritance, findings or friendly donations, purchase, conquest, lending at interest, performance of works and acceptance of gifts. According to him, learning, mechanical arts, work for wages, services, rearing cattle, traffic, agriculture, contentment with little, alms and receiving interest of money are the modes of subsistence permitted to all men in times of distress. But neither a Brāhmaṇa nor a Kṣatriya should lend money in normal conditions. Only in exceptional circumstances they can do it, charging only a low rate of interest.[86]

It is interesting to note that among the items of sale forbidden to a Brāhmaṇa or a Kṣatriya, but not to a Vaiśya, there is the human being which undoubtedly refers to a slave. Though slavery was a recognised institution of ancient India there is a difference of opinion among he scholars in regard to its degree and extent. D.D. Kosambi rejected in unequivocal voice the social formation called slavery. But S.A. Dange, R.S. Sharma and D.R. Chanana have a different view, though each of them has his own definition of slavery. Thus Chanana defines a slave "to be a person who is under the full power of his master, liable to be beaten, branded or killed at the sweetwill of the latter".[87] Though instances of such slaves were

not rare in ancient India, Indian slavery was not of classical or Graeco-Roman type, but "domestic slavery", the term which even Dange was obliged to use. Though Megasthenes said that none of the Indians employ slaves,[88] the ninth rock edict of Aśoka admits the existence of slavery since it proclaims that the law of piety consists among other things in the kind and proper treatment of slaves and hired servants. Kauṭilya says that the *mlecchas* are not punishable if they sell or pledge their children but an Ārya cannot be reduced to slavery. Severe punishment he has prescribed for those who unlawfully sell or pledge a person. But under certain conditions an Ārya also could become a slave, such as one captured in battle, one who sells himself in distress, one who is born of a slave-woman, one so made for a debt or fine or court's degree.[89] Jaimini says that when a man makes a gift in the Viśvajit sacrifice of everything belonging to himself, he has no right to make a gift of the Śūdra who waits upon him as his duty.[90] According to Manu slaves are of seven kinds:

> There are slaves of seven kinds, viz., he who is made a captive under a standard (*dhvajāhṛta*), he who serves for his daily food (*bhaktadāsa*), he who is born in the house (*gṛhaja)*, he who is bought (*krīta)*, he who is given (*datrima*), he who is inherited from his ancestors (*paitrika)* and he who is enslaved by the way of punishment (*daṇḍadāsa*).[91]

Kauṭilya also makes a similar classification, but his attitude towards the slaves was basically different from that of Manu. Kauṭilya is more liberal and has prescribed various ways how they are to be set free from slavery. He is also very much concerned regarding the rights and privileges of the slaves. Kauṭilya says:

> The offspring of a man who has sold himself as a slave shall be an Ārya. A slave shall be entitled to enjoy not only whatever he has earned without prejudice to his master's

work, but also the interitance he has received from his father.

On paying the value for which one is enslaved, a slave shall regain his Āryahood. The same rule shall apply either to born or pledged slaves.

The ransom necessary for a slave to regain his freedoom is equal to what he has been sold for any person who has been enslaved for fines or court decrees shall earn the amount by work. An Ārya made captive in the war shall for his freedom pay an amount proportional to the dangerous work done at the time of his capture or half the amount...

The property of slave pass into the hands of his kinsmen; in the absence of any kinsman his master shall take it.

When a child is begotten on a female slave by her master, both the child and its mother shall at once be recognised as free. If, for the sake of subsistence the mother has to remain in her bondage, her brother and sister shall be liberated.[92]

By contrast Manu's attitude towards the slaves is not at all liberal. According to him:

A wife, a son and a slave, these three are declared to have no property; the wealth which they earn is acquired for him to whom they belong.

A Brāhmaṇa may confidently seize the goods of his Śūdra slave; for as that slave can have no property, his master may take his possessions.[93]

Manu says that the artisans, craftsmen, manual labourers and persons following various lower occupations mostly belonging to the Śūdra category will have to give one day's service in every month to the king. Though the Śūdras in the traditional sense constitute the fourth *varṇa*, Manu considered them as a conglomeration of numerous occupational subcastes and tried to explain their origins in terms of the *varṇasaṅkara*

or 'mixed caste' theory. Their social hierarchy in regard to rank and status may broadly be divided into three categories—high, middle and low. Those having moderate callings are placed in higher ranks than others and regarded as good hybrids born of hypergamic marriages in which the husband's caste is higher than that of his wife. Those having lower occupations are placed in the lower ranks and are regarded as bad hybrids born of hypergamic marriages in which the husband's caste is lower than that of his wife. Those coming between these two in regard to occupations are placed in the intermediary ranks and regarded as middle hybrids in which the caste-status of the husband and the wife is more or less the same. The invention of this *varṇasaṅkara* theory was designed to incorporate numerous detribalised and occupational castes into the Śūdra category of the fourfold system. According to this theory hybrid castes emerging from morganatic marriages produce many other hybrid caste of the second rank and they in their turn produce mixed castes of the third rank. Following this system innumerable functional social groups can be accommodated as mixed castes within the structure of the fourfold order. But since in reality such a scheme cannot be feasible, apart from suggesting an imaginary pedigree, what Manu and subsequent law-givers did was to classify the existing subcastes, mostly belonging to the Śūdra category, on the basis of the nature of their callings and place them in the scheme of the mixed castes.[94]

While dealing with the Śūdra subcastes Manu has taken into account as forming their substrata the occupational groups or guilds, a good many of which were constituted by detribalised peoples. In the *Ṛgveda*,[95] *Atharvaveda*,[96] *Taittirīya*,[97] *Vājasaneyi*[98] and *Kāṭhaka*[99] Saṃhitās and also in the Brāhmaṇa literature[100] we come across occupational groups like those of the barbers (*vaptā*), carpenters (*tvaṣṭā, takṣan*), physicians (*bhiṣak*), ironsmiths (*karmāra*), leather-workers (*carmamnā*), chariot-makers (*rathakāra*), reciters and charioteers (*sūta*), chamberlains (*kṣatr*), potters (*kaulāla, kulāla*), arrow-makers

(*iṣukṛt, iṣukāra)*, bow-makers (*dhanvakṛt*), string-makers (*jyākāra*), bards (*māgadha*), sowers (*vapa),* jewellers (*maṅikāra),* goatherds (*ajapāla*), keepers of ewes (*avipala),* dancers (*kāri*), cultivators (*kināsa*), fisherman (*kevarta, dhīvara*), blowers of bellows (*kośakārī*), servants (*dāsa*), hunters (*puñjiṣṭha, mṛgāyu, śvanin*), goldsmiths (*hiraṇyakāra*), wine-makers (*surākāra*), dyers (*rajayitri*), washer-woman (*vāsaḥpalpali*), rope-makers (*rajjusarga*), metal-smelter (*ayastāpa*), gamblers (*kitava*), wicker-workers (*bidalakāra*), cowherds (*gopāla*), etc. That many of such occupational groups were originally tribes is indicated simply by the tribal names of various castes, as we shall presently see; and the process of their transformation may be outlined with reference to the Niṣādas. Of the eight peoples forming the Niṣāda community, as we find in the Rudrādhyāya of the *Yajurveda,* the Vrātas, Puñjiṣṭhas, Śvanins and Mṛgāyus were hunters still clinging to food-gathering economy, while the Takṣans, Rathakāras, Kulālas and Karmāras left their tribal fold and settled in the Vedic society as members of castes belonging to the lower grades of the hierarchy having undertaken the occupations of carpenter, chariot-maker, potter and ironsmith respectively.

From the list of the occupational castes belonging to the Śūdra category, as found in the *Manusmṛti,* a social stratification of an uneven economic development is possible to make. At the lowest level were the food-gatherers who subsisted especially on hunting and fishing like the Arnadons of the Nilambur forest, the Chenchus of the Nallamallais, the Birhors, Koruas and Hill Marhias of Central India and other food-gathering tribes of modern times. At this level belonged Manu's Andhras, Kirātas, Caṇḍālas, Cuñcus, Medas, Madgus, Pulindas, Mataṅgas, Śabaras, Śvapacas, Lubdhakas, Mārgavas, Kaivartas, Dhīvaras, Mallas, etc. The next higher level, from an economic point and view, was constituted by the food-producers, the pastorals and the agriculturists as well as by craftsmen catering other needs of society. Though agriculture, cattle-rearing and trade were meant for the Vaiśyas and craftmanship

for the Śūdras, such hard and fast distinction could not be maintained. Manu called agriculture a low profession, but had not made it an occupation of the Śūdras, though the pastoral Ābhiras and their derivatives, the Gopas, Gopālakas, Golakas, etc., were placed in the Śūdra category. Among other professionals as is gleaned from the Dharmaśāstras in general and the *Manusmṛti* in particular, the Ambaṣṭhas were physicians: the Ayaskāra, Takṣans, Upakruṣṭas, Kāṃsakāras, Vardhakas, Suvarṇakāras, Sauvarṇikas, Hemakāras, Tāmropajīvins, etc., followed the occupations of blacksmiths, carpenters, goldsmiths, coppersmiths and so forth; the Kaulālas or Kumbhakāras were potters; the Tantuvāyas were weavers; the Tunnavāyas were tailors; the Rajakas, Udbandhakas and the Cailenirṇejikas were washermen; the Aiśvikas were horse-dealers; the Tailikas, Cakrīs and Cākrikas were oil-pressers; the Nartakas were dancers; the Tāmbulikas were dealers in betel-leaves; the Pāṇḍusopākas were bamboo-workers; the Mālākaras were flower-dealers; the Nāpitas or Kuntalakas were barbers; and so forth.

A process of historical determinism must have given a concrete shape to the caste system which came into existence as the result of a long social evolution extending over centuries. The working of this process did not escape the notice of Manu who was eager to incorporate conflicting tribes of various cultural grades within the framework of the idealised fourfold social order and to rationalise their existence in the prescribed set-up with the help of the *varṇasaṅkara* theory by which even the foreign tribes were inducted.[102] He tried to create a plural society by offering the detribalised castes special hereditary occupations and cultural freedom though he was not ready to give them equality of status and position. While Manu believed that such an ideal could be achieved by persuasive legislation, Kauṭilya thought that the use of force and pressure from outside was necessary to quicken the process. Kauṭilya who was the champion of organised statehood, categorically prescribed that the tribes should be destroyed by

any means—war, diplomacy, sabotage, bribery and any suitable corrupt practice—and that the tribals should be cut loose from their kinship-bond and engaged in various professions required by the larger society or by the state. Being dissociated from their original environment they would become occupational groups at the first stage and then transformed into castes of various status according to the importance of the their respective callings.[103]

We have already had the occasion to describe such a process of transformation with reference to the Niṣādas. The Ambaṣṭhas also offer a typical example. They were a well known tribe of the Punjab region that offered a stubborn resistance to Alexander, as has been recorded by the classical writers. Subsequently they migrated in different parts of the country. In the Purāṇas as also in the *Bṛhatsaṃhitā*[104] they are mentioned as tribes. Ptolemy refers to them as Ambastae.[105] Manu describes them as an *anuloma* hybrid sprung from the marriage of a Brāhmaṇa man with a Vaiśya woman[106] and prescribes the profession of medicine for them,[107] though later law-givers hold that they may subsist by agriculture or may be fire-dancers or heralds.[108] In some parts of India the Ambaṣṭhas had taken up lower professions and thus received a lower position in the caste-hierarchy, but in Bengal they had taken up the profession prescribed for them by Manu and as Vaidyas they were held in high esteem having almost the same position as the Brāhmaṇas.[109] Other law-givers[110] refer to a mixed caste called Bhiṣak, supposed to have sprung from clandestine union between a Brāhmaṇa male and Kṣatriya female, supporting itself by studying medicine, astrology, astronomy or mathematics. It is to be noted that the medicine-man occurs as *bhiṣak* in the *Ṛgveda.*[111] According to the *Vaikhānasa Smārta Sūtra.*[112] the offspring of the marriage of a Brāhmaṇa male with a Kṣatriya female is the foremost among the *anulomas* and is called *savarṇa* while the offspring of the clandestine union of these two is called *abhiṣikta.* If crowned he becomes a king, otherwise he subsists by studying medicine or

the science of ghosts, or astronomy, astrology and mathematics. The profession of medicine has been attributed to the Sūtas in some Purāṇas. The Ambaṣṭhas are also known as Bhṛjjakaṇṭakas.

The *pañcakṛṣṭi* of the *Ṛgveda*[113] has been explained by Yāska as five classes of men which included the four *varṇas* and the Niṣādas as the fifth.[114] Manu, however, says that there cannot be any fifth *varṇa*.[115] The commentator Mahīdhara explains the word Niṣāda as it occurs in the *Vājasaneyi Saṃhitā*[116] as denoting a Bhilla or Bhil. The Buddhist Jātakas describe them as hunters and foresters. The Purāṇas mention the Kirātas, Bhillas, Nāhālakas, Bhrāmaras and Pulindas as descendants of the Niṣādas and describe them as black, low-statured, short-armed, having high cheek-bones, a flattened nose, red eyes and copper-coloured hair—characteristics still conspicuous among many hill-tribes of India.[117] Niṣāda occurs in the *gaṇa-kulālādi* of Pāṇini[118] implying an occupational caste of tribal origin belonging to the level of the potters, etc. In the *Bṛhatsaṃhitā*[119] they are mentioned as a people of the south-east division in whose country pearls are found. The earliest epigraphic reference to the Niṣādas is found in the Junagadh inscription of Rudradāman.[120] The tribe perhaps lived at that time (c. A.D. 150) in the western Vindhya-Araballi region. According to Manu the Niṣādas were an *anuloma* caste having sprung from the union of Brāhmaṇa male and Śūdra female,[121] and they are the same as the Pārāsavas. Later legal texts maintain a kind of ambiguity in regard to the Niṣādas. It appears that originally the Niṣādas had a higher social position and that is why they were regarded as belonging to the *anuloma* order, but later on account of their adoption of lower occupations such as hunting, fishing and so forth, there was a marked decline in their social status. Vijñāneśvara[122] says that there are two kinds of Niṣādas. While the *anuloma* Niṣādas are good, the *pratiloma* Niṣādas living on fishing belong to a lower rank. The same is also said by Medhātithi.[123]

Among the detribalised castes belonging to the Niṣāda category subsisting on hunting, fishing and other lower avoca-

tions, Manu refers to the Pukkasas (Pulkasa or Paulkasa)—frequently mentioned in the Buddhist literature as a wild tribe subsisting on hunting—as the hybrid of a Niṣāda male and Śūdra female.[124] Manu prescribes catching and killing animals that live in holes as the occupation of Kṣatṛ, Ugra and Pukkasa.[125] The Kṣatṛs are regarded by Manu as a *pratiloma* caste sprung from a Śūdra father and a Kṣatriya mother and the same holds good in the case of the Ugras.[126] Other law-givers provide for the Pulkasas or Pukkasas the manufacture and selling of liquor[127] and for the Ugras the work of the staff-bearer of the king and of executing punishment on the offenders.[128] The *Āpastamba Dharmasūtra,* however, says that a Brāhmaṇa may accept gift from the Ugras. According to Manu, the Andhras, Medas, Cuñcus and Madgus—all *pratiloma* hybrids connected directly or indirectly with the Niṣādas—have the avocation of killing forest animals.[129] The Śvapacas or Śvapākas are produced by Kṣatṛ male and Ugra female and they have the same avocation as that of the Caṇḍālas.[130] The Antyas,[131] Antyajas[132] and Antyavasāyins[133] are generic appellation for all lowest castes like the Caṇḍālas. The Antyavasāyins are regarded as sprung from the union of a Caṇḍāla male and a Niṣāda female having occupations of the lowest type. Among castes having occupation of fishermen, the Dharmasūtra of Gautama[134] refers to the Dhīvaras described as the hybrid of Vaiśya male and Kṣatriya female. In the *Taittirīya Brāhmaṇa*[135] Dhīvara, Dāsa and Kaivarta are separately mentioned, though having the same profession of fishing. Regarding Dāsa, Manu says that "a Niṣāda begets on an Āyogava woman a Mārgava or Dāsa who subsist by working as a boatman and whom the inhabitants of Āryāvarta call a Kaivarta".[136] Śaṅkara on *Vedāntasūtra* II. 3.43 says that Dāsa and Kaivarta are the same. In the Jātakas it is said that fishermen who work with nets and baskets are called Kevatta.[137] The Jālopajivīns mentioned by Hārīta is probably the same as Kaivarta.[138]

Among the occupational castes, the Sutas who are described as the hybrids of Ksatriya male and Vaiśya female have

been given the avocation of the management of horses and chariots by Manu.[139] Kauṭilya is careful to add that the Suta who figures in the Purāṇas as the reciter is different from this.[140] According to the *Mahābhārata*[141] the Sutas are the attendants of the Brāhmaṇas and the Kṣatriyas. According to some Purāṇas[142] the Sutas were to preserve the genealogies of the kings and great men and traditions about learning or books, but they are not authorised to study the Vedas. The Āyogavas, probably the same as the Vedic Āyogu[143] are according to Manu[144] a *pratiloma* caste springing from the union of a Śūdra male and Vaiśya female whose avocation is carpentry. Some law-givers[145] say that the Āyogavas are weavers or subsist by making vessels of bronze or by cultivating paddy or by dealing in cloth or by going to the stage. Takṣans or Takṣakas are mentioned by Manu[146] as having the occupation of carpentry. They are also known as Vardhakī. According to Patañjali[147] Takṣan is a Śūdra and on the same level with Ayaskāra or ironsmith. The Karmāra or blacksmiths are mentioned by Manu.[148] The Dhigvanas are said to have sprung from the union of Brāhmaṇa male and Āyogava female who subsist by working on and sale of hides.[149] Kulluka on Manu X.49 quotes a text of Uśanas that Dhigvans subsist by working on hides and distinguishes them from Kārāvaras. Manu says that the Kārāvaras are a doubly mixed caste, having sprung from the union of a Niṣāda male and Vaidehi female and their calling is leather-workmanship.[150] The Ādhiṇḍikas are likewise the offspring of a Niṣāda male from a Vaidehi female and they belong to the craft of Carmakāra.[151] Kulluka says that their avocation is to prevent strangers from trespassing on places where offenders are kept imprisoned. Manu refers to Carmakāras or leather-workers in general and the specific term he uses is *carmavakartin*, i.e., cutters of hides.[152]

The Pāṇḍusopākas, according to Manu, have sprung from the union of a Caṇḍāla male and a Vaidehika female who maintain themselves by dealing in bamboos.[153] They are the same as the Burudas who are also workers in bamboo and are

mentioned in the *gaṇakulālādi* of Pāṇini.[154] The Veṇas or Vaiṇyas, according to Manu,[155] are born of the union of a Vaidehika male and an Ambaṣṭha female who make their livelihood by playing musical instruments. Kulluka on Manu IV. 215 says that Veṇa is one who maintains himself by splitting bamboos and that he is the same as Buruḍa according to Visvarūpa. Kauṭilya adds that the Veṇa or Vaiṇya follows the same profession as the Rathakāra.[156] Yājñavalkya refers to them as Vaiṇas which Vijñaneśvara explains as meaning those who maintain themselves by cutting or splitting bamboos.[157] The Karaṇas, also known as Khaśa, Naṭa and Jhalla, originate from a *vrātya* of the Kṣatriya caste, and though Manu does not assign any special calling to them,[158] according to some later law-givers they are the same as the Caraṇas or Vaitālikas whose business is to sing the praises of the kings and the Brāhmaṇas and study of the science of erotics. The Kāruṣas, according to Manu, sprang from the *vrātya* Vaiśyas.[159] The Kukkuṭas sprang from the union of a Śūdra male and a Niṣāda female.[160] Later sources state that their occupation was weapon-making. Among other occupational castes Manu mentions Śailuṣa or actors, Tunnavāya or tailors, Raṅgāvatāra or stage actors, Suvarṇa or goldsmith, Śauṇḍika or wine-dealer, Cailanirṇejika or washerman and Rañjaka or dyer.[161]

Among tribes inducted into the Śūdra category by the application of the mixed-caste theory the Māgadhas who gave their name to the Māgadha country and are mentioned in the *Atharvaveda*[162] and the *Taittirīya*[163] and *Vājasaneyi*[164] Saṃhitās, have been described as a *pratiloma* caste sprung from the union of a Vaiśya male and a Kṣatriya female.[165] The Vaidehikas likewise were a tribe mentioned in the Vedic literature whose territory which later developed into a kingdom that lay to the east of the river Sadānīrā.[166] They are described by Manu as sprung from the union of a Vaiśya male and Brāhmaṇa female.[167] According to Manu,[168] their peculiar work is to attend on and guard women while according to the later sources[169] their occupation is pastoralism. The Ābhiras, whose

kingdom in the north-western Deccan is mentioned in the Nasik inscriptions[170] and who are named among the tribes subjugated by Samudragupta[171] are described by Manu as sprung from the union of a Brāhmaṇa male and an Ambaṣṭha female[172] They might have been a foreign tribe and had settlement in different parts of India. One notable settlement mentioned by Ptolemy as Aberia or Abiria was a part of Indo-Scythia. They were pastoral peoples and are now represented by the Ahirs. The Āvantyas who resided in the Malwa region and created the kingdom of Avantī with capital at Ujjayinī (cf. inscriptions from Nasik and Ajanta, Junagadh inscription of Rudradāman)[173] are described by Manu as hybrids of Vrātya male and Brāhmaṇa female.[174] The Mallas and Licchavis as well as the Khaśas and Drāviḍas are mentioned as hybrids of Vrātya male and Kṣatriya female.[175]

The Mallas were a well known tribe of eastern India. They are frequently mentioned in the Buddhist and Jain texts and were constituted by nine confederated clans. From the Jain *Kalpasūtra* we learn that the Malla chiefs were among those who had instituted an illumination on the occasion of the death of Lord Mahāvīra.[176] The Licchavis of Vaiśalī were also a very important tribe famous for their republican constitution. In the subsequent political history of India they played a major role. The Khaśas were a powerful tribe of north-western India which survives even to this day. Drāviḍa is a general term to denote the south Indian tribes, though modern historians and philologists use the term to denote a speech-family mainly concentrated in the South Indian tribes, but having a few pockets in northern India as well. The Sātvatas who formed a clan of the Yādavas have been described by Manu as a hybrid of Vrātya male and Vaiśya female.[177] They are the same as the Kāruṣas. The Andhras, Pauṇḍras, Coḍas, Cuñcus and other tribes are also described as hybrids of various mixed castes of the lower order.[178] The Andhras are mentioned in the Vedic texts along with the Puṇḍras, Śabaras, Pulindas and Mutivas.[179] They lived between the Krishna and the Godavari and are

mentioned in a good number of inscriptions including those of Aśoka.[180] Later they formed an empire in the Daccan. The Pauṇḍras or Puṇḍras are located in the eastern division in the *Bṛahatsaṃhitā.*[181] Their country roughly corresponded to the Rajshahi division of northern Bengal. A Maurya inscription has ascertained the location of the capital of the Pauṇḍras at Mahasthan in the Bogra district.[182] The Coḍas were a southern tribe whose territory roughly corresponded to modern Trichinopoly and Tanjore districts. In Southern inscriptions the name appears in the forms of Cola, Coḷa and Coḍa. It is taken back to the third century B.C. by one of the edicts of Aśoka.[183] The Oḍras are also mentioned by Manu[184] who were a tribe of Orissa and responsible for naming a part of the country after their name. The Cuñcus of Manu[185] are same as modern Chenchus of the Nallamallais.

Even foreign tribes and those living in the border region such as the Kāmbojas, Yavanas, Śakas, Pāradas, Pallavas, Cīnas, Kirātas and Daradas have also been inducted by Manu into the category of the Śūdras. Manu says that formerly these peoples were Kṣatriyas, but in consequence of their omission of sacred rites and of their not-consulting of the Brāhmaṇas they have gradually sunk into the condition of the Śūdras.[186] The Kāmbojas are generally associated with Gandhāra in ancient literature and in the inscriptions of Aśoka.[187] They occupied roughly the province round about Rajaori or ancient Rājapura, including the Hazara district and probably extending as far as Kafiristan. The Daradas were the inhabitants of modern Dardistan, north of Kashmir on the Upper Indus. They ae mentioned in the *Mahābhārata*[188] and the Purāṇas.[189] The Cīnas are frequently mentioned in ancient Indian literature, but instead of the Chinese proper, the name generally denoted the Mongloid tribes of the north, especially those living beyond the Himalayas. In Sanskrit literature, tribes belonging to the Vindhyan region are often called Kirātas, Śabaras and Pulindas. The Kirātas are mentioned in the Puranic list of Janapadas as dwelling in the Udīcya or Utarāpatha region and also in the Paravatāśraya or

the Himalayan region. The *Periplus* refers to the Kirātas (Kirrhadae) living to the north of Dosarene (Tosali)[190] while Ptolemy locates them near the mount Maiandros, and one branch, the Airrhadoi, in the coastal region beyond the mouth of the Ganges.[191] The word Yavana was used in medieval Indian literature as a synonym of *mleccha* and indicated any foreigner. But as late as the early centuries of the Christian era it meant the Greeks only. The word was derived from the Old Persian form Yauna, signifying originally Ioniam Greeks, but later, all peoples of Greek nationality. The Śakas were the Scythians who were originally a tribe of Central Asian nomads. The Pahlavas (from the old Persian Parthava) are regarded as Parthians, but when the Pāradas are separately mentioned, as we find it in the *Manusmṛti*, the term Pahlava primarily indicates the Sassanians or Persians in general.

Manu has not mentioned the peculiar avocations of many of these well-known tribes because in the time when the present form of the *Manusmṛti* was composed they were mostly disintegrated and absorbed within the bigger fold of the Indian society with heterogeneous occupations. Only in the case of the royal dynasties the original tribal name was maintained. His doctrine of the 'mixted-caste' in terms of their occupational positions and vice versa is not, however, free from contradictions. Theoretically it has been suggested that the *anuloma* hybrids should have a better occupational position and status than the *pratiloma* hybrids. But this principle has not always been maintained. The *anuloma* Ugras, for example, have not a better position than the *pratiloma* Māgadhas. According to the logic or the mixed-caste theory, in the *pratiloma* order the Caṇḍālas should be given the first rank because they are said to have sprung from the union of Śūdra male and Brāhmaṇa female. But they are placed at the lowest. Manu says that the Caṇḍālas are the lowest among men beyond the pale of religious observances prescribed for the four Varṇas.[192] This intense dislike has its roots in the Vedic texts[193] in which the Candālas were regarded as the most

despised and untouchable caste and is also supported by the evidence of Buddhist literature and foreign accounts.[194] When it is said that all the mixed-caste have their origins in the morganatic marriage among the divinely ordained four *varṇas*, why then Manu and other law-givers, ignoring the norms set up by themselves, treated the Caṇḍālas in a different way? Was it a fact that they were too much sensitive in regard to the purity of Brāhmaṇa women? Did they want to make it a point that the Brāhmaṇa woman had been a taboo, and anyone attempting to seduce her would meet the same fate as that of a Caṇḍāla?

Manu has not made an exhaustive list of all the so-called mixed-castes or specify their actual occupations, status and role in society. He had perhaps no direct touch with the functional castes which were far more numerous than those known to him only conventionally. The same holds good in the case of Kauṭilya[195] whose list of mixed castes tallies almost entirely with Manu's. Commenting on the list of the mixed-castes, as found in the *Yājñavalkya Smṛti*, Vijñaneśvara says that the list is only exemplary; in reality mixed castes are endless. Historically speaking, the origin of most mixed-castes or subcastes was due to the growth of occupational divisions and specialisations as well as adoption of new occupations by groups of detribalised peoples who came into the bigger fold of the Hindu society. It has very little to do with morganatic marriages. In fact, the classification or gradation of the functional Śūdra castes on the basis of *varṇaśaṅkara* theory lacked credibility owing to its inconsistencies. Rather, the older division of the Śūdras into *aniravasita* (general professional) and *niravasita* (lower professional), as made by Pāṇini,[196] was more effective. Following this approach, another division of the Śūdras into those whose prepared food could be partaken by the Brāhmaṇas (*bhojyānna*) and those whose food could not be partaken by the Brāhmaṇas (*abhojyānna*) came into existence. In the first category were included one's own slave, one's cowherd, barber, family friend and one who shared with one crops reared on one's land.[197] The third and the well-known

classification found in later legal texts and Purāṇas was into Sat-Śūdra and Asat-Śūdra. The former class included those Śūdras who followed good occupations or trade, served the twice-born and had given up meat-eating and drinking.

The laws of Manu in relation to possession, contracts, debts, pledges, sale and purchase, partnership, gift, employer-employee relations, violation of compacts, boundary disputes, partition of property, inheritance, etc., convincingly prove that the concept of private property and individual ownership formed the basis of the economic infrastructure of social organisation. There is a theory that the king was the owner of lands and the subjects were only occupants. This theory was based on Vijñāneśvara's interpretation of a passage of Yājñāvalkya[198] which implied that the privileges of making a gift of land belonged only to the king. This theory was very much favoured by the British administrators. But Jaimini says that in the Viśvajit sacrifice the king may donate everything belonging to him but not the earth which is common to all.[199] Śabara clarifies this statement saying that others have as much right over the earth as the king, and the latter is entitled to have a share of crops produced from the earth for his duty of protection. Manu seems to hold that so far as lands already brought under cultivation are concerned, the ownership belongs to the cultivator and the king is only entitled to levy taxes for the protection he affords. We have already had the occasion to see that according to Manu the king should take a fiftieth part of the cattle and gold and a sixth, eighth or twelfth part of crops and a sixth part of other produces and in the time of emergency he may raise his demand to a fourth of the produce. But the means of production—land, labour, capital and organisation—belonged to the individual. In the case of treasure-trove found underneath the ground as in mines the king is entitled only to a share.[200] If the king were the owner of all land Manu would have declared that the king took all the mines and treasure found underneath the ground. Manu clearly states that a field belongs to him who uproots the stems

of trees and shrubs from the waste on uncultivated land.

> (Sages) who know the past call this earth even the wife of Pṛthu; they declare a field to belong to him who cleared away the timber and a deer to him who first wounded it.[201]

Manu's insistence on individual ownership is more clearly reflected in his laws in relation to partition and inheritance. There is a divergence of opinion among the later law-givers on the question whether ownership is only known from Śāstra or is a secular matter, but it has been admitted that ownership is a matter of ordinary usage. The next question is whether ownership arises from partition or whether partition takes place of what already belongs to oneself by birth. For at least thousand years there have been two schools that widely differ on the question of partition and inheritance. The Dāyabhāga school upholds the doctrine of *uparamasvatvavāda* (ownership arising on death) which does not recognise that the son, grandson or great-grandson acquires by birth any right of ownership in the ancestral property held by the father or other ancestor. The Mitākṣarā on the other hand insists on *janmasvatvavāda* which means that ownership arises by birth. According to this school every member of the family immediately on his birth is entitled to a share of the joint property. Both these schools were not started in themselves for the first time, but each had a respectable antiquity behind it. Law givers like Manu, Nārada and Devala had put forward the doctrine of *uparamasvatvavāda* while the *smṛtis* of Yājñavalkya, Viṣṇu and Bṛhaspati espoused the doctrine of *janmasvatvavāda*. The differences between these two schools have thus been summarised by Kane:

> (1) The Dāyabhāga denies the theory that property is by birth, while the Mitākṣarā accepts it; (2) the Dāyabhāga lays down that the right to inherit and the order of heirs is determined by the principle of religious efficacy, while the

> Mitākṣarā holds that blood relationship is the governing factor in this matter; (3) the Dāyabhāga holds that members of a joint family (such as brothers or cousins) hold their share in quasi-severalty and can dispose of them even when there is no partition by metes and bounds; (4) the Dāyabhāga holds that even in an undivided family the widow succeeds to her husband's share on his death without male issue, while the Mitākṣarā holds that she does not do so.[202]

The source of this Dāyabhāga may be traced to Manu's famous maxim that the sons have no power over their paternal estate so long as the parents are alive, but after death the brothers being assembled, may divide among themselves in equal shares the paternal and maternal property.[203] Kulluka commenting on this verse says that the father's estate is to be divided after the father's death and the mother's estate after the mother's death and that the equal division takes place if the eldest son does not desire to receive an additional share. Manu is evidently in favour of unequal division, because he says that as an alternative the eldest alone may take the whole paternal estate and the others have to live under him just as they lived under their father.[204] Unlimited *patria potestas* and the doctrine of primogeniture are thus Manu's primary concern. According to Manu if the paterfamilias dies without previously accomplishing the partition, his place will be taken by the eldest son who is either simply regarded as the heir or is at least considered to be the director of the household and has to look after his brothers and relations as father. Even where there is division of property the eldest has the lion's share. The eldest shall have one-twentieth of the estate as extra along with the best of all chattels. The middlemost will get half of that which is one-fortieth and the youngest will get half of that or the one-fourth of the eldest which is one-eightieth of the total. Those who are between the eldest and the youngest shall have the share prescribed for the middlemost. Among the goods the eldest will take the best article, the best of

animals.[205] In support of the doctrine of primogeniture Manu says that "if the eldest brother behaves as an eldest brother ought to do, he must be treated like a mother and like a father; but if he behaves in a manner unworthy of an eldest brother, he should yet be honoured like a kinsman".[206] 'Like a kinsman' means, according to Medhātithi and Kulluka, 'like a paternal or maternal uncle'.

Manu says that if, instead of remaining united, the brothers prefer to live separately, there is an increase of spiritual merit.[207] According to Medhātithi and Kulluka, it is due to the fact that, being separate, each of them has to kindle the sacred fire, offer Agnihotra and five great sacrifices and so forth, and hence each gains merit separately.[208] This shows that there was an option either to remain joint after the father's death or to become separate. Partition was generally made when all the coparceners were major, but there was no bar if a coparcener was minor.[209] The next question is what property is liable to be partitioned. Property may be divided into two classes—joint family property and separate property. Joint property is either ancestral property or property jointly acquired with or without the aid of ancestral property or property acquired separately but thrown into the common stock. According to Manu, whatever property the eldest son acquires by his own effort, a share of that should go to the younger brothers. But when the property is earned jointly by all the brothers the division will be equal. Property acquired by learning or as gift belong solely to him to whom it is given. If, any brother has a profitable calling and does not desire a share of the family property, he may be made separate by the others having offered a trifle out of his share. Property earned by a person without using the patrimony exclusively belongs to his own. If a father recovers lost ancestral property, there is no need of sharing it with his sons, because it is self-acquired. If the divided brothers begin to live together once again as coparceners in that case during second partition the division will be equal. If any brother is deprived of his share or dies, his share is not lost to his immediate heirs.[210]

Leaving aside other forms of inheritance, let us now come to the question of the inheritance and proprietary rights of women. In fact, a correct assessment of the social position of women can only be possible by a review of their economic rights and privileges.[211] The term *strīdhana,* i.e., the peculium of the female members of the family and their special privilege of inheriting the same is mentioned in the older Dharmasūtras.[212] Manu uses the word *pāriṇāhya* meaning 'household gear' and says

> Let the husband employ his wife in the collection and expenditure of his wealth, in keeping everything clean or in the fulfilment of religious duties, in the preparation of his food and in looking after the utensils.[213]

But this has nothing to do with economic rights. The *Taittirīya Saṃhitā*[214] says that "the wife of the sacrificer holds on to the cart, for the wife is the mistress of the household gear". Jaimini,[215] according to Śabara, refers to this passage of the *Taittirīya Saṃhitā* for establishing that women do own certain property. We have already had the occasion to quote a saying of Manu that "a wife, a son and a slave are declared to have no property, the wealth which they earn, is acquired for him to whom they belong".[216] According to Medhātithi, Govindarāja, Kulluka and Rāghavānanda the verse means only that these persons are unable to dispose of their property independently. The first categorical statement which seems to have some bearing on the proprietary rights of women as found in the *Manusmṛti* is as follows:

> But to the maiden sisters the brothers shall severally give portions of their shares, each out of his share one-forth part; those who refuse to give it, will become outcasts.[217]

This is no legal right. Here the brothers are simply asked to donate a portion from their share voluntarily; the sisters are

not inheriting from their father. According to all the commentators the meaning of the verse is that, if a man leaves children by wives of different castes, the brothers are to provide for the dowry of the unmarried sisters of the same caste, e.g., the son of a Brāhmaṇa wife for the daughter of the latter, that of Kṣatriya wife for the daughter of the latter, and so forth. The interpretation makes the whole, situation more complex. As regards the expression 'a fourth share' Medhātithi says that a brother shall receive three-fourths and the sister one-fourth, and that, if there are many sisters, they will receive one-fourth of the share of a brother of equal caste. Kulluka adds that even if there are many brothers and sisters of the same caste, but born of different mothers, one-fourth part must be given to the sisters of the full blood, i.e., by their full brothers. Thus direct inheritance of the father's property on the part of the daughters is out of question. But they may inherit their mother's property:

> But when the mother has died, all the uterine brothers and the uterine sisters shall equally divide the mother's estate.
>
> Even to the daughters of those daughters something should be given, as is seemly, out of the estate of their maternal grandmother, on the score of affection.[218]

Kulluka and Rāghavānanda restrict this rule to unmarried daughters and hold that married daughters receive merely a 'token of respect'. Nārāyaṇa says that the term 'the mother's estate refers to other property than *strīdhana*. The term *strīdhana* literally means 'women's property' but its real significance is restricted to certain special kinds of property given to a woman on certain occasions or at different stages of her life. The oldest extant definition of it is found in the *Manusmṛti*:

> What was given before the nupital fire (*adhyāgni*) what was given on the bridal procession (*adhyavāhanika*), what was given as token of love (*prītidatta*) and what was received

> from her brother (*bhrātṛdatta*), mother (*mātṛdatta*) or father (*pitṛdatta*) that is called the sixfold property of a woman.
>
> Such property, as well as a gift subsequent and what was given to her by the affectionate husband, shall go to her offspring, even if she dies in the lifetime of her husband.[219]

Kulluka states that both the separate property of a woman enumerated in the aforesaid verses descend to her children. Nārāyaṇa remarks that 'a gift subsequent' and the 'husband's affectionate gift' are not *strīdhana* or separate property and that hence the wife has no right of free disposal with respect to these two.

> It is ordained that the property of a woman married according to the Brāhma, the Daiva, the Ārṣa, the Gāndharva or the Prājāpatya rite shall belong to her husband alone, if she dies without an issue.
>
> But it is prescribed that the property which only may have been given to a wife on an Āsura marriage or one of the other blamable marriages shall go to her mother and to her father, if she dies without issue.[220]

These two verses are significant. In the Brāhma form of marriage the daughter is handed over as a gift to a man learned in the Vedas and of good conduct. In the Daiva form the daughter is also handed over as a gift to a priest at a sacrifice. When the father gives away the daughter after receiving from the bridegroom a cow and a bull or two pairs it is the Ārṣa form of marriage. The gift of a daughter by the father after he has addressed the couple 'may both of you perform together your duties' is called the Prājāpatya form. The voluntary union of a maiden and her lover is known as the Gāndharva form. When a bridegroom receives a maiden after having given as much wealth as he can afford to her kinsmen and to the bride herself is called the Āsura form. The forcible abduction of a maiden

is known as the Rākṣasa form of marriage and when a man by stealth seduces a girl who is sleeping, intoxicated or disordered by intellect, it is the Paiśāca form of marriage.[221] The commentators on Manu have no special interpretation of these eight forms of marriage. But one is tempted to ask how the forcible abduction of a girl or seducing her stealthily when she is not in senses, which have elsewhere been described by Manu as highly sinful acts, become valid forms of marriage. It appears that the original significance of the last four forms of marriage was different as is indirectly indicated in Manu III.21. Originally these forms might have pertained to certain people known as Gandharvas (still surviving as a caste in north India living on musical performances), Asuras, Rākṣasas and Piṣācas. For example, the Āsura form of marriage is a purely matrilocal marriage which is still current among the lower strata of Indian society. Pāṇḍu's marriage with Mādrī was a purely matrilocal marriage in which Bhisma as the guardian of Pāṇḍu offered various forms of wealth to Mādrī's brother Śalya saying that the *kuladharma* established from antiquity must be respected. The Asuras, as is known from the Vedic texts, were a cultured people living in Iran and Western Asia. And it is against this background of matrilocal marriage system, current among various peoples, that Manu said that in case where the system of marriage is not patriarchal, in which system, the girl is not considered as a commodity to be presented as gift, the *strīdhana*, after the death of the wife will go to the wife's own clan and not to her husband's clan.

The concept of *strīdhana* underwent significant changes in subsequent period. The Mitākṣarā[222] explains that the number six is intended to exclude a smaller number of the kinds of *strīdhana*. Yājñavalkya enumerates several kinds of *strīdhana* as follows: what is given by the father, mother, husband and brother, what is received before the nuptial fire, what is presented to her on her husband's marrying another wife, what is given by the cognate relations of the wife, the *sulka* and gifts subsequent to marriage.[223] Kauṭilya names *śulka*, *anvādheya*,

adhivedanika and *bandhudatta* (gifts from friends) as kinds of *strīdhana.*[224] Nārada has the same six kinds as Manu IX. 194, but reads *bhartṛdāya* (the husband's gift) for Manu's 'what is given as token of affection.'[225] Among later Smṛti writers Kātyāyana gives the most elaborate treatment of *strīdhana* in about 27 verses. The definition of Kātyāyana has been accepted by all digests including even the *Dāyabhāga.* Manu uses another term *yautuka* which has been defined by him as that form of present in wealth or kinds which goes directly from the mother to the maiden daughter.[226] So *yautuka* seems to be a synonym of *strīdhana* [226] in a technical sense. The succession to *strīdhana* varies according as the woman is unmarried or married, according as the marriage was an approved or an unapproved form and so forth. The views of Manu in relation to this succession have already been noted. Later law books and digests present a variety of opinions. It is to be observed in this connection that Manu and other law-givers only enumerate and describe certain kinds of *stridhana,* but they do not attempt to make a comprehensive list of it. It appears that the term *strīdhana* at first included only six kinds of property as described by Manu, then nine, and ultimately by the time of Kātyāyana it included all property, whether movable or immovable obtained by a woman, either as a maiden or at marriage or after marriage, from her parents, or the family or relatives, both agnate and cognate, husband and friends and what is obtained by her own labour.[227]

We shall conclude the chapter with reference to the economic position of the widows. In the Dharmasūtras there is no explicit reference to the wife's right to succeed to her deceased husband's estate. The *Āpastamba Dharmasūtra* states that in default of a son the nearest *sapiṇḍa* succeeds but does not expressly mention the wife as an heir.[228] Gautama appears to state that the estate should be taken by the *sapiṇḍas* of the departed one who is issueless, the *sagotras, sapravaras* or his wife.[229] Manu does not declare that the wife is the heir of sonless man and there are certain passages in the *Manusmṛti*

which impliedly exclude her. He says that if a man dies childless and has no brothers, it is his father who will have the inheritance of his son (but not his wife).[230] Elsewhere he says that a mother shall obtain the inheritance of a son who is dead leaving no issue, and if the mother is dead, the paternal grandmother shall take the estate.[231] The widow had, however, the right to retain the ornaments, for Manu says that the ornaments which may have been worn by women during their husbands' lifetime, his heirs cannot divide among themselves.[232] Manu has the following injunctions for the widows. They should emaciate their body by living on pure flowers, roots, and fruits; they should not think of any male person; should be self-controlled and chaste; and should control her thoughts, words and actions. But Manu has not discrouraged the *niyoga* system and says that a son legally begotten on an appointed widow shall inherit like a legitimate son,[234] though his commentators say that this rule does not hold good in the case of the *kali* age. In another place he says:

> If the widow of a man who died without leaving issue raises up to him a son by a member of the family, she shall deliver to that son the whole property which belonged to the deceased. But if two sons begotten by two different men contend for the property in the hand of their mother, each shall take, to the exclusion of the other, what belonged to his father.[235]

Such passages show that there was difference in theory and practice, at least in some cases widows could retain property and though Manu disfavoured widow remarriage, this did not cease to happen, though the remarried widows (*punarbhūs*) were socially looked down upon. Later law-givers, however, took a more liberal attitude towards the widows. Yājñavalkya was probably the first to clearly enunciate the rule that the wife was the foremost heir of a sonless man. Bṛhaspati says:

> In the Veda and in the doctrine of the Smṛtis and in popular usage the wife is declared to be half the body of the husband, equally sharing the consequences of good and evil acts. Of him whose wife is not dead half the body survives. How can another obtain the property, while half the body of the deceased lives?[236]

Kauṭilya has, however, a slightly different approach, and he seems to be more liberal than Manu, especially in the case of the widows. It is interesting no note that while, according to Manu, debt precedes all disputes, Kauṭilya holds that it is the marriage which determines all kinds of litigation. Like Manu, Kauṭilya also admits that in the case of matrilocal marriages such as the Āsura form of marriage, the parents of the bride receive money (*śulka*) paid by the bridegroom, and after their death the daughter inherits the amount in a natural way. But in the case of patrilocal marriages, represented by such forms as Brāhma, Ārṣa, Daiva and Prājāpatya, property of women or *strīdhana* consists of the means of subsistence (*vṛtti*) or jewellery (*ābadhya*). According to Kauṭilya[237] means of subsistence valued at above 2000 *paṇas* shall be endowed in the favour of the wife and there is no limit of jewellery. On the death of her husband a woman, desirous to lead a pious life, shall at once receive not only her endowment and jewellery but also the remainder of her husband's deposits due to her. If after obtaining these she remarries another person, in that case she shall be caused to pay that property back to the kinsmen of her former husband together with interest on its value. But if this remarriage has her first father-in-law's consent (which can be obtained under certain circumstances), in that case the amount is not to be returned. If she bears children to a *savarṇa* husband (i.e., a second husband belonging to the same *gotra* as that of the former husband) with a view to avoid the extinction of her race, she shall not be liable to contempt thereof. In that case she shall retain whatever either her former father-in-law or her former husband or both had given

to her. Otherwise no woman can succeed in her attempt to establish her title to the property of her deceased husband after her remarriage. Kauṭilya lays own elaborate rules not only about the remarriage of the widows but also about the second marriage of the married women which he allows under certain conditions.[238] Manu does not say anything about the remarriage of the widows, but in one passage he tells that if a woman has two sons by two husbands, each of them will receive the property of his real begetter.[239] In such a case Kauṭilya says that if a woman after her remarriage attempts to take the possession of the property of her former husband under the plea of maintaining her sons by her former husband, she shall be made to endow it in the name of the sons concerned. Kauṭilya is also silent on the vital question whether the daughters have the direct and natural right to inherit the share of the property of their father.

Manu's sociology should thus be studied from an economic point of view. There are many passages in the *Manusmṛti* in which it is stated that women should be honoured and their rights should be maintained.[240] Again there are passages where it is said the women do not care for beauty, quality or age; they are eager to give themselves to any one, basically faithless and unchaste in nature; and hence they are to be guarded.[241] In fact there are many verses which show a disparaging attitude towards the Śūdras, women and persons belonging to the lower ranks of social hierarchy. That is why many historians think that Manu was out and out a reactionary law-giver who advocated a social system based on oppression, inequality and injustice. On the other hand the admirers of Manu say that while Manu's preference to the Brāhmaṇas (in their opinion, those who were the representatives of ideal Brahmanism, and not the so called Brāhmaṇa castes of subcastes) admits of no doubt, some of his statements regarding the Śūdras and the womankind were interpolations. A universal law-giver like Manu cannot put on record such a statement that women are by nature promiscuous. Such passages were interpolations

made by some mysogynist. The same argument of interpolation they extend to the case of the Śūdras as well. According to them, instead of approaching the doctrine of the four *varṇas* as outlined in the *Manusmṛti* from a narrow viewpoint if one takes up a wider range of vision one has to admit that all men all over the earth naturally fall into one or the other of these four *varṇas* according to their inner or outer characteristics. It is a natural division and not an artificial division. But a close study of the *Manusmṛti* from an economic point of view shows that Manu was more concerned with the innumerable *jātis* or specialised occupational subcastes and their place in the fourfold system. In a country like India where races were many, languages were numerous, customs varied from region to region, Manu tried to form a social whole out of diverse and conflicting elements by insisting on a structure with hierarchical grades for various communities and with social duties and means of livelihood allotted to each of them. The principle of equality was sacrificed by him, but in its place the lower orders received a guarantee for the protection of life and property and chances for the maintenance of life.

NOTES

1. *Light on Early Indian Society and Economy*, Bombay 1966, pp. 1-18; also incorporated in his *Perspectives in Social and Economic History of Early India*, New Delhi, 1983, pp. 1-22; cf. R.S. Sharma and V.N. Jha, *Indian Society: Historical Probings*, New Delhi, 1974.
2. *Indian Historical Review*, VI, 1979-80, pp. 1-63.
3. K. Sundararama Aiyar, *Dharma and Life*, 2 Vols., Madras, 1924; Bhagwan Das, *Science of Social Organization or the Laws of Manu in the Light of Ātmavidyā*, Madras, 1932-33 (first published 1910); G.H. Mees, *Dharma and Society*, The Hague, 1935; Kewal Motwani, *Manu: A Study in Hindu Social Theory*, Madras, 1934; P.H. Prabhu, *Hindu Social Institutions*, Bombay, 1940; K.V.R. Aiyangar, *Aspects of Hindu View of Life According to the Dharmaśāstra*, Baroda, 1932; *Aspects of Social and Political Systems in the Manusmṛti*, Lucknow, 1949; S. Varadachariar, *The Hindu Social Theory*, Lucknow, 1946.
4. IV. 61 and Medhātithi's com. on it.
5. III. 3.6.

6. cf. *Matsya* CXLIV. 40, 43; *Liṅga* XL. 7.42; etc.
7. X. 81-83.
8. See D.D. Kosambi, *Introduction to the Study of Indian History*, Bombay, 1956, pp. 176-226; R.S. Sharma, *Perspectives*, pp. 128-36; R.B. Chakravarti, *Warfare for Wealth*, Calcutta, 1986, pp. 46-76.
9. II. 1; II. 8;
10. XII. 119.16: XII. 133 contains an eulogy of *Koṣa*.
11. II. 61.17.
12. VII. 65.
13. I.327-28.
14. *The Hindu Revenue System*, Calcutta, 1929, reprint 1972. pp. 19ff.
15. *Gautama* X. 27; *Vasiṣṭha* I. 42; *Baudhāyana* I.10.18.1; etc.
16. Ghoshal, *op. cit.*, pp. 24-25.
17. VIII. 304-08.
18. VIII. 40.
19. *Raghuvaṃśa* I. 18.
20. X. 119.
21. XII. 16, 41.
22. VII. 127-28.
23. XII. 87. 13-14.
24. VII. 129.
25. VII. 140.
26. IX. 305.
27. V. 34, 17-18.
28. XII. 87. 20-22.
29. V. 2.
30. II. 1.
31. VIII. 170-71.
32. Kane,: *HD*, III, pp.184-86.
33. Ghoshal, *op. cit.*, p. 33.
34. VII. 6.5: X. 173.6.
35. Cf. *Ait. Br.* XXXV.3: *Taitt. Br.* II. 7.18.3.
36. Fick, p. 119.
37. *CII.* I. p. 164.
38. VII. 80.
39. VII. 130-31, VIII. 305.
40. VII. 128-29.
41. VII. 137.
42. VIII. 198.
43. VIII. 307.
44. *Manusmṛti*, Vol. IV, pt. II, p. 340.
45. Ghoshal, *op. cit.*, p. 78.
46. Baroda, 1928, p. 102.
48. CCIII. 2.

49. VII. 62.
50. VII. 81.
51. VIII. 399; cf. Yājñavalkya II. 261.
52. VIII. 400-402.
53. VII. 130-32, 137-38; cf. *Āpas. Dh.S.* II. 26.9; *Gaut.Dh.S.* X. 24-27, 31; *Vas. Dh. S.* XIX. 26-28; *Baudh. Dh. S.* I. 18.1.13.15.
54. VIII. 403.
55. VIII. 404-06.
56. IX. 221-28. 258.
57. II. 200-03.
58. XVI. 8.
59. VII. 138.
60. VII. 62.
61. VIII. 39.
62. VIII. 35-38.
63. V. 2.
64. X. 120.
65. V. 2.
66. *Ep. Ind.* VII. p. 36.
67. VIII. 131.
68. VIII. 132-34.
69. II. 3.2.1.
70. VIII. 135-37.
71. For works on ancient Indian economic condition see N.S. Subha Rao, *The Economic and Political Conditions in Ancient India*, Mysore, 1911; J.N. Samaddar, *Economic Condition of Ancient India*, Calcutta, 1922; N.C. Bandyopadhyaya, *Economic Life and Progress in India*, Calcutta, 1925; S.K.Das, *Economic History of India*, Calcutta, 1925; Pran Nath, *A Study in the Economic Condition of Ancient India*, London, 1929; U.N. Ghoshal, *Contributions to the History of the Hindu Revenue System*, Calcutta, 1929; *The Agrarian System in Ancient India*, Calcutta, 1931; K.V.R. Aiyangar, *Aspects of Ancient Indian Economic Thought*, Benaras, 1934; A.N. Bose, *Social and Rural Economy of Northern India*, 2 Vols., Calcutta, 1942-43; B.N. Dutta, *Dialectics of Land Economics in India*, Calcutta, 1952; B.P. Majumdar, *Socio-economic Life in Ancient India*, Calcutta, 1960; P. Neogi, *Economic History of Northern India*, Calcutta, 1962; L. Gopal, *Economic Life of Northern India*, Benaras, 1965; G.L. Adhya, *Early Indian Economics*, Bombay, 1966; R.S. Sharma, *Indian Feudalism*, Calcutta, 1965; *Light on Early Indian Society and Economy*, Bombay, 1966; B.C. Sen, *Economics in Kauṭilya*, Calcutta, 1967; D.R. Das, *Economic History of Deccan*, New Delhi, 1969; D.N. Jha, *Revenue System in the Post-Maurya and Gupta Times*, Calcutta, 1967; S.K. Maity, *Economic Life in Northern India in the Gupta Period*, Delhi, 1970; B.N. Mukherjee, *Economic Factors in the Kuṣāṇa History*, Calcutta, 1970;

G.K. Rai, *Involuntary Labour in Ancient India*, Allahabad, 1981; R.K. Chaudhuri, *Economic History of Ancient India*, Patna, 1982; B.P. Roy, *Later Vedic Economy*, Patna, 1984; B.D. Chattopadhyaya (ed.), *Essays in Indian Economic History*, New Delhi, 1987; Om Prakash, *Early Land Grants and State Economy*, Allahabad, 1988.

72. IV. 147.
73. III. 152.
74. X. 81-82: cf. *Vas. Dh. S.* II. 22; *Yāj.* III.35.
75. IX. 2.
76. VIII. 348.
77. IX. 326-33.
78. X. 83-84.
79. I. 5.10.
80. Ferrington, *Greek Science*, I, pp. 105-06.
81. X. 85.
82. X. 86-89.
83. VII. 8.15.
84. Cf. *Āpas. Dh. S.* I. 7.20. 12-131, *Baudh.Dh. S.*II. 1.77-78; *Vas. Dh.S.* II. 24-29; etc.
85. X. 94.
86. X. 115-17.
87. *L'esclavage dans I'Inde ancienne d'après les textes Palis et Sanskritis*, Pondicherry, 1957; Eng. trans. *Slavery in Ancient India*, New Delhi, 1960, p. XIII. It is based mostly on Buddhist sources.
88. Cf. Strabo, XV. 1.54.
89. Kauṭilya III.13.
90. VI. 7-6.
91. VIII. 415.
92. Shamasastry, pp. 209-10.
93. VIII. 416-17.
94. Books and articles on the Caste system are more than five thousand. For a general review of the major works see M.N. Srinivas, 'Caste: A Trend Report and Bibliography' in *Current Sociology*, VIII(3), 1969, pp. 135-85; also Suvira Jaiswal in *IHR*, VI, 1979-80, pp. 1-63. There are numerous field studies in historical perspectives pertaining to various regions made by Crooke, Enthoven, Ibbetson, Nesfield, Thurston and Rangachari, Russel and Hiralal, Risley, Nanjundayya, Ananthakrishan Iyer, etc., besides the Gazetteers and Census Reports. Among other important works see E.W. Hopkins, *Mutual Relations of the Four Castes in Manu*, Leipzig, 1881; *Social and Military Position of the Ruling Caste in Ancient India*, New Haven, 1889; J.N. Bhattacharya, *Hindu Castes and Sects*, Calcutta, 1886; J.C. Ghosh, *Brahmanism and Śūdra*, Calcutta, 1902; S.V. Ketkar, *History of Caste in India*, 2 Vols., New York, 1909, Calcutta, 1911; E. Senart, *Caste in India*, Eng. trans.,

London, 1930; R. Fick, *Social Organisation of Northeastern India,* trans., S.K. Mitra, Calcutta, 1930; N.K. Dutta, *Origin and Growth of Caste in India,* Calcutta, 1931, 1933; E.A.H. Blunt, *Caste System of Northern India,* London, 1931; G.S. Ghurye, *Caste and Race in India,* London, 1932; *Caste and Class in India,* Bombay, 1950; A.M. Hocart, Les Castes, Paris, 1938; J.H. Hutton, *Caste in India,* revised ed. London, 1951; P.N. Prabu, *Hindu Social Institutions,* Bombay, 1940; H.V. Rao, *Indian Caste System,* Bangalore, 1951; R.S. Sharma, *Some Economic Aspects of the Caste System in Ancient India,* Patna, 1952; *Śūdras in Ancient India,* Delhi, 1952; L. Dumont, *Homo Hierarchichus,* Delhi, 1970; P. Misra, *Evolution of the Brāhmaṇa Class,* Varanasi, 1978; G.P. Upadhyay, *Brāhmaṇas in Ancient India,* New Delhi, 1979; etc.

95. I. 61.4: VII.32. 20; VIII. 5.38: IX. 112. 1-3: X. 72.2: X. 119. 5: X. 142.4.
96. III. 5.6-7.
97. IV. 5.4.2.
98. XVI. 26-28: XXX.5-13.
99. XVII. 13.
100. *Taittirīya* III. 4.1ff; *Tāṇḍya* III. 4; etc.
101. Cf. *Kāṭhaka Saṃ.* XVIII. 13; *Taitt. Sam.* IV. 5.4.2: *Mait. Sam.* XVI. 27; *Ait. Br.* VIII. II; *Pañcaviṃśa Br.* XVI. 6-8.
102. This process is nicely described in N.K. Bose's small Bengali work *Hindu Samājer Gaḍan.* See also D.P. Chattopadhyaya, *Lokāyata,* Delhi, 1959, pp. 171ff; N.N. Bhattacharyya, *Ancient Indian History and Civilization: Trends and Perspectives,* New Delhi, 1988, pp. 34ff., 150ff.
103. Kauṭilya XI. Saṅghavṛtta.
104. XI. 19, XIV. 7: XVI. 22.
105. VII. 1.66.
106. X. 8: cf. *Baudh Dh. S.* I. 9.3: *Yāj.* I. 91.
107. X. 47.
108. cf. *Uśanas* 31-32.
109. Risley, *Peoples of India,* p. 114.
110. Cf. *Uśanas,* 26-27.
111. X. 112.1.3.
112. X. 12.
113. X. 53.4.
114. *Nirukta* III.8: cf. *Bṛhaddevatā* VII. 69.
115. X. 4.
116. XVI. 27: XXX. 8.
117. *Vāyu* II. 1.120-21; *Viṣṇu* I. 13; *Bhāgavata* IV. 14.44.
118. IV. 3.118.
119. V. 76: XIV. 10.18.
120. *Ind. Ant.* VII. p. 262.
121. X. 8: cf. *Baudh Dh. S.* I.9.3; II.2.33; *Vas Dh.S.*XVIII.8; *Mbh.* XIII.48.5; *Yāj.* I. 91; *Kauṭilya* III. 7.

122. *Mit.* on *Yāj.* I. 91.
123. On Manu X. 8.
124. X. 18.
125. X.49.
126. X. 9.12-13, 16; cf. Kauṭilya III. 7; *Baudh. Dh.S.* I. 95.
127. Gautama IV. 17; Uśanas 17; etc.
128. Cf. Uśana, 41, *Vaikhānasa* X.13.
129. X. 36. 49.
130. X. 19: X. 51-56.
131. IV. 79.
132. IV. 61: VIII. 279.
133. IV. 71: IX. 39.
134. IV. 17.
135. III.4.12.
136. X. 34.
137. Fick, p. 302.
138. Quoted by Aparārka, p. 279.
139. X. 47.
140. III. 7.
141. VIII. 32.48.
142. Cf. *Vāyu.* I. 1.33-38.
143. *Taitt. Br.* III. 4.1.
144. X. 12.
145. *Viṣṇu Dh. S.* XVI. 8; *Uśanas* 13.
146. IV. 210.
147. On Pāṇini II. 4.10.
148. IV. 215.
149. X. 15; X. 49.
150. X. 36.
151. X. 37.
152. IV. 218.
153. X. 37.
154. IV. 3.118.
155. X.19; cf. *Baudh Dh.S.* I. 9.13.
156. III. 7.
157. I. 161.
158. X. 22.
159. X. 23.
160. X. 18.
161. IV. 214-16.
162. V. 22.14.
163. III. 4.1.1.
164. XXX. 5.22.
165. X. II, 17; Kauṭilya III. 7; *Mbh.* XIII. 48.12; *Yāj.* I. 93.

166. Cf. *Śat. Br.*I. 1.4.10ff; *Ait Br.* VIII. 14; *Śāṅ. S.S.* XVI. 29.5; *Br. Up.* III. 8.2.
167. X. 11,13,17; Kauṭilya III. 7; *Yāj.* I. 93; *Mbh.* XIII. 48.10.
168. X. 47; cf. *Agni Pu.* CLI. 14.
169. Uśanas 20-21; *Vaikhānasa* X. 14.
170. *ASWI,* IV, p. 104.
171. *CII,* III, p. 14.
172. X. 15.
173. *ASWI,* IV, pp. 109, 117; *Ind. And,* VII, p. 262.
174. X. 21.
175. X. 22.
176. *SBE.* XXII, p. 266.
177. X. 23.
178. X. 36ff.
179. *Ait. Br.* VIII. 18; *Śāṅ.S.S.* XV. 26.
180. *Ind. Ant.* XX, pp. 239ff; *CII,* III. p. 230; *ASWI.* IV, p. 127; etc.
181. V. 70ff; IX. 15; X. 14; XIV. 3; LXXX.7.
182. *IHQ.* IX. pp. 722-23.
183. *Ind. Ant.* XX, pp. 39ff.
184. X. 43-44.
185. X. 48.
186. X. 43-44.
187. *Ind. Ant.* XX. pp. 239ff.
188. VI. 9. 67.
189. Cf. *Mārkaṇḍeya,* XVII.
190. Sec. LXII.
191. VII. 2.2.
192. X. 12.
193. *Vāj. Sam* XXX.17; *Taitt. Br.* III. 4.14.17; *Chānd Up.* V. 10.7.
194. e.g., Fa-hien's Account, See *Records of the Buddhist Kingdoms,* Eng. Trans. J. Legge, London, 1886, p. 43.
195. III. 7.
196. II. 4.10.
197. Cf. *Yāj.* I. 166.
198. I. 318.
199. VI. 7.3.
200. VIII. 39.
201. IX. 144.
202. *HD,* III, pp. 558-59.
203. IX. 104.
204. IX. 105; cf. *Baudh. Dh. S.* II. 3.12; *Gaut. Dh.S.* XXVIII.3.
205. IX. 112-14.
206. IX. 110.
207. IX. 111; cf. *Gaut. Dh. S.* XXVIII. 4.

208. Cf. Manu III. 67.
209. Cf. Kauṭilya III. 5; *Baudh. Dh. S.* II. 2.42.
210. Manu. IX. 204-12.
211. See. Gurudas Banerjee, *Hindu Law of Marriage and Strīdhana*, 5th ed., Calcutta, 1923, pp. 319-519; J. Jolly, *Adoption, Inheritance and Partition*, TLL, Calcutta, 1885, pp. 226-70.
212. Cf. *Gaut. Dh. S.* XXXVIII. 24 ff.
213. IX. 11.
214. VI. 2.1.1.
215. VI. 1.16.
216. VIII. 416.
217. IX. 118; cf. Yāj. II. 124.
218. IX. 192-93.
219. IX. 194-95.
220. IX. 196-97.
221. III. 27-34.
222. On *Yāj.* II. 143.
223. II. 143-44.
224. III. 2.
225. *Dāyabhāga.* 8.
226. IX. 131.
227. *Kātyayana*, 594ff.; *Nārada* XIII. 8-9.
228. II. 6.14.2 ff.
229. XXVIII. 19.
230. IX. 185.
231. IX. 217.
232. IX. 200.
233. V. 157-60, 165 ff.
234. IX. 145 ff.
235. IX. 190-91.
236. *HD.* III. P. 703.
237. III. 2.
238. III. 5.
239. IX. 191.
240. III. 55-59.
241. IX. 14-15.

Bibliography

I. ORIGINAL SOURCES

Agni Purāṇa, ed. by R.L. Mitra, Bib. Ind., Calcutta, 1873-79; also Ānandāśrama Press edn., Poona, 1957; Eng. trans. by M.N. Dutt, Calcutta, 1901.

Aitareya Brāhmaṇa, ed. with Sāyaṇa's com. by Satyavrata Sāmaśramī, Bib. Ind., Calcutta, 1894-1906; Eng. trans. by A.B. Keith, HOS, Cambridge Mass, XXV, 1920.

Aitareya Upaniṣad, see under Upaniṣads.

Aṅgiras Smṛti, Ānandāśrama Press, Poona, 1905; ed. Jīvānanda, Calcutta, 1876; also pub. in *Ārya Śāstra* Series, Calcutta.

Āpastamba Dharmasūtra, ed. by G. Bühler, Bombay Sanskrit Series, 1892, 1894; ed. with Haradatta's *Ujjvala* com. by Mahadeva Sastri and K. Raṅgācārya, Mysore, 1898; Eng. trans. by G. Bühler in *SBE,* II, Oxford, 1897.

Apastamba Gṛhyasūtra, ed. by M. Winternitz, Vienna, 1887; Eng. trans. by H. Oldenberg, in *SBE,* XXX.

Āpastamba Smṛti, Ānandāśrama Press, Poona, 1905, ed. by Jīvānanda, Calcutta, 1876.

Āpastamba Śrautasūtra, ed. with Rudradutta's com. by R. Garbe, Bib. Ind., Calcutta, 1881-1903; books I-VII translated into German by W. Caland, Gottingen, 1921.

Arthaśāstra of Kauṭilya, ed. by R. Shamasastry, Mysore, 1919; Eng. trans. by the same, Mysore, 1929; ed. and Eng. trans. pts. I-III by R.P. Kangle, Bombay, 1960-65; ed. with Bengali trans. by R.G. Basak, Calcutta, 1964.

Āśvalāyana Gṛhyasūtra, ed. with com. of Gārgya Nārāyaṇa by R.N. Vidyāratna and A.C. Vedāntavāgīśa, Bib. Ind., Calcutta, 1866-69; with com. of Haradatta by Gaṇapati Śāstrī, TSS, No. 78, Trivandrum, 1923; Eng. trans. by H. Oldenberg, *SBE,* XXIX.

Āśvalāyana Śrautasūtra, ed. with Gārgya Nārāyaṇa's com. by R.N. Vidyaratna, Bib. Ind., Calcutta, 1864-74.

Atharvaveda, Eng. trans. in part by M. Bloomfield in *SBE,* XLII, Oxford, 1887; by W.D. Whitney, Cambridge Mass, 1905.

Atri Smṛti, Ānandāśrama Press, Poona, 1905; ed. by Jīvānanda, Calcutta, 1826; also in *Ārya Śāstra* series, Calcutta.

Āvaśyaka Sutra, ed. with *Niryukti* of Bhadrabāhu and com. of Malayagiri, Āgamodaya Samiti, 56, Bombay, 1928.

Baudhāyana Dharmasūtra, Eng. trans. by G. Bühler in *SBE,* XIV, Oxford, 1882.

Baudhayana Gṛhyasūtra, ed. R. Shamasastry, Mysore, 1920.

Baudhāyana Śrautasūtra, ed. W. Caland, Bib. Ind., Calcutta, 1904-23.

Bhagavadgītā, Eng. trans. by K.T. Telang in *SBE,* VIII, Oxford, 1882.

Bhāgavata Purāṇa, Eng. trans. by G.T. Tagara, Delhi, 1976.

Bhagavatīsūtra, Āgamodaya Samiti, 3 Vols., Bombay, 1918-21.

Bhāradvāja Gṛhyasūtra, ed. E. Solomon, Leiden, 1913.

Brahmāṇḍa Purāṇa, Veṅkateśvara Press, Bombay, 1913. Text with Bengali trans. in Vaṅgavāsī edn., Calcutta, 1910.

Brahma Purāṇa, Ānandāśrama Press, Poona, 1896.

Brahmasūtra of Bādarāyana, Eng. trans with com. of Śaṅkara and Rāmānuja by G. Thibaut in *SBE,* 34, 38, 1890-1904.

Bṛhadāranyaka Upaniṣad, see under Upaniṣads.

Bṛhaspati Smṛti, Eng. trans. by J. Jolly in *SBE,* XXXIII, Oxford, 1889.

Bṛhatsaṃhitā, ed. by H.Kern, Bib. Ind., Calcutta, 1865; Eng. trans. by the same in *JRAS,* IV-VII; ed. and trans. by V. Subrahmanya Sastri, Bangalore, 1947.

Caraka Saṃhitā, ed. by N.N. Sengupta, Calcutta, 1927.

Chāndogya Upaniṣad, see under Upaniṣads.

Dhammapada, ed. by S.S. Sastri, PTS, London, 1914; Eng. trans. by F. Max Müller in *SBE,* X, Oxford, 1898.

Garuḍa Purāṇa, Eng. trans. by M.N. Dutt, Calcutta, 1908.

Gautama Dharmasūtra, Eng. trans. by G. Bühler in *SBE,* II, Oxford, 1892.

Gobhila Grhyasūtra, ed. C. Tarkālaṅkāra, Bib. Ind., Calcutta, 1907-8; Eng. trans. by H. Oldenberg in *SBE,* XXX.

Gopatha Brāhmaṇa, ed. R. Mitra and H.C. Vidyābhuṣana, Bib. Ind., Calcutta, 1870-72.

Harivaṃśa, ed. with Nīlakaṇṭha's com. by Gopal Narayan, Bombay, 1895; Eng. trans. by M.N. Dutt, Calcutta, 1897.

Hiraṇyakeśi Gṛhyasūtra, Eng. trans. by H. Oldenberg in *SBE,* XXX.

Īśā Upaniṣad, see under Upaniṣads.

Kālikā Purāṇa, ed. by P. Tarkaratna, Vaṅgavāsi Press, Calcutta, 1907.

Kalpasūtra of Bhadrabāhu, ed. H. Jacobi, 1879 and Eng. trans. by the same in *SBE,* XXII.

Kāmandakīya Nītisara, ed. by R.L. Mitra, Calcutta, 1861, rep. with R.L. Mitra's trans. by S.K. Mitra, Calcutta, 1982.

Kāmusūtra of Vātsyāyana, Eng. trans. by S.C. Upadhyaya, Bombay, 1961.

Kāṭhaka Saṃhitā, ed. by L. Von Schroeder, Leipzig, 1900-1910; A.B. Keith in *JRAS,* 1910, 517ff; 1912, 1095ff.

Kaṭha Upaniṣad, see under Upaniṣads.

Kātyāyana Smṛti, ed. and trans. by P.V. Kane, Bombay, 1933.

Kauṣītaki Brāhmaṇa, Eng. trans. by A.B. Keith, HOS, XXV, Cambridge Mass, 1920.

Khadira Gṛhyasūtra, Eng. trans. by H. Oldenberg in *SBE,* XXIX.

Kūrma Purāṇa, ed. with Bengali trans. by P. Tarkaratna, Vaṅgavāsi Press, Calcutta, 1914.

Kuṭāra Mānava, ed. E.C.G. Jonker, Leiden, 1885.

Mahābhārata, critical ed., Poona, 1927ff; Eng. trans. by K.M. Ganguly, pub. by P.C. Roy, Calcutta, 1884-96; rep. Calcutta, 1926.

Mahābhāṣya of Patañjali, ed. by Kielhorn, 3 Vols., Bombay Sanskrit Series, 1880-85.

Mahāvaṃsa, Eng. trans., *The Great Chronicle of Ceylon,* by W. Geiger, London, 1912.

Maitrī Upaniṣad, see under Upaniṣads.

Mānava Gṛhyasūtra, ed. by F. Knauer, St. Petersburg, 1897; pub. with com. of Aṣṭāvakra in GOS, Baroda, 1926; trans. by Dresden, Groningen, 1941.

Manusmṛti, for Sanskrit editions see under J.H. Dave, J. Jolly, N. Kurundakara, V.N. Mandlik, K. Motwani and L. Sternback in the Bibliography. Also see Ch.I. Eng. trans. by Sir William Jones, Calcutta, 1794; by G.C. Haughton, Madras, 1863; by A.C. Burnell and E.W. Hopkins, London, 1884; by G. Bühler in *SBE,* XXV, Oxford, 1886; ed. with trans. and notes in 5 vols. by G.N. Jha, Calcutta University, 1922-29. For other translations see under J.D.M. Derrett, M.N. Dutt, J. Jolly, Loiseleur-Deslongchamps, G. Strehly and W. Doniger in the bibliography.

Manuṭīkāsaṃgraha, ed. J. Jolly, Bib. Ind., Calcutta, 1889.

Mārkaṇḍeya Purāṇa, Eng. trans. by F.E. Pargiter, Calcutta, 1904.

Matsya Purāṇa, Eng. trans., ed. by S.B. Shastri, Delhi, 1972.

Medhātithibhāṣya on Manu, ed. and Beng. trans. by Bhūtanath Saptatīrtha, 5 Vols.

Muṇḍaka Upaniṣad, see under Upaniṣads.

Nārada Smṛti, ed. with extracts from com. of Asahāya and others by J. Jolly, Bib. Ind., Calcutta, 1885; trans. by the same in *SBE,* XXXIII, 1880; trans. of a shorter text by the same, London, 1876.

Nirukta of Yāska, ed. with Eng. trans. by Lakshman Sarup, 2 Vols., Lahore, 1922.

Nyāya Sūtra, ed. with Eng. trans. by S.C. Vidyābhuṣana in *SBH* Series, Allahabad, 1911.

Parāśaramādhava, ed. by V.S. Islampurkar, Bombay Sanskrit Series.

Pāraśara Smṛti, Eng. trans. by K.K. Bhattacharyya, Bib. Ind., Calcutta, 1887.

Pāraskara Gṛhyasūtra, Eng. trans. by H. Oldenberg in *SBE,* XXIX.

Praśna Upaniṣad, see under Upaniṣads.

Raghuvaṃśa, ed. with Eng. trans. by G.R. Nandargikar, Bombay, 1897.

Rājataraṅgiṇī of Kalhaṇa, Eng. trans. by M.A. Stein, London, 1990.

Rāmāyaṇa, Eng. trans. by M.N. Dutt, Calcutta, 1893-94.

Ṛgveda, Eng. trans. by R.T.H. Griffith, Benares, 1896-97; F. Max Müller in *SBE,* XXXII, 1891; H. Oldenberg in *SBE,* XLVI, Oxford, 1897.

Saṃskāraprakāśa, pub. in Chowkhamba Sanskrit Series, Varanasi.

Sāṅkhya Kārikā, Eng. and Beng. trans. by H.T. Colebrooke and H.H. Wilson, Calcutta, 1837.

Sāṅkhya Pravacana Bhāṣya, ed. by R. Garbe, HOS, Cambridge Mass., 1895.

Sāṅkhya Sūtra, ed. with Vijñānbhikṣus com. and trans. by J.R. Ballantyne, Calcutta, 1862-64; ed. with Aniruddha's com. and trans. by R. Garbe, Calcutta, 1892.

Śāṅkhyāyana Gṛhyasūtra, Eng. trans. by H. Oldenberg in *SBE,* XXIX.

Śāṅkhyāyana Śrautasūtra, Eng. trans. by W. Caland, Nagpur, 1953 (rep.).

Śatapatha Brāhmaṇa, Eng. trans. by J. Eggelling in *SBE,* XII, XXVI, XLI, XLIII, XLIV, Oxford, 1882-1960.

Skanda Purāṇa, ed. by G.P. Ravuker, Veṅkateśvara Press, Bombay, 1909-11.

Ślokavārtika, Eng. trans. by G.N. Jha, Bib. Ind., Calcutta, 1900.

Smṛticandrikā, Eng. trans. by J.R. Gharapure, Bombay, 1940-46.

Sūryasiddhānta, Eng. trans. by J. Burgess in *JAOS,* XI.

Susrutasaṃhitā, Eng. trans. by V.C. Dutta and A.C. Chattopadhyaya, Bib. Ind., Calcutta, 1891.

Śvetāśvatara Upaniṣad, see under Upaniṣads.

Taittirīya Āraṇyaka, ed. by R.L. Mitra, Bib. Ind., Calcutta, 1872.

Taittirīya Brāhmaṇa, ed. by R.L. Mitra, Bib. Ind., Calcutta, 1890.

Taittirīya Saṃhitā, Eng. trans. by A.B. Keith, Cambridge, 1914.

Tāṇḍa Māhā Brāhmaṇa, ed. by A.C. Vedāntavāgīśa, Bib. Ind., Calcutta, 1874.

Tantravārtika, Eng. trans. by G.N. Jha, Bib. Ind., Calcutta, 1903.

Upaniṣads Īśādiviṃśottara-śatopaniṣadāḥ (Texts of 120 Upaniṣads), ed. by Ācārya Nārāyaṇa Rāma, Nirṇaya Sāgar Press, Bombay, 1948; R.E. Hume, *Thirteen Principal Upaniṣads,* Oxford, 1921; K. Narayanaswami Aiyar, *Thirty Minor Upaniṣads,* Madras, 1914; S. Radhakrishnan, *Principal Upaniṣads,* London, 1953.

Vaikhānasa Smārta Sūtra, Eng. trans. by W. Caland, Bib. Ind., Calcutta, 1929; *Śrautasūtra,* ed. by the same, Bib. Ind., Calcutta, 1941.

Vaiśeṣika Sūtra, Eng. trans. by A.E. Gough, Benares, 1873.

Vājasaneyi Saṃhitā, ed. with Mahīdhara's com. by A. Weber, London, 1852.

Vāmana Purāṇa, ed. P. Tarkaratna, Vangabāsi Press, Calcutta, 1908.

Varāha Purāṇa, ed. H.P. Sastri, Bib. Ind., Calcutta, 1887.

Vasiṣṭha Dharmasūtra, Eng. trans. by G. Bühler in *SBE,* XIV, Oxford, 1882.

Vāyu Purāṇa, ed. P. Tarkaratna, Vaṅgavāsi Press, Calcutta, 1921.

Vedānta Sūtra, see under Brahmasūtra.

Vinaya Piṭaka, Eng. trans. by T.W. Rhys Davids and H. Oldenberg in *SBE,* 1881-85.

Vīramitrodaya, Eng. trans. by G.C. Sarkar, Calcutta, 1879.

Viṣṇu Dharmaśāstra, Eng. trans. by J. Jolly in *SBE,* VII, Oxford, 1880.

Viṣṇu Purāṇa, Eng. trans. by M.N. Dutta, Varanasi, 1912.

Vyavahāramayukha, ed. and trans. by V.N. Mandlik, Bombay, 1880.

Yājñavalkya Smṛti, Eng. trans. by G.C. Basu and S.N. Naraharayya in *SBH,* Allahabad, 1913, 1918; trans. with coms. of Vijñāneśvara, Mitramiśra and Śūlapāṇi by J.R. Gharpure, Bombay, 1936-42.

II. SECONDARY SOURCES: BOOKS

Achyutan, M. *Educational Practices in Manu, Pāṇini and Kauṭilya,* Trivandrum, 1975.

Adhya, G.L. *Early Indian Economics,* Bombay, 1966.

Agarwala, V.S. *India as Known to Pāṇini,* Lucknow, 1953; *India as Known to Manu,* Varanasi, 1970.

Aiyangar, K.V.R. *Some Aspects of Ancient Indian Polity,* Calcutta, 1914; *Some Aspects of Hindu View of Life according to the Dharmaśāstras,* Baroda, 1932; *Aspects of Ancient Indian Economic Thought,* Benares, 1934; *Indian Cameralism,* Madras, 1949; *Aspects of Social and Political System of the Manusmṛti,* Lucknow, 1949.

Aiyar, K.S. *Dharma and Life,* 2 Vols., Madras, 1924.

Aiyar, C.P.R. *Indian Political Theories,* Madras, 1937; *The Philosophical Basis of Indian Legal and Social Systems,* Madras, 1949.

Altekar, A.S. *The Position of Woman in Hindu Civilization,* Benares, 1938; *State and Government in Ancient India,* Benares, 1942; sec. edn., Benares,1958.

Ambedkar, B.R. *Who Were the Śūdras?* Bombay, 1948; *The Untouchables,* New Delhi, 1948.

Anjaria, J.J. *The Nature and Ground of Political Obligation in the Hindu State,* Calcutta, 1935.

Ayyar, R.S.V. *Manu's Land and Trade Laws,* Delhi, 1976.

Bader, C. *Women in Ancient India,* London, 1930.

Bandyopadhyaya, N.C. *Economic Life and Progress in India,* Calcutta, 1925; *Kauṭilya: An Exposition of His Social and Political Theories,* Calcutta, 1927; *Development of Hindu Polity and Political Theories;* 2 Vols., Calcutta, 1927, 1938; ed. in a single Vol. by N.N. Bhattacharyya, New Delhi, 1980.

Banerjee, N.N. *Manu and Modern Times,* New Delhi, 1975.

Banerjee, N.V. *Studies in the Dharmaśāstra of Manu,* New Delhi, 1980.

Banerjee, G.D. *Hindu Law of Marriage and Strīdhana,* Calcutta, 1878; fifth edn., Calcutta, 1923.

Banerjee, P.N. *Public Administration of Ancient India,* Calcutta, 1966; *International Law and Custom in Ancient India,* Calcutta, 1920.

Beaman, G.B. *On the Sources of the Dharmaśāstras of Manu and Yājñavalkya,* Leipzig, 1805.

Belvalkar, S.K. and R.D. Ranade, *History of Indian Philosophy,* Vol. II, Poona, 1927.

Bergaigne, A. *Inscriptions Sanscrites et du Cambodge.*

Betai, R.S. *A Reconstruction of the Original Interpretation of the Manusmṛti,* Ahmedabad, 1970.

Bhandarkar, D.R. *Some Aspects of Ancient Hindu Polity,* Benares, 1929.

Bhattacharyya, J.N. *Hindu Castes and Sects,* Calcutta, 1886.

Bhattacharyya, N.N. *Indian Puberty Rites,* Calcutta, 1968; *History of Indian Cosmogonical Ideas,* New Delhi, 1971; *Ancient Indian Rituals and Their Social Contents,* New Delhi, 1975; *Ancient Indian History and Civilization: Trends and Perspectives,* New Delhi, 1988.

Bhattacharjee, S.S. *The Hindu Theory of Cosmology,* Calcutta, 1978.

Bhattacharji, Sukumari. *The Indian Theogony,* Calcutta, 1970, sec. edn., Calcutta, 1978.

Blacker, C. and Loewe M. *Ancient Cosmologies,* London, 1976.

Blavtasky, M. *Secret Doctrines,* Adyar, ed.

Blunt, E.A. *Caste System in Northern India,* 1931.

Bose, A.N. *Social and Rural Economy of Northern India,* 2 Vols., Calcutta, 1942-45.

Bose, N.K. *Hindu Samājer Gaḍan,* in Bengali, Visvabharati.

Bose, P.P. *Indo-Aryan Polity,* London, 1925.

Bose, P.N. *Public Administration in Ancient India,* London, 1930.

Breasted, J.B. *History of Egypt,* London, 1906.

Bühler, G. *The Laws of Manu, SBE,* XXV, Oxford, 1885.

Burnell, A.C. and E.W. Hopkins. *The Ordinances of Manu,* London, 1884.

Chakladar, H.C. *Social Life in Ancient India: Studies in Vātsyāyana's Kāmasūtra,* Calcutta, 1929; 'Some Aspects of Social Life in Ancient India' in *Cultural Heritage of India,* Vol. II, Calcutta, 1962.

Chakraborty, G. *Espionage in Ancient India,* Calcutta, 1990.

Chakravarti, R. *Warfare for Wealth,* Calcutta, 1986.

Chanana, D.R. *Slavery in Ancient India,* New Delhi, 1960.

Chatterjee, H.N. *Studies in Some Aspects of Hindu Saṃskāras in Ancient India,* Calcutta, 1965.

Chatterjee, H. *International Law and Inter-State Relation in Ancient India,* Calcutta, 1958.

Chattopadhyay, B.D. *Essays in Indian Economic History* (ed.), New Delhi, 1987.

Chattopadhyay, D.P. *Lokāyata,* Delhi, 1959; *History and Society* (ed.), Calcutta, 1978.

Chaudhari, R.K. *Economic History of Ancient India,* Patna, 1982.

Colebrooke, H.T. *A Digest of Hindu Law,* 4 Vols., Calcutta, 1787-98.

Coomaraswamy, A.K. *Temporal Power in the Indian Theory of Government,* New Heaven, 1942; *Selected Papers,* ed. Roger Lepsey, Princeton, 1977.

Cornford, F.M. *The Republic of Plato,* Eng. trans., London, 1941; rep. 1972.

Cowell, E.B. *Hindu Law*, Calcutta, 1870.

Dandekar, R.N. *Vedic Mythological Tracts*, Delhi, 1979.

Dange, S.A. *India from Primitive Communism to Slavery*, Bombay, 1949.

Das, Bhagavan *Science of Social Organisation or the Laws of Manu in the Light of Ātmavidyā*, 2 Vols., 1910; sec. edn., Madras, 1932-34.

Das, R.M. *Women in Manu and His Seven Commentaries*, Varanasi, 1962.

Das, S.K. *The Economic History of Ancient India*, Calcutta, 1925; sec. edn., 1944.

Das, D.R. *Economic History of Deccan*, New Delhi, 1969.

Datta, H.N. *Manur Varṇāśramadharma*, in Bengali, Calcutta, 1968.

Datta, N.K. *Origin and Growth of Caste in India*, 2 Vols., Calcutta, 1931, 1933.

Davar, R.S. and K.D.P. Madan. *General Principles of Indian Law*, Bombay, 1950.

Dave, J.H. *Manusmṛti*, ed. with nine Commentaries, 5 Vols., Bharatiya Vidya Bhavan, Bombay, 1972.

Derrett, J.D.M. *Religion, Law and State in India*, London, 1968; *Essays on Classical and Modern Hindu Law*, Leiden, 1976; *Manuśāstravivaraṇa*, Verlag, 1975.

Diehl, C.G. *Instrument and Purpose: Studies on Rites and Rituals of South India*, Glecrup, 1956.

Dikshitar, V.R.R. *Hindu Administrative Institutions*, Madras, 1929; *Mauryan Polity*, Madras, 1932.

Doniger Wendy and Brian K. Smith. *The Laws of Manu*, Penguin, 1991.

Drekmeier, C. *Kingship and Community in Early India*, Stanford, 1962.

Dumont, L. *Homo Hierarchicus*, Delhi, 1970.

Dunning, W.A. *History of Political Theories: From Rousseau to Spencer*, Indian edn., Allahabad, 1970.

Durkheim, E. *Elementary Forms of Religious Life*, Eng. trans., London, 1912.

Dutt, B.N. *Studies in Indian Social Polity*, Calcutta, 1944; *Dialectics of Land Economics in India*, Calcutta, 1952; *Dialectics of Hindu Rituals*, 2 Vols., Calcutta, 1951, 1956, rep. 1965.

Dutta, M.N. *Manusmṛti*, Eng. trans. in *Hindu Religious Codes*, Vol. V, Calcutta, 1908.

Dutta, R.C. *A History of Civilization in Ancient India*, 3 Vols., Calcutta, 1889-90.

Eliade, M. *Birth and Rebirth*, London, 1958.

Farrington, B. *Greek Science*, 2 Vols., London, 1944.

Fick, R. *Social Organization of North East India in Buddha's Time,* Eng. trans., S.K. Mitra, Calcutta, 1920.

Fonten, Rose, J.E. *Ritual Theory of Myth,* London, 1966.

Forchhammer, E. *The Jardine Prize: An Essay to the Sources and Development of Burmese Law,* Rangoon, 1885; *King Wagaru's Manu Dhammasattham,* Rangoon, 1892.

Frazer, J.G. *The Golden Bough,* 13 Vols., London, 1913; abridged edn., London, 1951.

Gadd, C.J. *The Divine Rule in the East,* London, 1944.

Ganguly, N.C. *Indian Political Philosophy,* Calcutta, 1930.

Garbe, R. *Aniruddha's Commentary, etc.,* Calcutta, 1892.

Gernep, A. Van. *Les Rites de Passage,* Paris, 1909; Eng. trans., London, 1960.

Gharpure, J.R. *Manusmṛti with the Bhāṣya of Medhātithi,* Bombay, 1917.

Ghosh, J.C. *Brahmanism and Śūdra,* Calcutta, 1902; *Principles of Hindu Law,* Calcutta, 1906.

Ghosh, J.C. (ed.) *English Works of Raja Rammohun Roy,* 2 Vols., Calcutta, 1887.

Ghoshal, U.N. *Contributions to the History of Hindu Revenue System,* Calcutta, 1929; *The Agrarian System in Ancient India,* Calcutta, 1931; *A History of Hindu Political Theories,* Oxford, 1923; expanded edn., *A History of Indian Political Ideas,* Oxford, 1959; rep. with corrections, 1966.

Ghurye, G.S. *Caste and Race in India,* London, 1932; *Caste and Class in India,* Bombay, 1950.

Gibelin, E. *Etudes sur le droit civil des Hindous,* 2 Vols., Pondicherry, 1846-47.

Goldstucker, Th. *Literary Remains,* London, 1879.

Gonda, J. *Ancient Indian Kingship from Religious Point of View,* Leiden, 1966.

Gopal, L. *Economic Life in Northern India,* Benares, 1965; *The Śukranītisāra: A Nineteenth Century Text,* Varanasi, 1978.

Gupta, R.K. *Political Thought in Smṛti Literature,* Allahabad, 1961.

Harrison, J.E. *Prolegomena to the Study of Greek Religion,* Cambridge, 1908; *Ancient Art and Ritual,* Cambridge, 1913.

Hartland, E.S. *Ritual and Relief,* London, 1914.

Haughton, G.C. *Mānavadharmaśāstra,* Madras, 1863.

Heesterman, J.C. *Ancient Indian Royal Coronation,* The Hague, 1957.

Henri, F. *Kingship and Gods,* Chicago, 1908.

Hillebrandt, A. *Altindische Politik,* Jena, 1923.

Hocart, A.M. *Les Castes*, Paris, 1938.

Hooke, S.K. *Myth, Ritual and Kingship*, London, 1958.

Hopkins, E.W. *Mutual Relations of the Four Castes in Manu*, Leipzig, 1881; *Social and Military Position of the Ruling Caste in Ancient India*, New Haven, 1889; *The Great Epic of India*, New York, 1901.

Hutton, J.H. *Caste in India*, rev. edn., London, 1951.

Ingallas, D.H.H. *Authority and Law in Ancient India*, supp. to *JAOS*, XXXI, 1911.

Jahn, W. *Uber die Kosmognischen Grundunschauungen im Mānava-dharmaśāstram*, Leipzig, 1904.

Jain, C.R. *Jain Law*, Madras, 1926.

Jain, J.C. *Life in Ancient India as depicted in the Jain Canon*, Bombay, 1947.

Jaini, J.L. *The Jain Law*, Arrah, 1916.

James, E.O. *Prehistoric Religion*, New York, 1957.

Jastrow, J. *Berolzheimer's The World's Legal Philosophies*, Eng. trans., New York, 1929.

Jauhari, M. *Politics and Ethics in Ancient India*, Varanasi, 1968.

Jayaswal, K.P. *Manu and Yājñavalkya: A Comparison and a Contrast*, Calcutta, 1930; *Hindu Polity*, Calcutta, 1924.

Jha, D.N. *Revenue System in Post-Maurya and Gupta Times*, Calcutta, 1967.

Jha, G.N. *Manusmṛti* with Eng. trans., explanatory and comparative notes, 5 Vols., Calcutta University, 1922-29; *Hindu Law and its Sources*, Calcutta, 1930.

Johänntgen, E. *Über das Gesetzbuch des Manu*, Berlin, 1863.

Jolly, J. *Outlines of the History of the Hindu Law of Partition, Inheritance and Adoption*, TLL, Calcutta, 1885; *Recht and Sitte*, 1886; Eng. trans. by B.K. Ghosh, *Hindu Law and Custom*, Calcutta, 1928; *Mānavadharmaśāstra* with extracts from four commentaries, London, 1887.

Jones, W. *Institute of Hindu Laws or the Ordinances of Manu*, Calcutta, 1794.

Jonker, E.C.C. *Ean oud - javaansch wetboek vergelekan met indische rechtbronnen*, Leiden, 1885.

Kane, P.V. *History of Dharmasastra*, 5 Vols., Poona, 1930-62.

Karve, I. *Hindu Society: An Interpretation*, Poona, 1961.

Keith, A.B. *Ṛgveda Brāhmaṇas*, HOS, 1920, rep., New Delhi, 1971.

Ketkar, S.V. *History of Castes in India*, 2 Vols., New York, 1909, London, 1911.

Keer, D. *Dr. Ambedkar: Life and Mission*, third edn., New Delhi, 1981.

Kosambi, D.D. *An Introduction to the Study of Indian History*, Bombay, 1956; *Culture and Civilization in Ancient India in Historical Outline*, London, 1965.

Krishna Rao, M.V. *Studies in Kauṭilya*, Delhi, 1958; rep. 1979.

Kurundakara, N. *Manusmṛti* (ed.), Bombay, 1983.

Lang, A. *Myth, Ritual and Religion*, London, 1899.

Laszlo, F. *Die Parallelversion der Manusmṛti im Bhaviṣya Purāṇa*, Wiesbaden, 1971.

Law, N.N. *Aspects of Ancient Indian Polity*, Oxford, 1921.

Legge, J. *Records of the Biddhist Kingdoms*, London, 1886.

Levi-Straus, C. *Structural Anthropology*, New York, 1964.

Loiseleur-Deslongchamps, A. *Lois de Manou*, Paris, 1833.

Mabbet, I.W. *Truth, Myth and Politics in Ancient India*, Delhi, 1971.

Macdonell, A. *Sanskrit Literature*, London, 1900.

Macfie, J.M. *The Laws of Manu: A Summary in English*, Madras, 1921.

Mahalingam, T.V. *South Indian Polity*, Madras, 1955.

Maine, H. *Ancient Law*, London, 1861.

Maity, S.K. *Economic Life in Northern India in the Gupta Period*, Calcutta, 1958; rep. Delhi, 1970.

Majumdar, B.P. *Socio-Economic Life in Ancient India*, Calcutta, 1960.

Majumdar, R.C. *Corporate Life in Ancient India*, Calcutta, 1922.

Mandlik, V.N. *Hindu Law*, Bombay, 1880; *The Mayukha and Yājñavalkya*, Bombay, 1880.

Manickam, T.M. *Dharma according to Manu and Moses*, Bangalore, 1977.

Marret, R.R. *The Threshold of Religion*, London, 1914.

Marsh, J. *Asiatic Memorial of the Creation, Fall, Deluge etc., from the Sacred Book of the Hindoos*, Winchester, 1823.

Mayne, J.D. *A Treatise of Hindu Law and Usage*, London, 1878.

Max Müller, F. *A History of Sanskrti Literature*, London, 1859; *India*, London, 1883.

Mees, G.H. *Dharma and Society*, The Hague, 1935.

Mercereau, H. *Le Droit positif chez les Hindous d'après le Mānava-dharmaśāstra*, Paris, 1925.

Meyr, A. *Das indische Recht*, Vienna, 1878.

Misra, B.B. *Polity in the Agni Purāṇa*, Calcutta, 1965.

Misra, P. *Evolution of the Brāhmaṇa Class*, Varanasi, 1978.

Misra, U. *Conception of Matter in Nyāya-Vaiśeṣika*, Allahabad, 1931.

Mitra, T. *The Hindu Widow*, Calcutta, 1881.

Mitter, D.N. *Position of Women in Hindu Law,* Calcutta, 1912.
Monier-Williams, M. *A Sanskrit-English Dictionary,* Oxford, 1899; *Indian Wisdom,* London, 1875.
Mookerji, R.K. *Local Government in Ancient India,* Oxford, 1919.
Motwani, K. *Manu: A Study in Hindu Social Theory,* Madras, 1934; *Manu Dharmaśāstra: A Sociological and Historical Study,* Madras, 1958; *Manu Dharma Śāstra* (ed.), Madras, 1959.
Muir, J. *Original Sanskrit Texts,* 5 Vols., London, 1858ff.
Mukherjee, B.N. *Economic Factors in the Kuṣāṇa History,* Calcutta, 1970.
Mulla, D.F. *Principles of Hindu Law,* Calcutta, 1912.
Naik, B.P. *Ideals of Ancient Hindu Politics,* Dharwar, 1932.
Niogy, P. *Economic History of Northern India,* Calcutta, 1962.
Nilakantha Sastri, K.A. *The Theory of Pre-Muslim Indian Polity,* Madras, 1912.
Om Prakash. *Early Land Grants and State Economy,* Allahabad, 1988.
Pal, R.B. *History of Hindu Law,* Calcutta, 1938.
Pande, R.B. *Hindu Saṃskāras,* Benares, 1949, rep., 1966.
Panikkar, K.M. *The Origin and Evolution of Kingship in India,* Baroda, 1938.
Paradkar, M.D. *Similes in Manusmṛti,* Delhi, 1960.
Patawardhan, M.V. *Manusmṛti, The Ideal Democratic Republic of Manu,* Delhi, 1968; *Manuvāda or the Hindu Socialistic Democracy,* Belgaum, 1973.
Pound, R. *An Introduction to the Philosophy of Law,* Lodon, 1946.
Prabhu, P.N. *Hindu Social Institution,* Bombay, 1940; *Hindu Social Organisation,* Bombay, 1958.
Pran Nath. *A Study in the Economic Condition in Ancient India,* London, 1929.
Prasad, Beni. *Political Theories of Ancient India,* Allahabad, 1927; *Theory of Government in Ancient India,* Allahabad, 1928; *State in Ancient India,* Allahabad, 1928.
Pratapgiri, R. *Problems of Indian Polity,* Bombay, 1935.
Pusalkar, A.D. *Bhāsa: A Study,* Delhi, 1968.
Radhakrishnan, S. *Principal Upanishads,* London, 1923.
Rai, G.K. *Involuntary Labour in Ancient India,* Allahabad, 1987.
Raman, N.S. Sundara. *Ethical Implications of Manu's Code,* Ph.D. dissertation, University of Rajasthan, 1955.
Rao, H.V. *Indian Caste System,* Bangalore, 1951.
Rislay, H. *Peoples of India,* Calcutta, 1908.

Roussel, A. *Cosmologie Hindoue d'après le Bhāgavata Purāṇa*, Paris, 1893.

Roy, B.P. *Later Vedic Economy*, Patna, 1984.

Roy, S.L. *Diplomacy in Ancient India*, Calcutta, 1978.

Salatore, B.A. *Ancient Indian Political Thought and Institutions*, London, 1963.

Samaddar, J.N. *Economic Condition of Ancient India*, Calcutta, 1922.

Sampurnanand. *Cosmogony in Indian Thought*, Benares, 1942.

Sangave, V.A. *Jain Community: A Social Survey*, Bombay, 1959.

Sangermano, Rev. *A Description of the Burmese Empire*, Rome, 1843; sec. edn., by J. Jardine, Rangoon, 1885.

Sarkar, B.K. *Hindu Sociology*, Allahabad, 1920; *Political Institutions and Theories of the Hindus*, Allahabad, 1921.

Sarkar, G.C. *Hindu Law of Adoption*, Calcutta, 1891.

Sarkar, H.B. *Dvīpamay Bhārater Prāchīn Sāhitya*, in Bengali, Calcutta, 1970.

Sarkar, S.C. *Some Aspects of the Earliest Social History of India*, London, 1928.

Sarvadhikari, R. *Law of Inheritance*, Calcutta, 1882.

Sastri, A.M. *India as seen in the Bṛhatsaṃhitā*, Delhi, 1969.

Sastry, K.R.R. *Manu and Thiruvalluvar: A Comparative Study*, Madras, 1973.

Sen, A.K. *Studies in Hindu Political Thoughts*, Calcutta, 1920.

Sen, B.C. *Economics in Kauṭilya*, Calcutta, 1967.

Sen, P.N. *General Principles of Hindu Jurisprudence*, Calcutta, 1918.

Senart, E. *Caste in India*, Eng. trans., London, 1930.

Sengupta, N.C. *Evolution of Ancient Indian Law*, Calcutta, 1953.

Shamasastry, R. *Evolution of Ancient Indian Polity*, Calcutta, 1920; *Kauṭilya's Arthaśāstra*, Eng. trans., eighth edn., Mysore, 1967.

Sharma, R.N. *Ancient India According to Manu*, Delhi, 1980.

Sharma, R.S. *Śudras in Ancient India*, Delhi, 1958, 1980; *Some Economic Aspects of the Caste System in Ancient India*, Patna, 1952; *Indian Feudalism*, Calcutta, 1965, Delhi, 1980; *Aspects of Political Ideas and Institutions in Ancient India*, Delhi, 1959, 1968; *Light on Early Indian Society and Economy*, Patna, 1966 (rep. as *Perspectives in Social and Economic History of Early India*, New Delhi, 1983); *Social Changes in Early Medieval India*, Delhi, 1969, 1986; ed. with V.N. Jha, *Indian Society: Historical Probings*, New Delhi, 1974, 1977.

Shastri, J.L. *Political Thoughts in the Purāṇas*, Lahore, 1944.

Sinha, H.N. *Sovereignty in Ancient India,* London, 1938.
Sinha, P. *Smṛti: Political and Legal System: A Socio-Economic Study,* New Delhi, 1982.
Sil, N.P. *Kauṭilya's Arthaśāstra: A Comparative Study,* Calcutta, 1985.
Spellman, J.W. *Political Theory of Ancient India,* Oxford, 1964.
Sternbach, L. *Judicial Studies in Ancient Indian Laws,* London, 1965-67; *The Mānava Dharmaśāstra* I-III, and *The Bhaviṣya Purāna,* Varanasi, 1974.
Strange, T. *Hindu Law,* London, 1830.
Strehly, G. *Les Lois de Manou,* Paris, 1893.
Stokes, W. *Hindu Law Books,* Madras, 1865.
Subha Rao, N.S. *The Economic and Political Conditions in Ancient India,* Mysore, 1911.
Suda, J.P. *Manu, Marx and Gandhi,* Meerut, 1967.
Thakur, V.K. *Urbanisation in Ancient India,* New Delhi, 1981.
Thapar, R. *Ancient Indian Social History,* Delhi, 1978.
Thomson, G. *Aschylus and Athens,* London, 1950.
Tiwari, Chitra. *Śūdras in Manu,* Delhi, 1963.
Tylor, E.B. *Primitive Culture,* 2 Vols., London, 1871.
Upadhyaya, G.P. *Brāhmaṇas in Ancient India,* New Delhi, 1978.
Varadachariar, S. *Hindu Judicial System,* Lucknow, 1946; *The Hindu Social Theory,* Lucknow, 1946.
Varma, V.P. *Studies in Hindu Political Thought and its Metaphysical Foundation,* Delhi, 1954.
Venkateswar, S.V. *Public Life and Political Institutions,* London, 1932.
Visvanathan, S.V. *International Law in Ancient India,* London, 1925.
Wagle, N.K. *Society in the Time of Buddha,* Bombay, 1966.
Wallis, H.W. *Cosmology of Ṛgveda,* London, 1887.
Weber, A. *History of Indian Literature,* Eng. trans. by J. Mann and Th. Zachariae, London, 1882.
Webster, H. *Primitive Secret Societies,* New York, 1932.
West, W. and H. Bühler. *Digest of Hindu Law,* Bombay, 1867-69.
Wilson, H.H. *Glossary of Judicial and Revenue Terms,* London, 1855.
Yadava, B.N.S. *Society and Culture in North India in the Twelfth Century,* Allahabad, 1973.
Yogi, H. *Saṃskāras: The Genius Behind Rites,* Madras, 1951.

III. ARTICLES

Betai, R.S. 'Criminal Law from Manu to Yājñavalkya to Nārada: A Positive Transition', *JOI,* XXII, 1973, 265-89; State of Criminal Law in Manusmṛti', *JGJRI,* XXIV, 1968, 279-98; 'Revisions of the

Manusmṛti', *Ibid.*, XXII, 1966, 193-201; 'The Textual Problem of Manusmṛti', *JGRS*, XXIV, 271-76.

Bose, H.A. 'Manu's Mixed Castes', *Ind. An.*, 1923, 24-29.

Bloomfield, W. 'Contribution to the Interpretation of the Veda', *JAOS*, XV, 1893.

Brown, C.M. 'Some Modern Views of the Manusaṃhitā' *ALB*, XXXI (20), 1967-68, 95ff.

Brown, N. 'Theories of Creation in the Ṛgveda' *JAOS*, LXXXV, 1965.

Chakladar, W.C. 'Some Aspects of Social Life in Ancient India', *CHI*, II, 1962.

Chattopadhyay, B.D. 'Trade and Urban Centres in Early Medieval North India', *IHR*, I, 1974, 203-19.

Coomaraswamy, A.K. 'Hindu Theory of State and Social Compact', *Hindustan Review*, 1918.

Furnival, J.S. 'Manu in Burma', Journal of the Burmese Research Society, XXX (2), 1940.

Ganguly, J.N.C. 'Hindu Theory of Property' and 'Philosophy of Law', *IHQ*, I-II, 1925-26.

Ghosh, B.K. 'Age of the Manusaṃhitā', *IHQ*, III, 1927, 803-13.

Ghoshal, M.M. 'On Some Recent Interpretations of the Mahābhārata Theory of Kingship', *IHQ*, XXXI, 1965.

Ghoshal, U.N. 'The Status of Śūdras in the Dharmasūtras', *IC*, XIV (1), 21-27; 'The Status of Brāhmaṇas in the Dharmasūtras', *IHQ*, XXIII (2), 1947, 83-92.

Glucklich, A. 'Dharma and Social Justice in the Criminal Code of Manu', *Contributions to Indian Sociology* (N.S.), XVI (1), 1982, 57-78.

Gopal, Ram. 'Manu's Indebtedness to Śāṅkhyāyana', *Poona Orientalist*, XXVII, 1962, 39-44.

Goswami, K.G. 'The Mānava Principle in Manu and Nietzche's Appraisal', *Dr. Satkari Mookerji Felicitation Volume*, Varanasi, 1969, 685-95.

Gupta, A.S. 'Manu on the Duties of Kings', *JIH*, XLVIII (2), 1970, 399-404.

Hazra, R.C. 'Dharma: Its Early Meaning and Scope', *OH*, VII(1), 1959, 15-35; VIII (1), 1960, 7-34; 'The Sources of Dharma', *OH*, II(2), 1954, 249-63; III(1), 1955, 65-88; III (2), 1955, 221-38; V(2), 1957, 87-102.

Hopkins, E.W. 'On the Professed Quotations from Manu found in the Mahābhārata', *JAOS*, XI, 1885, 239-75; 'Social and Military

Position of the Ruling Caste in Ancient India', *JAOS,* VII, 157-376.

Jha, V.N. 'Varṇasaṅkaras in the Dharmasūtras: Theory and Practice', *JESHO,* XIII (3), 1970, 273-88.

Jaiswal, S. 'Studies in Early Social History: Trends and Possibilities', *IHR,* VI, 1979-80, 1-63.

Jolly, J. 'Arthaśāstra and Dharmaśāstra', *ZDMG,* LXXVII, 1913, 49-96.

Kangle, R.P. 'Manu and Kauṭilya', *Ind. Ant* (N.S.) I(1), 1964.

Laine, J.W. 'The Creation Account in the Manusmṛti', *ABORI,* LXII, 1981, 157-68.

Lingat, R. 'The Buddhist Manu on the Propagation of Hindu Law in Hinayanist Indo-China', *ABORI,* XXX, 1949-50, 284-97: 'Time and the Dharma: On Manu I 85-86', *Contributions to Indian Sociology,* VI, 1962, 7-16.

Majumdar, R.C. 'Hindu Law in Java and Bali', *S. Krishnaswamy Aiyanger Presentation Volume.*

Mukherji, P. 'Property Rights of Women as recorded in Kauṭilya Arthaśāstra and Manu', *OH,* IX(1), 1961, 49-60; 'Widowhood and Niyoga in the Arthaśāstra and Manusmṛti', *OH,* XI, 1963, 1-15.

Nandi, R.N. 'Client, Ritual and Conflict in Early Brahmanical Order', *IHR,* VI, 1979-80.

Orenstein, H. 'Logical Consequence in Hindu Social Law: Another Interpretation', *Contributions to Indian Sociology* (N.S.) IV, 1970, 22-34.

Raghavan, V. 'The Manusmṛti', *CHI,* 1959, II, 335-63; 'Rājavidyā: Manu and the Bhagavadgītā', *T.M.P. Mahadevan Commemorative Volume,* Madras, 1963.

Ramamoorthy, R. 'Concept of Punishment under Manusmṛti', *IPQ,* II(1), 1974, 51-64.

Rocher, L. 'Ancient Indian Criminal Law', *Journal of Oriental Research,* XXV, 1955, 15-34; 'Schools of Hindu Law', *India Maior* (Gonda. Fel. Vol.), Leiden, 1972, 167-76.

Sastri, A. Chinnaswami. 'On the Date and Authorship of Manu', *OH,* I(2), 1953, 107-16.

Shah, H.A. 'The Manu Smṛti in the Light of some Recently Published Texts', *Ind. Ant.,* 1916, 112-15, 125-26; 1917, 95.

Shah, K.J. 'Concept of Dharma', *Journal of Indian Academy of Philosophy,* XII(1), 1973, 35-45.

Sharma, S.D. 'The Concept of Justice in Manu', *Indian Sociological*

Journal, 1976, 47-68.

Shreedhara, B.H. 'Manu's Theory of Kingship', *The Journal of the Karnataka University*, XV, 1971, 43-50.

Sinha, B.P. 'The Kauṭilyan State', *JBRS*, XI, No. 3.

Srinivasa, M.N. 'Caste: A Trend Report and Bibliography', *Current Sociology*, VIII (3), 1969.

Tadpatrikar, S.N. 'Cosmic Account in Manusmṛti', *ABORI*, XXXI, 1950-51, 297ff.

Verma, P. 'Family as a Social Institution in the Mahābhārata and the Manu Smṛti', *Vedanta Kesar*, LXIV(4), 123-27.

Index